'A gripping account of the .... turous
life as a .... oking,
prolific p .... Diego
when vis .... ardian

D0177380

0 02

'In a bittersweet tale of love, loss and longing, al-Shaykh retells the remarkable story of her courageous, spirited mother' *London Review of Books*

'Hanan al-Shaykh's fictionalized account of her mother's life burns with truth ... It's about true love, the way a young girl's dreams of the cinema can teach her to use her beauty as both shield and weapon, and how family obligations can weigh down a life. The language is lustrous ... Her book has a warmth that crosses cultures and feels like a pure, shining blast of sun' *LA Times*

'The writing is flawless, the story is completely captivating, and the fact that it's all true is remarkable ... For all of us, this story can be one of healing – of seeing our parents for the children they once were and for the obstacles they had to overcome' Bookreporter.com

'An amazing read' *The Lady*

'Deeply reflective and moving ... al-Shaykh climbs into the body of her mother, skilfully re-creating the voice of a talented and charismatic storyteller ... Our unconventional mothers may make choices that damage our hearts, but as al-Shaykh shows us, those same choices can ultimately save us from a fate such as theirs. We can honor them by holding the nuances of their lives up to the light. We can become what they could not become. In doing so, we set them free' *San Francisco Chronicle*

'The writer masterfully blends Arabic parable and Western resolve to enter her illiterate mother's mind and heart, writing what [her mother] could not. *The Locust and the Bird* conquers the distance between mother and daughter, revealing the tragedies that can ensue when cultural machismo forces brave women into impossible choices' *More*

'The author beautifully captures her mother's impish character, her ability to turn every occasion into a laugh. Her inability to manage money is ever present, as is her warmth and her humanity' *Irish Examiner*

'Astonishing ... Spectacular ... [*The Locust and the Bird*] is Hanan al-Shaykh's masterpiece. Kamila is Hanan's most extraordinary character' *Jakarta Post*

'Hanan puts aside her old resentments to tell her mother's remarkable and poignant story, and gradually comes to understand all her mother has been through, and how she survived' *Booklist*

'The author's journalistic talent reveals itself in her ability to get past her own abandonment to paint Kamila as a vivid, wilful girl who lived as though she were the heroine of a great film' *Publishers Weekly*

'Hanan al-Shaykh is one of the most courageous writers of the Arab world. Her novels, chock full of marvelous characters, conventional and unconventional, have drastically changed how women in the Middle East are perceived. This memoir, the story of her irrepressible mother, might help explain the origins of Hanan al-Shaykh's singular ability to trail-blaze' Rabih Alameddine, author of *The Hakawati*

'*The Locust and the Bird* puts to rest, with much gentleness and ease, every stereotype about the Arab world and its women to which we have long grown attached' *An-Nahar* (Beirut)

'An exceptional book, beautifully and painstakingly crafted to make the reader laugh and cry; sometimes funny, sometimes heartbreakingly cruel ... It is an unforgettable story of family, of tragedy and joy, a story' *Middle East* magazine

'Comic, tender and mischievous ... A fearless, pioneering writer' *Independent*

THE LOCUST AND THE BIRD

MY MOTHER'S STORY

HANAN AL-SHAYKH

Translated from the Arabic

BLOOMSBURY

LONDON · BERLIN · NEW YORK

Bloomsbury Publishing Plc
36 Soho Square
London WID 3QY

www.bloomsbury.com/hananal-shaykh

Bloomsbury Publishing, London, New York and Berlin
A CIP catalogue record for this book is available from the British Library

ISBN 978 1 408 80084 3

Typeset by Hewer Text UK Ltd, Edinburgh
Printed in Great Britain by Clays Limited, St Ives plc

To my sisters and brothers

ONCE UPON A time, a king was taking a stroll in his garden when a locust flew into the wide sleeve of his robe. A bird, in hot pursuit, flew in after it. The king sewed up the sleeve, sat on his throne and asked his people, 'What is up my sleeve?'

No one knew the answer. But it so happened that a man named Bird, who was desperately in love with a woman called Locust, was standing in the crowd. He came forward, only the face of his beloved in his mind, and proclaimed to his king, 'Wails and tales. My life story is one long revelation. Only the locust can capture the bird.'

DRAMATIS PERSONAE

Kamila	my mother
Kamil	Kamila's brother
Hasan	Kamila's half-brother (the lute lover)
Ibrahim	Kamila's half-brother (Mr Gloomy)
Khadija	Ibrahim's wife
Manifa	Kamila's half-sister and first wife of Abu-Hussein. Mother of Hussein the Ideologue, Hasan and Ali, Kamila's nephews and later stepsons
Raoufa	Kamila's half-sister (married to the gambler)
Abu-Hussein	Kamila's brother-in-law through his first marriage to Manifa and later her husband (the Haji)
Maryam & Inaam	Kamila's nieces (Raoufa's daughters)
Fatme	the seamstress
Fatima & Hanan	Kamila's daughters to Abu-Hussein
Fadila	Kamila's friend
Muhammad	Kamila's second husband
Miskiah	Muhammad's sister
Ali	one of Muhammad's brothers
Ahlam, Majida & Kadsuma	Kamila's three daughters to Muhammad
Toufic & Muhammad Kamal	Kamila's two sons to Muhammad

HANAN

Prologue

I AM IN ONE of three black limousines roaring through the streets of New York City, like barracudas on speed. I see the lights and hear the clamour. There are white roses in my daughter's dark hair, and an ivory one in the buttonhole of her fiancé, whose hair I now see combed for the first time. Today is their wedding day.

I had never imagined a wedding in the presence of hundreds of guests. Nor that my children would be choosing a theme for such an event, as has become the fashion with so many Arab weddings. (Botticelli's *Birth of Venus* is one example I remember, where the bride rose from a vast shell as it opened electronically.) But I also hadn't imagined that my daughter would marry just as I had thirty-two years earlier, with neither a wedding party nor a white dress.

My daughter is not in the white-leather dress she imagined designing for her wedding, long before she fell in love and thought seriously of marriage. She is not wearing the veil of white lace, which, years before, she made her father buy for her for Halloween. That veil was eventually given to our Moroccan au pair, herself about to be married. (It may still be in Morocco, being handed on from one bride to another.) I used to smile, thinking of that veil, perhaps the only English one to cover the face of a shy Berber bride, waiting anxiously as the hands of her groom lift it to see her face for the first time.

Instead, my daughter has chosen a suit for her wedding day: short jacket and knee-length skirt of soft blue, with traces of pink and beige. My own wedding dress was a plain ordinary blue, short and very sixties. It occurs to me that my mother wore a white gown on the day of her own wedding. My mother's wedding day! No, I cannot call it that. It was the day on which she was sacrificed.

I try not to think of Mother now. Yet I no longer see the lights of New York. I don't hear its crash and roar. I see my mother being forced into a white wedding dress, a tiara of artificial flowers being placed on her head. She pulls it off, along with a chunk of her hair. She tears the dress off, grabbing a jute sack used to wipe the floor, wrapping her body in it, racing to the stove, blackening her face with soot, howling and howling as she tries to push away the hands that surround her. She is a tiny fish, netted.

My daughter blows me a kiss. My son-in-law brings me back to this day of happiness with a kiss of his own. I banish my mother's agony with sudden guilt. Why didn't I tell her when I myself was getting married?

But then, I didn't really live with my mother. I can count the times I saw her as a child. When I did, it was as though she was a wild, chaotic neighbour. She had no authority over me. If she was upset about something I had done during my rare visits – like the time I played 'La Poupée qui fait non' on my portable gramophone for the tenth time – all she could do was wail.

Is it right, though, for children to marry in secret, in the absence of those who gave them life? I married in secret. No party. My father learned of my marriage when a friend congratulated him. As the expression on his face changed from embarrassment to suspicion to confusion to panic, they showed him the newspaper I worked for and read out the news item. My father slapped his face with both hands and wept. He pounded his chest and wept again. When he got home, he found a telegram stuck to the door. He rushed to a neighbour and asked that they read it for him, because he read nothing but the Quran. 'Dear Father STOP Married STOP My love STOP Hanan.'

A devout Shia Muslim, my father had long since reconciled himself to the fact that I would not marry a man of faith, as he had once hoped before I revealed my true colours, as a rebel at heart. Nevertheless, to have chosen to marry a man from another faith – a Christian – was as unimaginable to him as a trip to the moon.

My mother, on the other hand, was ecstatic when my sister told her I had eloped. She ululated and danced, breathing a sigh of relief, although I was only twenty-three years old. When we met, two months after my wedding, she took me in her arms and tried to lift me. Laughing, she told me how she had stretched out her hand and asked the statue of a poet who shared my husband's name for some money. 'We're relatives now!' she told it.

My marriage was my mother's victory. With it, she triumphed over everyone who had never failed to remind my older sister and me that we wouldn't find good husbands – not only because of our humble background but because of what our mother had done. Like mother, like daughter … In Arabic the words are harsher: 'Tip the jar on to its mouth [stand it upside down] and the daughter like the mother goes south.'

My mother fell in love with a man who was not her husband. My mother left home.

I wasn't good marriage-material either. Too independent. Too liberated. At eighteen I went alone to Cairo to study. I caused a scandal there and in Lebanon – I had a love affair, of course, with a well-known, well-married Egyptian novelist twice my age.

My mother couldn't have cared less that I married a Christian. In fact, she may have believed that my reflected glory would improve her own social standing. I had married a man – the man who is still my husband – from a family famous enough to have its line charted by historians.

So why didn't I tell her? The truth is that it didn't occur to me that she might want to share in my happiness. It had been years since my mother had entered my thoughts. When she left home, I tucked her out of sight, in a box in my head. I was seven years old. I decided that a voice had given birth to me.

A voice kept me company. A voice whispered to me, described things and emotions, asked questions. A voice taught me how to take care of myself. My own hands dressed me, put my shoes on, braided my hair. I found myself detaching from my father, too. As loving as he was, he stayed much closer to God than to my sister and me. He prayed constantly, his tearful eyes like red coals, his forehead imprinted from his prostrations, his arms and mind raised towards heaven. The more my father trembled before God, the bolder I became.

But the voice understood only too well my mother's absence from the house. It made me stare at the cupboard in the bedroom my sister shared with my father and his wife. I would look at my stepmother's belongings. I would wonder how the tiles, with a pattern like a smiling Japanese face, could continue to smile when my stepmother's only pair of shoes lay there, instead of my mother's.

The same voice put a pen in my hand, so that I could describe how my mother and the man she loved became one against me, my father, my maternal grandmother and my uncle's family – but never against my sister. Somehow she remained joined to them, always excited, always anticipating when and where she might next see them.

I used my mother's absence to encourage people to take an interest in me. One of them was the music teacher who took me to see *Never Say Goodbye*, a film about a mother who abandons her daughter. I was terribly proud that, unlike the other children in my neighbourhood, my life was the stuff of movies.

At that time Lebanese coins had a hole in the centre. I threaded some into a bracelet and, each time my hand brushed against a table, their jingling sound promised me maturity, control, freedom; promised me that I could cope with the neighbourhood children's taunts about my absent mother. The voice helped me to seduce them. I was like a magician: I told stories and did funny imitations. I could make them laugh. I could show how little I cared about our mother's desertion. But her absence was a kind of presence, like a photograph that fell down and shattered into a million pieces, leaving its dusty contours etched for ever on the wall where it had hung.

I longed to escape. When finally my father's prayer beads told him that I could go away to study, I left for school in Sidon. There I met and eventually shared a room with Leila Khaled, the Palestinian who, years later, in 1969, would become the first woman to hijack a plane. We became close, moving our beds into the room used for storage, away from the other girls. If I think now of what bound us two girls together and made us happy to occupy that damp storeroom which was inhabited by many snails, what comes back to me is a sense of alienation, of not belonging. Leila had grown up in a refugee camp; I was running away from my family.

Two years later, at the age of eighteen, the voice challenged me to travel to Egypt. I had heard the song, 'Take me back to Cairo ... beside the River Nile ...' and when I met a Lebanese student who told me about a school in Cairo that didn't insist on geometry and algebra, I began to hear that song, over and over.

To raise money I persuaded the editors of literary magazines and newspapers to give me the chance to interview politicians about their first love, showing them the articles I'd written in the student pages of a newspaper. Two months later I'd managed many interviews, and I had some money. My father did not consult his prayer beads this time. I showed him the money and recited the Prophet's Hadith: 'Seek knowledge from the cradle to the grave; and seek knowledge even if you have to go to China.'

Egypt was much closer than China. My father tried to convince me that there would be no stigma in arriving in Cairo with my things in a cardboard box, but I knocked at one neighbour's door after another until someone lent me a suitcase. I went.

Back in Beirut, four years later, the voice helped me to control my feelings of suffocation and to see life differently: my home as free lodging, my stepmother simply as an unpleasant, childless employee, my loving father as a Sufi living in his own shrine. His tears were tears of love – he couldn't bear to think of me rotting in hell because of my refusal to pray, cover my hair, or wear long sleeves.

As soon as I could afford it, I left home. I lived in a women's hostel in a district by the sea. Mine was a fully independent life, away from family, from my neighbourhood, working long hours as a journalist and broadcaster. And the voice stayed with me until I turned twenty-three, fell in love, and decided to marry.

It was the voice, not my father, not my mother, that gave me away, at the moment when the man I loved asked about my parents and I answered, 'Don't worry about them,' and held his hand.

Little did I know then that, many years later, my mother would convince me to reconsider that dismissive anger of mine, to surrender fully to the past, to meet her as if for the first time in my life. On one of my yearly trips to Lebanon, I sat with my mother on her balcony overlooking Nourwairi Street. Taxis were beeping at pedestrians. Cars were beeping at taxis. Through loudspeakers small-truck vendors were announcing to the world, 'Best onions. Best potatoes.'

On her balcony Mother had created a garden: potted plants were everywhere, alongside a frangipani apparently unchanged in forty years, still not fully grown. A family friend appeared, accompanied by a daughter who was about sixteen. My mother welcomed them as if she were surprised by their visit. Somehow I guessed this wasn't the complete truth. My mother knew that I preferred to see her on her own, not in a sitting room filled with neighbours, relatives, friends and their friends.

The guest came straight to the point. Could I talk to his daughter, give her some advice about being a writer? She wanted to become one. He snatched the exercise book that she had been clutching, along with her sunglasses, and handed it to me, confident that his mission was virtually complete. He then joked with my mother, shook me by the hand and left. I winked at my mother. I understood her ploy. We both smiled.

I asked the girl when she had begun to write. She mumbled something and then, to my surprise, she asked me if I could remember the first thing I had written.

I laughed and said, 'Yes, I can. I wrote about a fruit fly that flew up Muhammad's nose and drove him crazy.'

Turning to my mother, I asked, 'Do you remember, Mama, how as soon as he entered your father's tent – wearing his beautiful suit even in the boiling heat – the fly went straight for Muhammad's nostril. He sneezed and sneezed!'

My mother laughed. I laughed too.

She said, not unkindly, 'A man like Muhammad, thinking of himself as so strong and mighty, so important, and then a fly no bigger than a mustard seed manages to throw him off balance.'

I opened the girl's exercise book. She had written the title of her story in red ink, the text in blue, and her signature at the end in a purple flourish. I couldn't get past a few sentences. I turned the page and saw that she had copied someone's drawing of the singer, Madonna.

'Do you also like drawing?'

The girl was pink with anxiety.

'I like to write, draw, act, sing, dance, but writing is what I like best.'

I gave her exercise book back to her.

'Writing will be your best friend.'

I knew that my mother would want me to praise the girl's writing, but I couldn't. My mother shifted her gaze, looking at me now.

'Have you written about Muhammad and the fly in one of your books?'

'Maybe somewhere … I forget.'

The girl stood up, kissed my mother and then me on both cheeks and left, clutching her exercise book.

Still standing, my mother looked intently at me again.

'What about my life story? When are you going to write that?'

When I became a journalist, Mother would have family or friends read aloud what I had written. Illiterate, she couldn't read for herself anything that I wrote. However, it was a series of articles about prominent women that got to her. The articles featured Lebanese society matriarchs and *grandes dames* who were politically active, both openly and behind the scenes. The articles had attracted a lot of attention and my mother was among the first to criticise them.

'Those women were privileged. Maybe nobody encouraged them to do what they did, but at least they were not oppressed. But what about the women who are treated as less than human because they are born female? You don't need to go out looking for such women. Here I am, right in front of you! Why don't you interview me? I could tell you how my father sold me for ten gold coins. I could tell you how I was forced into marriage at the age of fourteen, how I was promised to your father when I was only eleven years old.'

As she spoke to the young journalist I then was, her passionate words fell on me like drops of rain on to a waterproof coat, sliding away without trace.

I grew accustomed to my mother's pleas, each time a new novel or even a major short story of mine came out. 'Why don't you write my life story?' she'd say. 'It might be more beautiful or more magical than whatever you have just had published.'

I was deaf. I believed I already knew everything about my mother. She was forced to marry my father, fell in love with another man, and left our home. That was it.

In 2001 the Arabic edition of my novel, *Only in London*, was published in Beirut. I invited my mother to the book launch. She asked me what the novel was about and when I began to describe to her the book's theme of Arab women negotiating contemporary London and things not being as they seemed, she cut me short.

'Why are you still nibbling from other people's dishes?'

I rushed to my own defence.

'Don't I tell you often enough how you inspire me? Don't I come to you to remember proverbs? Don't I take your advice about the characters in my books?'

Again she cut me short.

'I don't want you to be inspired. It only means that you see things from your perspective, not mine. Take that story of yours, "The Persian Carpet". The mother in it is depicted as a thief. She steals the carpet not caring that suspicion lands on Elya, the blind cane-chair repairer. I loved Elya! I used to give him food and sing to him. No, you don't say anything about the mother having given up everything to get away from an ascetic more than twice her age, a man she was forced to marry. You don't say that the husband sold all of his wife's jewellery to save his shop …'

'Mama,' I began, 'that story is about the little girl and her fascination with Elya because he manages to mend the chairs even though he can't see.' I stopped. I couldn't continue. In my story the little girl trembled with burning rage when she spotted the lost Persian rug spread on the floor of her mother's new house, when she visited her for the first time after her parents had divorced. Not only did she wish that she could throw off her mother's arms from around her, she also wanted to sink her teeth into her mother's white flesh. How could she have taken the rug and let the blame fall on the blind man?

My mother protested, 'Isn't it fair for the divorced mother to be attached to a little rug? Doesn't the rug belong to her also?'

To myself I thought: Shouldn't the question be why the divorced mother was not sufficiently attached to her two daughters? Didn't *they* belong to her as well? Can my mother tell me why she didn't try to fight for custody, even if she was sure it was hopeless?

I almost spoke, almost snapped, but instead offered her the cliché about fiction: that the instant we put characters on the page, even when they are based on people we know, they become fictional. Art.

My mother listened carefully. She lit a cigarette. She puffed and puffed as I imagined her lungs filling with smoke, ready to explode at any second.

'But if characters become different, how come Muhammad and me, and you yourself, didn't change at all in *The Story of Zahra*? It was obvious you copied episodes, incidents and places exactly. The only difference is that your Uncle Ibrahim took the character of your father. Let's not talk about this book any more. I suffered enough when it was read to me. My heart felt like it was in a mincing machine.'

Before I could say anything my mother sighed, lifted her hand to shoo away an insect as it buzzed between her and me.

'There's nothing for you here,' she told it. 'Go to the kitchen. You will find all the crumbs you need.'

This made me laugh and sigh in great relief.

'Mama, didn't you throw cheese to the little mice in the attic?'

She giggled, and slapped her hand.

'I stopped when I was told they would grow into fat rats.'

But then she said, 'In *The Story of Zahra*, Muhammad and I made you weep. You wrote that you wept so loudly that the whole world heard your cries, and sobbed. Except us. Although we weren't far away, you showed us as selfish and heartless. So much bitterness from my own daughter!'

I stood up, eager to leave, but then I registered my mother's despair. I knew she would suffer, believing that she had upset me.

I sat down and she changed the subject to the girl who had shown her writing to me.

'Did you notice her shoes, like lamp posts ... huge and high?'

I hugged her.

'You are so clever and witty.'

But she had started me thinking. Was that really what I had written? My question went into the void, into the noise and commotion of the street, to my mother, to the book itself. More than twenty years ago: Who was I then? What was I thinking? And wanting to say?

In the winter of 1976 I sat down in a small furnished flat in London and wrote the novel that became *The Story of Zahra*. With two suitcases and my two-year-old son, barely a toddler, and my six-month-old baby daughter, I had fled the war in Lebanon. My husband was in Saudi Arabia organising new work opportunities. And for two months I didn't unpack, hoping we could all go home to Lebanon.

We did return – every evening for a few seconds, accompanied by the commentary on British television. I saw Beirut wrapped in a black cloud, transformed by balls of fire, overrun by fighters, the Lebanese people fleeing in terror, hiding in shelters, in corners, lying dead on roads, killed by snipers. They spouted everywhere, mysterious creatures that exhaled only when their human targets fell to the ground. I had been certain that I was going to be killed by one of them no matter where I hid. That, combined with my fear for my children, was reason enough for me to flee not only Beirut but also Lebanon.

In a new country, with a new culture and language, I began for the first time to think about where I had come from, about the culture in which I had been raised, about what I had left behind. To understand the violence and why Beirut had become a demon playground – a bleak name even for the Lebanese to utter – I needed to write. Yet, to my horror and bewilderment, each time I sat down to write I saw myself as a five-year-old, hiding in the dark behind a door with my mother, shaking with fear, my mother's hand covering my mouth as a face spied on us. The image kept recurring.

I was scratching at old scars. Why, in London of all places, had the war inside me erupted? I had been confident that I had released my mother from that box inside my mind; and that marrying and having my own children had mended the rupture between us. And now I was being taken by my fountain pen from the cold of London to the haze of that room in Beirut where we had hidden behind the door. I felt again the confusion that bubbled inside me each time we took a different and unfamiliar route, rather than the one to the doctor's, even though at home I had heard my mother announcing that she was off to get a calcium injection to help straighten my bow legs. Yet instead of seeing the rough wrought-iron grilles over the frosted-glass door of the surgery and coloured shadows behind the door, I saw a room engulfed in darkness, with brown furniture. And instead of the round, flat face of the doctor, his thin ginger hair combed like rows of vermicelli, I saw a tall man, with thick, brown, straight hair, wearing a black-and-white houndstooth tweed jacket, who handed me a hairless pink rubber doll, no bigger than my finger.

Eventually the time came when I realised that my mother wanted us to be inseparable, as close as the orange and its navel – but only when she was meeting the man with thick brown hair. I was sharing her secrets. I was to be witness to her lies and fabrications, but unaware that she meant me to confuse faces and places, and doctors with lovers.

Take the memory that begins under the walnut tree. In the background, I can see the desolate mountains, valleys, hills, red stones and thorny bramble bushes of Bhamdoun. I am tiny, running with my older sister, with my mother – not very much older than my sister and me – and with my cousin, Maryam. Then I see the tall man, with the brown straight hair, talking with my mother in Asfouri and I cannot understand a word. We call it the language of birds, so why are they speaking in words and not chirping and tweeting as canaries do? I see him lying with his head on my mother's lap. His eyes are the colour of quince jam. They are half-open. Is he sleeping, or trying to sleep? I didn't know then that eyes like his are called dreamy, passionate. My mother is singing to him, 'Oh sleepy love'. I ask myself: Why is she lulling a grown-up man to sleep? Why did we have to run so fast to meet him? Couldn't she wait to sing her song?

A photograph was taken that day. I saw it with other photos when my mother took them out of her bra to show them to Maryam, who lived with us. In the photo, my sister and I stand side by side looking at my mother and at the man who, that day, is wearing a white blazer. I am trying to understand the game. He is standing now and lifting her up in his arms as though she were a baby. Each of them takes turns being a baby. Years later I saw the photo again, this time with a stab of agony. The rocks, the walnut tree, the summer sky, my mother's laughter, and her frail shoe almost falling off her foot – they were all there. But where my sister and I had once stood was a blank spot.

Was I really there with my sister? Did I really hear my mother singing to that man 'Oh sleepy love'? I held another photograph. In it my mother, my own family and the family of my uncle are gathered on the rooftop of our house, surrounding my cousin who was about to take the boat for America. I thought of rubbing my mother's face out of the photograph, just as she had done to my sister and me. I didn't, though. It wasn't until much later that I understood what held me back. It was because, although she is looking at the camera, it is as if she cannot see it. It is as if she is already far away from us. In the midst of her family, she is gazing off at the future.

'So,' my mother persisted, 'you haven't answered my question. My life story – why don't you write it? Perhaps you are not curious to know about my childhood, and why I left you?'

We were still sitting on her extremely noisy balcony. The ashtray cradled her many cigarette butts. No, I had never wanted to hear her story. And whether from fear of pity or sadness, I didn't want to intensify the past. It was gone and the distant years had faded away.

'Listen, Hanan, listen to me, *habibti* [darling], I don't think I can bear keeping my story to myself any more. I am warning you, if you are not going to listen to me, I will tell it to the walls – or maybe to that girl with the lamp posts on her feet.'

I wasn't ready. I was afraid that she would seduce me, as powerfully as the ocean tempts someone to plunge into its cool on a hot day. I feared that she would weave her charm around me, creating a web made from sugar. I would succumb like so many before me: old, young, women and men. I would find myself believing every word, even when I should doubt her. I knew perfectly well why she wanted to tell me her story. She sought forgiveness. But how could I betray that first realisation of mine as a child that it was *places* that snatched away loved ones, that it was that fake doctor's surgery that took away my mother?

How could I forget the times when I heard thunder – and wondered if my mother was also hearing it? Or when I saw lightning and wondered if she had seen it at the same moment I had? Or when I shouted, 'He ha ho!' and didn't know whether the breeze carried my voice across the neighbourhood to where she lived? How could I hush her voice, when she had held my doll to her breast, crying and singing to it as though it were her own beloved child:

> Go to bed my little doll
> so the little bird can come
> to wake you up at dawn …

And what about the moments when it was not I who wanted to bite my mother's flesh, but my mother who was biting me, leaving a circle of teeth marks on my hand like a perfect drawing – for in those days she was a child herself, and would bite in anger. Beatings were for older mothers.

But now, neither of us were children. My mother handed me a cigarette, knowing that I didn't smoke, and in fact that I'd never given up pleading with her to stop.

I asked her if she wanted to go to a café by the sea.

Her answer was, 'I was never so desperate to read and write as I am now, if for no other reason but to write my story. Let me tell you how it hurts when a piece of wood and a piece of lead defeat me.'

When I asked her what she meant, she said, 'Isn't a pencil made of wood and lead?'

I looked at my hand. No teeth marks.

My hand was ready to pick up a pen. For the first time I was ready to hold up our past against the light.

Finally I said it.

'Let's begin.'

In classical Arabic, as though she had memorised it over and over again, my mother offered her first words.

'Wails and tales. My life story is one long revelation. Only the locust can capture the bird.'

KAMILA

1932: Ever Since I can Remember

I T ALL BEGAN on the day that my brother Kamil and I chased after Father, with Mother's curses ringing in our ears. I hoped and prayed God would take vengeance on him. He'd fallen in love with another woman, deserted us, and married her.

Mother had been to court in Nabatiyeh[1] to seek child-support payments, but it did no good. Kamil and I were hunting for him so that he would buy us food. We ran over the rocky ground to the next village where he lived. We searched in the market at Nabatiyeh, asking people where we might find him. The sound of his voice and his loud laugh finally led us to him; he was too short to spot in a crowd, much shorter than Mother. Following her instructions, we asked him to buy us sugar and meat. He agreed immediately, telling us to follow him. We tagged along, our eyes glued to his back, terrified of losing him among the piled-up sacks of burghul[2] and lentils, camels, donkeys, sheep and chickens, hawkers and vendors peddling their wares. At times he disappeared and we'd panic, thinking we had lost him for ever; then he'd reappear and our spirits would soar. Finally he gave up trying to lose us. He told us that he had no money and could buy us nothing.

---

1 A town in the inland part of southern Lebanon where a large percentage of Shiites live. It is divided into 'Upper' and 'Lower' districts.
2 Cracked wheat.

He described how to find our uncle's cobbler's stall near by and then he vanished.

Kamil yelled Father's name as loudly as he could above the vendors' cries and the bleating of the animals.

'Listen, boy,' said a man selling sheepskins. 'That voice of yours is about as much use as a fart in a workshop full of metal beaters!'

We made our way back to Mother. She was waiting with her brother at his cobbler's stall. When she saw we were empty-handed, she frowned and swore she'd go back to court. We arrived home with no meat, no rice, no sugar. Mother made us tomato *Kibbeh*[3] without meat. She squeezed the tomatoes and the red juice oozed between her fingers. Did the tomato pips feel pain and try to escape, I wondered? Didn't Mother say that Father had crushed her heart?

Mother kneaded the *Kibbeh*.

'Look how red it is, and there's burghul in it, just like real *Kibbeh*,' she said brightly.

Like real *Kibbeh*? Who was she fooling? Where was the raw meat to be tenderised? Where was our wooden mortar and pestle, which I would recognise out of a thousand? Real *Kibbeh*? Then why wasn't Mother extracting those white, sinew-like bits of thread and making a pile of them, leaving the meat looking like peeled figs?

The next day Mother took us to court and talked to a man called a sheikh, who wore a turban shaped like a melon.

'My husband's refusing to support them,' she told him, pushing us forward. 'How am I supposed to feed my children? By cutting off a piece of my own hand? How am I supposed to clothe them? By flaying my own skin?'

---

3 A popular Lebanese dish made of ground lamb, grated onion and cracked wheat.

We listened as the man in the turban talked to Mother. He used one phrase that stuck in my mind: 'The payment due to you will be sitting right there, in the middle of your home.' I thought he meant it would happen literally; I didn't realise it was a figure of speech. The moment we got home I started pacing the floor, the way I'd seen older people measure things, even graves. When I'd calculated the exact middle of our home, I sat by the spot and waited for the lira to appear.

A neighbour came in to offer Mother advice.

'Let him have the children,' she said. 'Stop torturing yourself!'

'Get out of my sight!' Mother yelled, and chased her to the door. 'Before I throw you into the prickly pear bush!'

Needless to say, the money never appeared, not in the middle of the house or anywhere else. One day, Kamil and I were playing with some children at the front of the house. Mother was busy in the vegetable plot picking some of the beans she'd planted and hunting for wild endive and chard. Father arrived and asked us to go with him to the market so he could buy us clothes, meat, sugar, molasses and sweetmeats. We were so hungry and excited that we forgot to tell Mother. Without even putting on our shoes, we rushed to Father and ran along behind him.

As we walked he kept adding to his promises.

'I want to buy you some new shoes as well. They'll be so shiny you'll see your faces in them!' he said.

He took us along a path between rocks, thorns and a few trees. But we knew this wasn't the way to the market; the path led to the neighbouring village, where he and his new wife lived.

'So she thinks she's smarter than me?' he told his new wife when we arrived at their house. 'They can live here. Then there'll be no expense and no headaches either.'

It was a long night. We tossed and turned, yearning for Mother. I worried that she must be imagining a hyena had pissed on our legs, enchanting us and stealing us away to its lair, where it would tear the flesh from our bones. Or perhaps she thought that the earth had opened up and swallowed us. But my brother assured me that the children we'd been playing with would tell her that we'd gone with Father. We fell asleep clutching each other, listening to each other's heartbeats, missing the sound of our cows in the night.

In the morning, I found I could not read Father's wife's expression. But at home, I had no trouble understanding Mother. I knew that I loved her. I also knew that, because Mother didn't like Father's wife, I wasn't obliged to like her either. I stared at her eyes, trying to discover the secret of their green colour – they were the first eyes I'd seen that weren't black. Did she put green kohl around them? Mother had black eyes – she ground black stones and used the grinds to line her eyes. We missed Mother so much that we couldn't swallow our breakfast of molasses and sugar. We had to sip tea with each mouthful.

My brother and I sat close to each other, staring and yawning, waiting for evening. Time passed slowly. It was the summer holidays and Father wasn't teaching in the second room of his house, so we didn't even sit and watch the lessons. We had never asked if Mother could send us to a teacher in Nabatiyeh; we knew that she couldn't afford it.

We made up our minds to run away just before sunset. There was no forethought; it was just the idea of another night in bed without Mother sleeping between us, a hand stretched out to touch each child, that made us leave. We waited on the porch until Father's wife put down a dish of lentils by the stone bread-oven. As soon as she disappeared inside to knead her dough, my brother grabbed the dish of lentils and poured the contents into his djellabah, gasping at the heat. Then we ran barefoot, back the way we'd come, over the brown and red stones, over the sparse vegetation, never stopping to worry about thorns or the scalding lentils. We kept running – not hand in hand as my mother used to instruct us. 'Promise me, you won't let anybody separate your hands, even angels,' she would say. I didn't even stop when I spotted, amid the rocks, a bush bearing a tomato the colour of anemones. Only when the fig trees and the big pond came into view did we slow down and begin to relax. When we spotted a grey rock called the camel (because it looked like one) we were certain we were on the way home. Thorns got inside my dress; they pricked my skin and hurt like hornet stings, but I wanted to see Mother and eat some of those lentils so badly that I ran even faster, as though I was swallowing the ground itself.

Darkness fell suddenly, as if the camel had blocked out the sun. We were terrified that Ali Atrash was going to jump out at us. Ali Atrash was the local madman; he walked with a wooden box tied so tightly against his chest that it seemed almost a part of him. When he breathed or cried out, the box jerked up and down. People said he'd once had a stash of gold coins, but awoke one morning to find them gone from the wooden box in which he hid them. When suspicion fell on his own brother, Ali Atrash went out of his mind. From that day on, he was scared of young children throwing stones at him. But they did it because they feared his madness. He would yell at them, nonsensical things like, 'Gold from the earth, gold from the earth!'

I tried to reassure my brother, telling him that Ali Atrash wouldn't harm us because he knew we were the children of a woman the locals called Little Miss Bashful. She had always treated him kindly, taken his hand when she met him, brought him to her house, sat him down on the threshold, bent over his shoeless feet and pulled out the thorns with her eyebrow tweezers, and given him food and drink.

Could he see us in the dark, we wondered? We each held our breath until we saw our house in the distance and knew for sure we were home. But before our joy could be fulfilled, we spied a figure wandering back and forth. I was sure it was Ali Atrash, but instead it was Mother waiting for us. When she saw us, she cried out and burst into tears. We whooped with pleasure.

'We've come home, Mother!' yelled Kamil. 'We've brought some lentils. I want you to have them.'

Mother began to sing, as if she was keening, and wrung her hands. She ran towards us, and we to her, until she wrapped us in her arms, weeping, kissing us and inhaling our scent.

'The bastard kidnapped you,' she kept saying. 'May God snatch him away too!'

She took us inside, and my brother scooped the lentils on to a plate. Mother had prepared some green beans and we ate with gusto. Then the three of us settled on the mattress. Mother sat, blowing on my brother's scalded thighs and my bleeding feet.

'Mother,' I asked, 'how did you know we would run away and come home?'

'I'm your mother, aren't I?'

I lay there, listening to the cows mooing in the back yard. I reminded myself that they snorted whether or not I was home, without knowing what was going on. Their huge eyes stared into the darkness as they lay down for the night. I stared hard through the darkness too, anxious to reassure myself that I was with Mother in the house and not with Father and his wife. This house would always stay where it was; I could see the bureau, the mirror, the living room, and the window.

I only felt sleepy when Mother finally lay down between me and my brother. The wind whistled and brushed the trees. The mooing soothed me to sleep, as if the cows were singing me a lullaby.

Door of Secrets

WHEN I AWOKE in the morning, the first thing I noticed was the moulding on the window frame. I could see a branch of the fig tree, trying to climb in through the window from outside. In Nabatiyeh, windows were called *bab al-sirr*, doors of secrets – maybe because we never knew what went on behind them. Mother reached out and picked some figs, rolled them on some moistened bread crusts, and shook a few grains of sugar on them, before handing them to us to eat. She propped our mattress against the wall and then we headed out to the field by the eucalyptus trees.

She told us to hurry.

'Get on with it before anyone sees us!' she said.

Why must we sneak our way into the wheat field? I wondered. The wheat had been cut and the field was empty. Mother bent over the red soil and picked up the leftover grain that was scattered on the ground, after the reapers had done their work the previous afternoon. I copied her every move. Spreading my skirt, I collected grain from the ground. The wheat gleamed like tiny bits of gold. But I was scared of the snakes that lazed in the shade under the stalks.

I asked Mother if the harvesters had left these bits for us, but she didn't answer. It took a few days for me to realise why it was left. After the farmers had reaped the wheat ears and transported them to the silo in bulging sacks, they abandoned everything else as worthless.

When we returned home, we were the same colour as the earth itself. We poured our caches of wheat grain on to a straw tray, which Mother had cleaned with both damp and dry cloths in case a lizard had slithered across it. She sent me outside to collect twigs from the thorn bushes. Mother used to say that my untamed curly hair looked like these bushes when I wouldn't let her smear oil on it after it was washed. When I returned, Mother had mashed the wheat with a small grinder and kneaded it into little loaves. She used the thorn twigs as kindling, put the loaves on the fire and baked them. When they were cooked we gorged on them, one after another.

Just before sunset she took us to another field to pick mushrooms that nestled between the wheat sheaves and the grass. We sang, 'Come on, mushrooms, pile yourselves up, get into heaps!' Mother fried them for us with some eggs.

Months had passed since we'd run away from Father with his lentils. We hadn't seen him since, but we heard village gossip. Mother assumed that he, in turn, must have heard how we lived on wheat left for the birds; and that we rarely visited the village shop, other than the time when I went in and burst into tears, begging for some treacle, and then returned home with most of it already licked off the aluminium plate. Mother remained determined to get the child-support payments she was due.

One day she put Kamil into new navy-blue trousers and made me wear a clean dress, which my half-sister – my mother's daughter with her late first husband – had sent from Beirut. We stood outside waiting, feeling proud and happy because we were off to market to get some meat, sugar, and treacle; and look for Father. When a peasant walked past with a tiny donkey as white as milk, Kamil latched on to it, grabbing its ears, and hugging it. The peasant told him he could have the donkey in exchange for his trousers. My brother accepted the deal on the spot. He took off his trousers, handed them over, and went back to hugging and kissing the donkey – as if the stray dog that now slept beside him under the covers wasn't enough. Mother was angry, but she took us to the market all the same, my brother riding on the donkey in his underpants. By the time we reached the market in Nabatiyeh, it was not meat I had on my mind, but coloured plastic bracelets and scarves called birds' feet, because they tapered into coloured threads that looked like the feet of hundreds of tiny birds.

We searched everywhere for Father.

A man praying on his rosary took pity on us.

'The moment your husband saw you coming he took off,' he told Mother. 'He melted away like a cube of salt, as the saying goes.'

'And I hope God melts him too,' Mother muttered.

It was my turn to ride the donkey as we headed home empty-handed. Each time someone stopped Mother to ask whether she'd managed to force Father to pay up, she'd reply, 'Good heavens, no! His heart's made of stone. I might as well think of him as dead and put my trust in God!'

Lying in bed that night with the dog and Kamil snuggled next to me, happy to be home, I wondered whether the cows were aware there was a donkey with them and whether they minded. I grabbed the dog's ear and began to sing the song I'd thought of when I saw the empty wheat field:

Do not rejoice, oh long-haired wheat,
Tomorrow comes the scythe
To do a merry dance and tickle your stomach,
To cut off those long tresses.
The songs of the fields will fade when the locks are all
    gone.

Eventually, we lost all hope that Father would help us. My mother did not have the heart to sell the cows so instead she found work picking oranges and lemons in the big citrus orchards. Mostly she took me with her and left my brother with a neighbour. On the way there we kept to the fields, crossing public roads and going down into the valleys. Time and again I would stop, so tired and my feet aching so much that I wanted to lie down to rest. But Mother would keep going and I knew I had to keep up. When we reached the field, Mother would find me a place under a tree, clear the ground of insects and anything damp, then spread out a sack for me to sit on. When she finished picking the fruit from the trees close by, she moved me along with her to keep me near. I had no sense of time; I kept singing, eating oranges, lounging about and listening to the songs of the workers and the gentle rustle of fruit being picked from the trees. I poked ants with a twig but left hornets alone.

Sometimes, instead of going straight home, Mother would take me to the River Litani to bathe. We made our way through the hills and valleys till the river appeared amidst the curving lines of rock and sparse foliage. When we reached the oleander trees – each one candy pink in colour and looking almost like an entire house made up of branches – we would stop. I would dash to the river and stand on the bank among the rocks, while Mother searched for a pumice stone with which to scrub me. Then she would grab my hand and we would wade in, until the water was up to my knees. My skin was white against the rocks and trees. Mother was terrified I would slip and get swept away. Her fear was infectious. I'd stand, petrified, as she scrubbed her own tall body through an opening in her dress.

Mother seldom smiled and I rarely heard her laugh. But on the last day that we visited the Litani, as she stood in the cool river, to my utter amazement she began to sing:

Oh compassionate friend,
Come and sing with me, and we'll comfort one another.

I remember how she poured water over me that day, saying, 'In the name of God,' and, 'Thanks be to God,' then smiled as she poured water over herself. Her black hair reached almost to her waist. And when she opened her eyes they were big and shining, as if the water had washed away her cares and the monstrous image of Father that hung over us. We came out of the river and walked along the bank collecting blades of lemon grass, folding them into bread with a little salt, and downing them hungrily. Once again Mother gave thanks to God.

It was the last time I heard my mother thank God before we left our home, the cows, the dog, the donkey, the fields, the Litani, and my friend Apple; before we went to live in Beirut.

For shortly after that last trip to the river she sat me and my brother down and said, 'It's time for us to leave the Litani behind. I'm taking you to Beirut. You can't spend your whole life eating chard and endive! So say goodbye to everything, because we can't take it with us.'

I didn't know what to think. I was curious to see Beirut, the place that made my mother cry, but at the same time I didn't want to leave Nabatiyeh. But true to her word, there came the day when she sold the cows, though she cried as she bade them farewell; and she gave the donkey to our Bedouin neighbour Rabiha. Her name meant 'winner', which she assured us meant that she always managed to come out on top. The dog seemed to realise his time with us was up and found himself another home.

It was time for me to say goodbye to my friend Apple, with whom I'd skipped and played jacks with sheep's knucklebones. Sometimes we would beat on sticks that we'd put up our noses and yell, 'Karkamah, Karkamah, Lord, let my blood flow.' And blood would indeed flow as we'd get nosebleeds. This made us terribly happy, because God had responded to our prayers and we knew we'd go to heaven for sure. I told Apple I wouldn't be away long, but she still began to cry.

'OK,' I said, 'I'll be away for as many days as I have teeth and not one day more,' an expression I'd heard the old people use.

I gave her everything *dah*, a word we used to describe pretty things: a red comb missing most of its teeth; a rattle and a baby's dummy; and bits of broken dishes that I'd collected from the village for playing house.

'Remember,' I warned Apple, 'the holy martyrs Imam Ali and Imam al-Hussein[4] will be your enemies if you play with anyone else besides me!'

'By God, I shall miss you so much, Kamila,' she sobbed. 'Make sure you never forget me!'

'I'll miss you too, Apple,' I cried back. 'Make sure nobody eats you before I'm back!'

I wondered if there'd be eucalyptus trees in Beirut like the ones I liked to cling to with one hand, while clutching my hair with the other, praying to God to make my hair as long as the tree and as soft and smooth as its leaves. I wondered too if I could pick damask roses in Beirut, just as the older girls did here. Like them I'd put the petals in a dish with some water and leave it outside the door overnight so the petals would catch the morning dew. Then I'd use the rose

---

4 Ali, the Prophet Muhammad's cousin, married the Prophet's daughter, Fatima. After Ali, the fourth Caliph, had been assassinated in 40 AH (661 CE), his two sons, al-Hasan and al-Hussein, became the figureheads of the 'Shiat Ali' (Ali's party), which was to become the Shia community within Islam. Al-Hussein was killed at the Battle of Karbala in 61 AH (680 CE).

water to wipe my face, and stand before the mirror. 'God,' I would tell myself. 'I'm so pretty!'

On our last night I slunk out to our garden plot to see if the cows had returned. Earlier in the day, when I was hunting for the cows' new home so I could say goodbye to them, Apple told me her mother had said that cows are like doves: they always return to where they came from. But they weren't there.

1934: Beirut

WE HEADED FOR Beirut in a Ford, not on foot, the way Mother would go when she felt a yearning to see her other four children who lived in the city. For these journeys, she left us with her only sister in Nabatiyeh and then walked for four days to get there. When she came back, her feet would be covered in blisters; they'd burst like balloons, but without making a sound.

I knew I had other siblings, two half-brothers and two half-sisters by Mother's first husband, who had been killed. If someone mentioned the word 'Beirut', Mother would put her hands to her cheeks and sing, 'Beirut, Beirut, you stole my children away from me!'

This confused me and Kamil.

'But nobody stole them. They all married there, didn't they?' Kamil would ask.

I hadn't met my half-brothers and half-sisters more than a few times, but I had a clear image of all four of them in my mind, with their olive-brown skin that was so different from mine and Kamil's. Even my mother was a shade or two lighter. The few times I heard one of them call her 'Mother', my heart missed a beat. I couldn't imagine Mother hugging anyone but Kamil and me. How could I accept that she had given birth to these others before us?

Mother's story came to me in bits and pieces. She had been married to a man from an illustrious family in Nabatiyeh that could trace its origins all the way back to the Crusaders, who once upon a time occupied southern Lebanon. The men in the family were renowned for their valour and for wearing golden gloves. By trade, Mother's husband was a muleteer who travelled between southern villages and the city of Beirut transporting goods. Together they built a house and had four children. They all lived happily together till the First World War began. Then the Ottoman authorities cut off supplies, confiscated the harvest, and people began to starve. Locusts gobbled up anything green in the fields and on the trees. When Turkey introduced general conscription, every single man within its starving domains had to join the army. Mother and her husband decided to make their escape. Mother left her valuables with her husband's family: an amber necklace and two hairgrips made of gold coins that she would twist in her braids. They hid their gold English 'Ottoman' guineas underneath their provisions in the bottom of the box strapped to one of their three mules, in case they were menaced by thieves and highwaymen on the remote paths.

They took the most rugged tracks through mountains and valleys, to avoid the normal Ottoman routes to Ma'an in Jordan. But before the family reached safety they were attacked by a gang, who stole the mule, along with the box containing the hidden gold. They didn't complain to the authorities at once, and when they did my bashful mother could not bring herself to look at the men the authorities paraded before them; and her husband was unable to pick out a culprit.

Under the cover of night, one of the gang members came back and killed Mother's husband. Any doubts about the man's guilt were resolved, but it marked the start of a life of misery for Mother. With her children and the two remaining mules, she joined a caravan on its way back to Lebanon. She hurried to her husband's family's house to collect her valuables, but the family shut the door in her face, claiming the valuables had been left as a guarantee for a debt owed by their now dead son. But Mother did not give up easily. She knocked on the door again and asked them to help her; she only abandoned hope when she was beaten and turned away.

She returned to her own house, cursing fate but grateful she and her children still had a refuge, only to discover that during her absence her home had been stripped of its furnishings. So she started work in the only way she knew: on the earth, in the fields with the crops. But however hard she struggled, she couldn't provide for her family. She took to knocking on the doors of feudal families and politicians, telling them her story. One offered to get the children admitted to an American charitable boarding school in the interior city of Sidon.

Mother agreed. But only one visit a month was permitted and she had to walk for two or three hours to reach them. Mother would stand below the girls' dormitory, shouting her daughters' names. As soon as they appeared at the window, she would burst into tears. Then she'd go to the boys' dormitory and call out the names of her sons. If they failed to appear, she would throw pebbles up to the balcony. The moment she saw the boys, there would be floods of tears.

Eventually things changed for Mother. A sheikh who had graduated from Azhar University of Theology in Cairo – the oldest Islamic university in the world – came back to his birthplace in south Lebanon and opened a school. He rented two rooms in Mother's house and moved in with his wife, a Turkish beauty called Hanim. As soon as she arrived in Nabatiyeh, women from all over the region came to get a glimpse of her lovely white complexion and luxuriant black hair, and to hear her Turkish accent. Soon the sheikh's diminutive son arrived to run the school for his father. Before long he was flirting with Mother, drawn by her height, her bright eyes and jet-black hair. She was attracted to him because he was so different from any of the men she knew. He was literate and witty, and could improvise poetry and recite early Arabic odes. Although she was ten years older, she felt sure he would help her take care of her four children. He began to call her Khadija bint Khuwaylid.[5]

After they got married, Mother decided to bring her four children back to live with her. One night she went to the school in Sidon and shouted for them one by one, urging them to jump over the school wall and come home. But they found it impossible to accept Mother's tiny new husband. What hope could there possibly be for them when she'd married a clown who wore a red fez in order to make himself appear taller? They grieved for their dead father and for the loss of their school. Soon each one left home again.

Easy-going Hasan, the elder son, left first to find work in Beirut. Serious Ibrahim lasted longer, helping Mother's husband, who travelled the villages working as a cobbler in the summer when the school was closed. One night Mother's husband decided to play a prank on him. He disguised himself in a cloak and jumped out at Ibrahim, yelling, 'Give me everything you have or I'll kill you!' Ibrahim panicked, the memory of his father's murder still fresh in his mind, and didn't laugh when his stepfather revealed himself. Furious and upset, he followed Hasan to Beirut.

A few months later the two girls joined their brothers. They left the house in Nabatiyeh to Mother, her new husband and my brother Kamil. Three years later I was born.

Beirut, I thought, as we travelled in the car, must lie beyond that mountain, that valley, that blue line. I watched

5 The first wife of the Prophet Muhammad, who was older than her husband.

as everything disappeared behind me. I saw the blue sea
for the first time and decided it was brother to the sky. I
watched them merge and dissolve into the distance. The sea
proceeded on its way and then stretched off into the horizon.
I wondered if the wind that struck my hand outside the car
window stayed the same or if it changed as the car sped
towards Beirut.

Eventually we arrived. Beirut was larger than the market
in Nabatiyeh; to me it seemed like the great wide world
itself. But I didn't see sacks spilling over with rice and sugar
as I'd imagined; nor did I spy people helping themselves to
treacle straight from the barrel. Instead they walked to and
fro, not stopping to greet each other as they did in Nabatiyeh.
Everything seemed strange to me, even the balconies. At first
I didn't realise they were connected to the rest of the house;
I thought they were separate houses. How could people live
in them, I wondered, when they had no roof? The houses
themselves were roofed with red tiles, one on top of the
other, just like pomegranate seeds. Large, tall apertures were
referred to as windows, not doors of secrets, or *bab-al-sirr*, as
we called them in the south. And Beirut's trees weren't like
the ones at home, although it wasn't long before I learned all
their names: azedarach, date, mulberry and locust.

We went to the home of my half-sister Manifa, and
her husband Abu-Hussein. We carried with us all that we
possessed in Mother's wooden box inlaid with velvet, brass
and tin: our clothes, hyssop, flower blossoms and marjoram.
We were soon joined by my half-brother Ibrahim and his
wife, who emerged from a house that was separated from
Manifa's by a small garden.

Now that we were in Beirut, Mother no longer needed to
go out at night to hunt for scraps of chard and endive with
which to make our dinner; instead we sat on the floor around
a tray containing a stew of potatoes and meat. Mother, Kamil

and I were very tentative about helping ourselves, even though there was much more food than we'd ever had in the south.

My brother-in-law instructed us in our manners and showed us how to eat.

'Lean your face over the tray. What a shame, such a little piece of bread!' (I'd taken the tiniest possible morsel.)

I thought: What a peculiar accent, and I couldn't help noticing that he was nearly as short as my father, although much thinner. My half-brother Hasan arrived and kissed Mother's hand. He brought with him a long loaf of bread that looked just like a rolling pin and was called a French stick. Then my other half-sister, Raoufa, came in. When she saw Mother, she hugged her and began to cry. She told everybody about her husband, who was addicted to gambling and horse racing. Her children were starving and homeless. I couldn't understand how such a thing could happen in Beirut.

As the days passed I didn't take much notice of my extended family. Instead I focused all my attention on sweets. I was totally absorbed by their variety, beauty, and their delightful names: white candyfloss, hazels, sesames. The vendor kept them in a glass-covered cart and went from street to street, calling, 'Wonderful hazels for sale!' I tried to get Mother to give me half a piastre; I went crying to Manifa; I rushed across to the vendor and stood before him in my wooden clogs, watching the boys and girls with shoes buying sweets and sucking on them with relish. I wore a pleading, hungry look on my face, my saliva flowing like a dog's.

'Why don't you buy some?' the vendor asked.

'I'm just looking,' I replied. But when he wouldn't relent and give me anything, I told him, 'No one will give me a piastre. I'm from the south and Father's dead.'

The vendor stared at me as though I hadn't spoken. I began to hate him. I tried to wheedle a coin from anyone who called at my sister's, but the only answer I got was, 'Oh, I wish I could. Tomorrow, perhaps. I wish I had something with me.' The one person I didn't dare ask was Ibrahim, whom I nicknamed Mr Gloomy. When he frowned, his eyebrows met like a black stick over his eyes. He didn't talk much to Mother and when he did he seemed angry and abrupt. He kept a watchful eye on me and muttered under his breath if I reached out for anything, even a nut or a bunch of grapes. I sensed that he hated me and I could not understand why.

Lying in bed one night, with Mother asleep between us, I asked Kamil if he'd have preferred to stay in Nabatiyeh.

'If we'd stayed there, you'd have died a thousand times over before you got to taste any treacle,' he said.

I stayed quiet and didn't ask if he'd noticed how Mother had changed. Although she still slept with us, I no longer felt her warmth. She'd begun to tell me off, something she'd never done before. She scolded me for walking too fast, for jumping, for saying I was hungry. I noticed how little she had to say apart from that; it was as though she'd become a table or a chair, one that could only sigh and moan and say, 'Oh God!' I decided that since we'd only left Nabatiyeh because there was no meat for us to eat, I should have been able to prevent our departure. I could have distracted the butcher, drawn out a knife and cut off a piece of the lamb hanging from his hook. Then we'd still be back there in our house in the south and Mother would still belong to us.

I watched other girls my own age and longed to play with them. There was one in particular who stared at me with contempt, perhaps because of my wooden clogs and my dress, which looked nothing like those the Beirut girls wore.

I tried to gain her sympathy.

'I'm not from Beirut,' I told her. 'Father's dead. Nobody will give me a piastre.'

'Your family's poor,' she said, and she turned her back on me.

Everyone in the house was expected to work for their food. Mother helped Manifa raise the children and manage the household. Manifa herself spent all day bent over the sewing machine making clothes or embroidering birds' feet on coloured headscarves for her husband to sell in the markets.

When my brother-in-law Abu-Hussein heard me begging for piastres, he announced that it was time I began work too. I was to wander the nearby streets, selling rubber bibs for nursing babies. Kamil was already working for Abu-Hussein, helping at his haberdashery stall downtown.

Very reluctantly, I listened to my brother-in-law's instructions after Mother made me feel guilty.

'Your sister and her husband are not obliged to take care of us. It's good of them to feed us and let us live with them,' she said.

So I made the rounds of the neighbourhood. I climbed stairs and entered gardens. I knocked on front doors and offered my rubber bibs. I forced them on people, pleading poverty; I wouldn't budge until they either bought one or shut the door in my face. I moved from house to house with a lump in my throat and, when I saw a pond with a fountain in the middle, it would remind me of how happy I used to be when I peed in the wilderness of Nabatiyeh, making patterns in the dust.

One day a woman opened her door and smiled. When I asked her to buy a bib, she was horrified.

'Who sent you?' she asked. When I told her, she clasped her hands to her head. 'Yay, yay!' she said in an accent I'd never heard before. 'I don't believe it! Aren't your family scared to death for you? Such a pretty girl! And how old are you?'

'Nine years old,' I answered.

She called out to another woman and told her my story. She clasped her head again.

'Yay, yay,' she said again. 'I can't believe it. Good God, show mercy on your servants! I've never in my life seen girls going around houses selling things! What kind of family must she come from? Don't you want to go to school?'

With that she purchased everything I had to sell, and gently pinched my cheek, and told me to take care of myself.

'Listen, my pretty girl,' she said. 'Look after yourself, do you understand? Don't let anyone fool around with you. If a man opens the door to you, run off quickly.'

I hurried home and told Mother what the woman had said. I asked her why no one had told me to watch out for myself or explained that I was to run off if a man opened the door. I said I wanted to go to school. But all Mother could do was sigh.

I began to cry and moan and beat my chest like an adult.

'I want to go to school; I want to go to school!' I shouted.

But Mother and Manifa only bustled round, hushing me to be quiet.

'Watch out,' they said, warning me against Abu-Hussein. 'Or he'll get you!'

It was just the kind of thing we used to say in Nabatiyeh to scare each other: watch out or else gremlins, hyenas, or the Devil himself will catch you.

Even Pigeons Go to School

'IT'S THE HONEST truth, by God, the Prophet, and Imam Ali,' I told Mother. 'In Beirut even pigeons go to school.'

Ever since we'd arrived in Beirut I had been watching the flocks of pigeons circling in the skies, splitting up, gathering together, diving then soaring up and down, and all in response to the orders of their owner, who cracked his whip on the concrete, blew his whistles, and gestured to the birds with a black cloth tied to a stick. This trainer, known as the pigeon-fancier, was a relative of the girl who had treated me with such contempt. When she finally deigned to talk to me, she said she'd be my friend only if I wore shoes instead of wooden clogs.

How I longed to wear proper shoes and dresses and be a pupil at school, sitting in a class with other girls my age, with real pens and notebooks! I begged my oldest brother Hasan to intercede on my behalf and get my family to send me to school, but he didn't want to get involved. He said he wished he was making a quarter of what Ibrahim and Abu-Hussein did, so he could pay for me to go. I realised that, although I was still young, the only way I could survive was to depend upon myself.

I knew that if I wanted to buy something I would have to steal some lira. So the following day, when my sister told me to go up to the attic and bring down five bibs to sell, I brought down ten bibs, keeping five of them hidden around my waist. I made my usual rounds, playing on people's sympathies and working hard. When I'd sold them all, I hurried to look for the sweet seller, handed over the extra money I'd collected, and bought hazels, gumdrops and candyfloss. Then I rushed over to the girl who had sneered at me, showed her what I had in my hand, and said I'd share them with her. I prayed with all my might to Imam Ali that she'd take some and become my friend. She took everything I'd bought and ate the lot. Then, regardless of my wooden clogs, she played with me for a little while before running off.

By this time I was sure that Mother no longer loved me. She did whatever Manifa, Abu-Hussein and Ibrahim told her to do and carried all the family problems on her shoulders. If my nephew became constipated, she'd fly into a panic; or, when Hasan failed to visit us for two days in a row, she imagined he'd been burned in the bakery where he worked. And as she became increasingly anxious, Ibrahim's frown deepened.

All day I would long for the night, when I could get into bed with Mother and bask in her warmth and affection like I had back in Nabatiyeh. Only then was I free of my household responsibilities. Since my sister had given birth to a new baby boy, my workload had increased. Now I had to take my two nephews to their respective schools each day, before returning home to the bibs and scarves. Having made my rounds peddling the bibs, I then had to bring the boys their lunches. Back home again, I helped my sister – rock the cradle, wash the nappies, hang them on the line. Next I'd hurry back to the schools, collect the boys and bring them home, where they'd be given sweets. Because I was with them I got some too. Then we'd play ball near the house.

One day when we were playing, I picked up the ball and held it close to my chest, ignoring the boys who were yelling at me to throw it to them. I held on to it tight, hoping that the neighbourhood children would see me and assume my parents had bought it for me – parents who lived, perhaps, in one of the huge houses with wide, wrought-iron balconies and windowpanes of coloured glass. I found myself waving up at a balcony, even though it was empty, until the shouts of my nephews brought me down to earth again.

As the Adha feast day[6] drew near, I heard the local girls chattering about their new dresses. I asked Mother about my dress for the feast, but she told me to be patient: my brother-in-law and Ibrahim were discussing the matter. Ibrahim suggested they share the cost of a piece of cloth and my sister could make me a dress, but Abu-Hussein insisted they buy me a second-hand one, because my sister was too busy. But when I saw the dress – with brown patches under the arms and a yellow line round the neck – I burst into tears. They also bought me a pair of second-hand shoes with huge soles and steel tips. I screamed and cried and swore by the Prophet Muhammad and Imam Ali that I would boycott the feast altogether.

I took out all my anger and distress on Mother.

'Tell them to buy me a new dress,' I screamed as I pounded her with my fists. 'Go on, tell them!'

Abu-Hussein began to scold me.

'Listen,' he said, 'every day is a feast day. Every day that God is not defied is a feast day.'

Then I had an idea. I remembered how Khadija, Ibrahim's wife, had made me take their daughter, who was three at the time but hadn't yet learned to walk, with me 'begging'. She hoped that, if I begged from strangers, a miracle would occur and my niece would get to her feet and walk. I had been afraid that this custom was observed only in Nabatiyeh; it was quite normal in the south to visit seven houses asking for a

6 Or Eid: religious festival for breaking the fast of the month of Ramadan.

piece of bread to get rid of a sty. But to my utter amazement, no one in Beirut was surprised at my request. They gave my little niece food, fruit and sweets without fail.

If only I could find someone to push me from house to house in a pram, asking, 'Please give this little girl a nice dress for the feast so she'll start walking'; or, 'Please give this late walker some shoes for the feast so she can stand up'; or, 'Please give this deprived child some white stockings and a wicker purse for the feast'. But who would push me, and where would I get a pram big enough? I was defeated.

It was the custom for the adults to give children money on feast days. My mother and Manifa gave me a little money; Ibrahim and Abu-Hussein declined. So, on the day of the feast, I put my money in my pocket, grabbed my nephew Hussein and, pretending we were off to visit my brother Hasan, set out for the Beirut pine forest, where the children's activities were being held. I knew I'd be in trouble if I got caught, because it was much too far away for me to walk. On the way there the girl who'd eaten all my sweets pointed a finger at me and began to sing, 'We're enemies now. If you talk to me, you'll die.'

I didn't want her to see me anyway, in that awful dress and those embarrassing shoes, so I walked behind her with Hussein, who was just five years old. We walked between the high trees, watching the world pass by. I grazed on pickled cucumber and parsnips and bought everything for us to share – even fresco, a sorbet made of crushed ice and syrup. I rode the swing with him at my side. As it soared up the children all yelled, 'We're the champions, yah, yah!'

Before we headed home, I cleaned our shoes lest the red earth give us away. Our trip to the pine forest must remain a secret, I warned Hussein, or I'd be punished.

The White Rose

IT WAS A while before I was allowed into the city centre, but finally one day Kamil took me to Burj Square, where he sold sewing materials from a stall alongside Abu-Hussein and Ibrahim's haberdashery stall.

'Hey, Kamil!' I shouted. 'This is the real Beirut; not like our neighbourhood. This is the one we always imagined!'

I took everything in: the tram that my brother Ibrahim drove in the mornings before going to work with Abu-Hussein at their stall, the cars with horns blaring, the horse-drawn carts, the liquorice-juice seller clanging his little cymbals, women without headscarves and men wearing sirwals,[7] just as they did in the south. I didn't know where to look next. I wanted to touch everything: cheeses of every sort and colour, chocolate, dresses, and shops selling gold. I was enchanted; it was as if I'd become a character in the huge billboard above the square, which showed a sad-eyed woman facing a man wearing a fez, with a white rose blossoming between them.

The poster was as tall as a building.

'That's a movie,' Kamil explained.

I was rooted to the spot, completely immobilised, enthralled by the woman's beauty. She was smiling and her white teeth were dazzling. She was wearing proper lipstick, she hadn't made do with rubbing a peeled walnut on her lips

---

7 Peasant's baggy trousers.

the way Apple and I used to, and her hair fell around her
face. I took off the sheer white headscarf that Abu-Hussein
insisted I wear, and tried to replicate her hairdo, till Kamil
grew impatient, gave me a punch and dragged me down a
side street. But I couldn't stop thinking about the face on the
billboard, especially the tears on her cheeks, which looked
just like soap bubbles.

I hurried home to tell my sister, who was still busy sewing,
about all I'd seen in Burj Square, especially the huge poster.
Manifa told me that everyone was going crazy over the film,
which was called *The White Rose*, in particular over the
famous singer Abdal-Wahhab who starred in it. With every
waking minute, every hour, every day that passed, I pestered
Manifa to take me to see it. Eventually she gave in, as long
as I promised not to tell a soul, not even Mother. When I
heard her telling her husband that she was off to visit her
sister Raoufa, and was taking me with her, I was astonished
and relieved. Maybe I wouldn't burn in hellfire after all for
telling lies. Even my sister, who prayed and fasted regularly,
lied to her husband.

It was dark in the cinema, but I managed to see the large
space, with seats close together. When the music started I
couldn't tell where it came from – I couldn't see a radio.
Then suddenly there was a light on the wall with lines on
it. I looked around but couldn't make out how the lines
were changing along with the light and music. Everything
seemed to come from a narrow beam of light, accompanied
by streams of dust, shining from a hole in the wall behind
us. Then a woman, a cat and some people moving around
appeared in front of me.

I whispered to my sister, 'It's just like a magic-lantern
show, only these people are moving!'

The heroine, Raja, played with her cat and another
woman scolded her. A man kissed Raja, his daughter, then

kissed the woman who had been scolding her. A young man named Jalal (played by Abdal-Wahhab) arrived wearing a fez, and found Raja kneeling to pick up her broken necklace.

He knelt down beside her and began to sing, 'No jacket, it makes me weep.'

After the film ended, the cinema remained dark. Manifa tried to hurry us out, but I wouldn't budge. I wanted to stay in my seat. Why had the actors spoken with such a funny accent, I asked; I had understood little. They were talking in Egyptian dialect, Manifa said.

'What is Egyptian?' I asked.

'There is a country called Egypt where all the films come from,' she answered.

I wanted to tell her I'd like to get a jacket for Abdal-Wahhab, because he kept singing and crying, 'No jacket, it makes me weep,' but I was scared she wouldn't let me. Could I steal Ibrahim's tram driver's jacket? I thought of its drab khaki colour and the sweat stains under the arms. Should I steal Abu-Hussein's jacket? The sleeves would have been too short for Abdal-Wahhab and it wouldn't even have reached his waist. Quite apart from these considerations, my brother-in-law prayed and read the Quran, whereas in the film Abdal-Wahhab actually spoke to a woman, sang to her, embraced her, then whistled as he hurried on his way. Such different men could never wear the same jacket.

That film, *The White Rose*, stayed with me. If I changed my name from Kamila, which means 'perfect', to Warda, which means 'rose', I told myself, I would be closer to the people in the film. I decided the movies were better than eating a whole tin of treacle, better even than talking to the Beirut girl or playing house in the vegetable patch with Apple.

After my trip to the cinema, I saw my easy-going brother Hasan in a new light. I nicknamed him the lute lover because he was obsessed with the lute. He loved to play it for Manifa and me when we visited him in his tiny room. I asked him in a whisper if he'd seen *The White Rose* and if he could sing like Abdal-Wahhab? He looked to left and right, then asked Manifa if her husband and brother Ibrahim were about. When she signalled no with a laugh, he began to hum and pretended to pluck a lute. Then he sang:

> Oh thou rose of pure love,
> God bless the hands that have nourished you!
> I wonder, oh I wonder, oh I wonder.

Then he mimed holding a rose in his hand and gazing at the flower.

I asked if he understood the Egyptian dialect, because I hadn't. Who had taken me to the film? Hasan asked, amazed. I lied and told him that I hadn't seen it, but our sister laughed and admitted she'd taken me. From this I understood that she was not afraid of Hasan; unlike her husband or our gloomy brother Ibrahim. In fact, she joked with Hasan and laughed in his presence.

Some time later, when my memories of the film had faded, Mother took me to visit my poor sister Raoufa, whose husband beat her whenever she criticised him or asked about the money he lost on betting on horses. I was astonished when Raoufa broke down to Mother.

'He's left us here on the mat and betted away everything. Dear God, I've actually thought about going out on the street and begging,' she said.

Despite Raoufa's distress, Mother never offered to seek help from Manifa's husband, nor from Ibrahim or Hasan, who had no money but might have brought her some bread from the bakery. I was so upset that I decided I should run away and live with the actors from the movie, in a place where people spoke to each other kindly and were concerned for each other's welfare. I knew for sure that they were cut from a different cloth than me, because they had all been to school.

Stone-Bearing Donkeys

IN THE SPACE of a night and a day, our house turned into a home of weeping and wailing. Manifa died very suddenly of fever. She was bitten by a rabid rat that was hiding in the pile of wood we used to heat the boiler.

Mother blamed herself for my sister's death. Coming to Beirut and staying at her house had brought bad luck, she said. She gnawed on her fingers, wishing it had been she who'd gone to collect wood that evening, not Manifa. She blamed the doctor too, for not connecting the bite with her fever; and for not realising till too late that Manifa had rabies.

My brother-in-law hugged his children and cried. It was the first time I'd seen a man crying, simply dissolving into tears, except for the men playing Imam al-Hussein in Nabatiyeh Square during the Ashura[8] commemoration. They would wail when Imam al-Hussein held his baby son and bade him farewell, knowing the end was near, as the enemies' arrow had struck the baby in the chest.

After Manifa's death I became a stone-bearing donkey. I was just like those beasts of burden that carried stones between the villages, with bleeding sores on their sides. Back

---

8 The Day of Ashura is on the 10th day of Muharram in the Islamic calendar. It is commemorated by the Shia as a day of mourning for the martyrdom of Imam al-Hussein, the grandson of the Prophet Muhammad, at the Battle of Karbala on 10 Muharram in the year 61 AH (10 October 680 CE). During the battle, fought over the succession of the caliphate, al-Hussein fought with seventy-two men against a thousand.

in Nabatiyeh, Apple's mother had given barley to them. 'You donkeys have to heave stones all day,' she would say to them, 'so here's something to soothe your weary legs and backs.' The donkeys would stop their braying and devour the barley. So what was my reward to be, I wondered?

The other adults in the family urged me to help Mother take care of my three nephews, lest they begin to feel the loss of their mother – particularly the youngest, who was not yet one and a half. Khadija, Ibrahim's wife, had been nursing and looking after him as though he were her own child.

Mother was overcome with grief, and she found it difficult to take care of the boys, although now that I was older I could see that she simply wasn't much good at household chores. I often overheard adults remark that she wasn't pulling her weight, or that she was lazy, like a closed book. They even told a joke about her: that one day when she'd bid farewell to her first husband as he got on his mule to go to work, she'd yelled out, 'Wait a minute, wait a minute, I was just going to bake you some bread.' But I was still only ten. My narrow shoulders could not bear the burden of the responsibility for the three boys and Mother.

Manifa's tragic death was not the only cruel twist of fate Mother suffered. Just a year later, Raoufa, my other sister, caught a fever and died within days. This time the cause wasn't a rat bite but a burst appendix. On her neighbours' advice she hadn't consulted a doctor, but instead had applied strips of boiled onion-peel and cumin to her abdomen. She left behind five children: two daughters and three sons, one of whom had survived polio and had a wooden leg.

A year after this second tragedy, Abu-Hussein and Ibrahim decided we should all live together, as Mother and I couldn't cope with looking after my three nephews on our own. So we all moved to a house, or rather a large apartment, in Ra's al-Nab, one of the more refined districts of Beirut – its name meant 'the source of a spring'. But there was no spring, only a tap gushing water outside a grocery shop.

Now we had my sister-in-law Khadija to help us and she was capable, intelligent and astute. She was also an energetic housekeeper. I loved her and she loved me. She combed out my curly hair – an act demanding patience and time – and came to my defence when Ibrahim yelled at me.

By this time Abu-Hussein's business had improved considerably. He'd withdrawn from partnership with Ibrahim, who now worked full-time as a tram driver, and joined with a fellow merchant to become co-owner of a shop selling imported men's clothing. This new business partner was very clever and my brother-in-law believed everything he said. They began to pay off Ibrahim's share in instalments, which made Ibrahim even more gloomy and angry. He could only watch as yet another opportunity slipped from his grasp – a pattern that had begun when Mother took him out of school.

Our new home was high up. To get to it we climbed a staircase with a black wrought-iron railing woven into a pattern that looked like children holding hands. Inside was a huge apartment, so wide that anyone would have thought it was a separate house. The walls stretched up very high too, and in the middle, at the very top, there were some nice decorated-glass skylights, which added to the light flooding through the many windows. Entering by the big wooden front door, we came into a large room called the lounge; to the right was my brother-in-law's room, which had a window overlooking the neighbouring garden. There were two other rooms, one bedroom shared by my nephews and Kamil, and another for Ibrahim's family. Between these bedrooms there was a corner where Mother and I slept; I thought of this space as my own house and often played there on the big mattress we spread out on the floor at night. Other visitors to

Beirut from the south – relatives and friends – would share our corner with us. For by this time our house had become a staging post for anyone on a trip to the city.

My favourite spot was the roof. When we went up the stairs into the open air it was as though we were in a lofty garden overlooking the other buildings. From up there we could see the fountain in a garden below, and a few trees scattered about, especially the luxuriant azedarach.

The move and our new good fortune only made Mother more depressed. She lamented the fact that Manifa, who had supported her husband so loyally, and worked so hard in the early days of their marriage, wasn't there to enjoy life now. Abu-Hussein's name was on the tip of every tongue from the south, whether they were settled in Beirut or only visiting. All spoke of his probity and hard work; they were so proud of this orphan boy who had risen to owning a business in Souq Sursouq[9] itself. Abu-Hussein's father abandoned his mother when he was just three years old. His stepmother tormented him and pulled his ears, and so he would run away and walk for hours to see his mother, who had remarried and moved to another village. When he was six, his father died. He had lost contact with his mother by then, and so a relative took him to the house of the most learned Shiite Muslim scholar in Nabatiyeh.

The sheikh taught him the Quran and how to be a devout Muslim and in return Abu-Hussein looked after his horse. When he was twelve he decided to leave the sheikh and the south and try his luck in Beirut. He began as an errand boy to a Beiruti family, and then became a peddler and finally a merchant.

In our new home, Mother grew sadder, but I was seldom unhappy. The windows were always wide open and songs

9 A famous bazaar in downtown Beirut. Sursouq is named after a family that owned a number of nineteenth-century mansions.

and music from neighbourhood radios worked their way inside. I used to hum the tunes and sing along with them. I was beginning to understand them now, and their language was the language of books, unlike the crude words of the songs I'd learned from women and men in the fields of the south.

> It's not Mother or Father I need,
> What I really desire is my olive-skinned lover.

'You are Hereby My Witness'

I WAS UP ON the roof one day when Mother and Khadija called to me to come. They told me I must go into the boys' bedroom and say the words, 'You are hereby my witness.' Then I could go back to playing.

Khadija gave me a white headscarf to wear. I went into the room and found myself facing a group of men in red fezzes and another man in a turban shaped like a melon, just like the one worn by the sheikh whom Mother went to see about her child support in Nabatiyeh. I tried to say, 'You are hereby my witness,' so I could run out of the room, but I was nailed to the spot, unable to speak. The man in the turban stared at the floor and mouthed sentences. What I could understand sounded like prayers: 'In the name of God,' and, 'May God pray for and bless the Prophet Muhammad and his family.' When he said this, the men repeated it after him.

Suddenly the man in the turban asked my age and Ibrahim answered, 'She's eleven years old.'

Then the man recited something again and I heard my name and Abu-Hussein's. Then he asked me to repeat after him, 'You are hereby my witness.'

I mumbled the words and rushed to the door, opened it, and found Mother and Khadija standing right there as though they had been listening.

I was afraid they would change their minds and stop me going back up to the roof to play, so I said, 'OK, it's done.

I said it. "You are hereby my witness." What more do you want?' Then I ran back up to the roof.

I was surprised that the grown-ups had been wasting their time listening to me repeat what the man in the turban told me to say. I was equally surprised that they were letting me play, rather than making me sweep the floor, clean the dishes – or telling me off.

I forgot all about what had happened that day and the words I'd uttered until nearly two years later when I met a young man who looked like a film star at the home of Fatme the seamstress.

Abu-Hussein had sent me to Fatme's to learn to cut and sew, because I'd been pestering them about school again. I was too old, they told me; the younger children at school would laugh at me. 'Let them laugh,' I said, but Mother replied that school lasted all day. Who would take the boys to school? Who would deliver my brother-in-law his lunch? Who would help with the washing? So instead I was taken to Fatme's house. She welcomed me with a big smile and, as soon as my brother-in-law left, I could feel her opening her heart to me.

I adored her. She was different from any woman I'd ever met. She talked loudly with a Beiruti accent, cursing, swearing and laughing – her laughter went on and on, just like the cry of the hyenas. There was always a cigarette dangling from her lips, and she would blow smoke in my face when she exhaled through her long nose. She had big eyes that could be gentle and furious at the same time. She never cried. She turned up the volume on the radio and drank coffee all day, one cup after another. Her teeth were as brown as dates, and she smoked and swayed to the music while she bent over the sewing machine or sat on the ground in the courtyard, with fabric spread out over her heavy thighs. Once, she sent me out for a pack of cigarettes and I was amazed at the way she pulled notes casually from her pocket. I told her that she was the only person I knew who did that; my brother and brother-in-law were so stingy that if they could they would've hidden their cash inside the crop of a chicken. She laughed, and told me to take off my headscarf, then grabbed my thick black hair. With the cigarette still dangling from her mouth, she told me how beautiful I was.

At the time, I didn't realise that the kindness and affection she showed me was because of her sympathy towards my plight. When I arrived late in the morning I would tell her what I'd been doing. 'I understand,' she'd say, 'I understand. You're like the stone-bearing donkey.' I wanted to live with her.

She told everyone who visited about my nice house and my brother-in-law who owned a shop in Souq Sursouq. She made me feel proud, but I still giggled as I acted out how Abu-Hussein walked, with his head down in case he stumbled over something in his path. I told her how he poked his nose into everything, like an old fussing hen.

I loved to watch Fatme's hands work their magic with the sewing machine. She taught me how to pleat, to gather, and to put on buttons. But the moment she left me to go into the kitchen and start cooking, I would sneak into her room, spread out her mother's prayer mat and slide underneath the brass bed, which stood high up off the floor.

There I'd sleep contentedly until she came in and scolded me.

'Come along you, get up. You're too spoilt!'

I was eager to get to Fatme's place every day. Needle in hand, I would sit there alone, far removed from the bustle of our house, from all the shouting and the demands for me to do this and not do that. Like the harvesters and farmers had in Nabatiyeh, I sang to myself as I worked, but not in the way I sang when I bathed at home. Then I had to sing quietly, so that Ibrahim or my brother-in-law would not hear me.

As I sang, I imagined myself as a heroine who embroidered while waiting for her beloved to return. He had been sent far away, because he was rich and she was poor:

> For love of you I have sacrificed my longing;
> Had I obeyed my heart,
> I would never have left you …

Then I would begin another song because I couldn't remember all the words of the first one:

> Oh thou rose of pure love,
> God bless the hands that have nourished you!
> I wonder, oh I wonder, oh I wonder.

One day, a young relative of Fatme's overheard me singing. He sat by the fountain in the garden, pretending to read, and waited until I appeared. I looked out of the window and saw a young man sitting by the edge of the fountain, as though a genie had conjured him out of the water and put him there. It looked like a scene from *The White Rose*, though this young man was not wearing a fez.

I listened as he asked Fatme in a gentle whisper, 'So where does this beautiful girl come from?'

'From Nabatiyeh,' Fatme replied.

He didn't look like any other young man I'd ever seen, either in Nabatiyeh or Beirut. Most of them had black curly hair and black eyes that were close together. They were either short or, if they were tall, then fat. The young man before me had straight brownish hair and eyes of a colour I could not name. And he was tall. He too had come from a village in the south, close to the sea. He went to school in Sidon. Fatme told me proudly that his family were what she called 'high-life'.

When it was obvious I had no idea what she meant, she added, 'Not the way it was down there. His family were notables and emirs. His father has been village mayor for the past thirty years. They own two race horses.'

I told her that my grandfather had owned a horse.

'Your grandfather owned a mule,' she replied with a smile. 'A horse is completely different.'

The word 'high-life' stuck in my mind. I was surrounded by people from the south who were struggling to make a living, while this young man's family (his name was Muhammad) made their horses race and earned money from them. I realised exactly what Raoufa's gambling husband had been up to: pawning everything they owned so he could bet on horses. I wondered whether that money had gone to Muhammad's family, and though I wanted to ask Fatme, I decided it was probably better not to. Instead I listened as she proudly and happily told me how the young man slept at her house once a month when he came from Sidon to Beirut.

From then on I waited for Muhammad to appear again in the garden with his book. When he appeared, I would watch as he gazed into the fountain and then at the house.

When eventually we did exchange a few words, the first thing I asked him was if he'd seen *The White Rose*. I stared straight at his jacket and asked if he owned another.

He hesitated a moment.

'Of course I do!' he replied. 'Why do you ask?'

I told him that I wanted to give Abdal-Wahhab a jacket, because in the film he sang, 'No jacket, it makes me weep,' with such passion.

Muhammad burst out laughing and began to sing the words as they really are: '*Ya ma shaakeit wa bakeit* ... [How long I wept and moaned. I witnessed joy and bliss and drank from the cup of desire].'

He asked me how old I was and I told him I was thirteen. He told me he was seventeen. He asked why I was learning to sew; did I really like embroidering and cutting so much?

'It's better than doing nothing,' I replied.

'If you'd gone to school,' he said, 'you'd know what Abdal-Wahhab was singing!'

I tried to hide my embarrassment.

'He was singing in Egyptian,' I hurriedly replied. 'That's why I didn't understand.'

'And how were you going to get the jacket to him?' he asked with a laugh.

Abdal-Wahhab must own a hundred jackets, he told me. I shouldn't really believe the things I saw on screen, even though such films were supposed to hold a mirror up to our society. *The White Rose* was the first Arabic film to contain singing, but the most striking thing about it, he told me, was that it showed how the rich never married the poor, or even middle-class people. The film's message was that this meant that love always suffered. He went on to tell me how Abdal-Wahhab's brother had beaten him because he loved singing and music so much. I told him in turn how my brother Hasan wanted to play the lute professionally but instead had to work in a bakery. I told him how, just like Abdal-Wahhab, he was scared to play the lute in front of his younger brother Ibrahim, who didn't approve of music. I also told him about Kamil and his lovely voice; that he wanted to become a singer but didn't know how to go about it.

I started looking forward to seeing Muhammad, especially after he said, 'God preserve that lovely dimple of yours!' He set me right on many things. When I told him how unfriendly my brother Ibrahim was to me, he said my brother was cross with Mother because she'd married my father and taken him out of school. His anger with her was channelled to me.

Muhammad began to offer me advice of all kinds; he did it with the utmost delicacy, as if tiptoeing on eggshells. Once he noticed how I kept my money in a pouch hung around my neck, under my clothes. He suggested I get myself a small handbag. As the weeks went by, he grew bolder and suggested I needed to wear a bra; and in fact I'd already noticed the way passers-by stared at my chest when I ran. When he saw me rubbing my teeth with salt and water, he gave me a toothbrush and toothpaste.

I watched as he did his homework, dipping his quill pen into the inkwell. I told him that the inkwell was just like a dark well and that the words looked like nails on the page. He nodded his head in amazement and asked where I'd heard the description. I told him I'd made it up and asked him to read what he'd written aloud. He read it aloud as if he was on the radio or was Abdal-Wahhab himself. I imagined he was the author of everything that he wrote, until he admitted that he copied things he liked from magazines.

> Oh life of the soul, oh soul of life.
> My heart is yours; is yours mine also?
> Tell me, I beg you, oh my life.

I asked Muhammad why there were gaps between the sentences; were they where the person dictating the letter had paused? Muhammad explained how poetry worked by leaving spaces between the verses.

I recited the song I'd thought up when I still lived in the south:

> Do not rejoice, oh long-haired wheat,
> Tomorrow comes the scythe
> To do a merry dance and tickle your stomach,
> To cut off those long tresses.
> The songs of the fields will fade when the locks are all
>   gone.

He made me swear the words I'd recited were my own. I could not understand why he wouldn't believe me. He'd once handed me the pen in order to teach me how to write my name and I couldn't even hold it properly. He was amazed that I composed things in my head when I could neither read nor write. He told me the image of the wheat stems being scythed down was beautiful. Describing it as an image when I hadn't drawn it seemed odd, but I nodded my head as if I understood.

The pieces of paper he kept hidden away in his pockets were not poems, but letters from his brothers, his family, and relatives in the village. I was desperate to know why they wrote to him. I thought that people only wrote letters when they'd emigrated to Brazil or Australia, not simply moved to Beirut. Why didn't Father write to us, asking after my health or that of my brother Kamil? After all, he was someone who composed poems and verses in the improvised form they called *zajal*. Why were Muhammad's family so concerned about each other, while those in my family only bothered about themselves? Why hadn't we received letters of condolence when my two sisters died? But then I thought about my uncle, the cobbler in the Nabatiyeh market, and my aunt who believed she had swallowed from a water pitcher a tiny snake, which was now living inside her. Neither of them had ever laid eyes on a pen and paper.

I asked Muhammad to read me some of his letters, so I could hear what his family told each other. 'Please,' I begged him.

He began to read me a letter from one of his brothers, and I concentrated on his mouth and eyes, as though I was observing a miracle.

My dear Muhammad,

How handsome you are and how beautiful your name! You are beautiful, and your body has been crowned

with that wonderful name. You have become beauty
personified, and now all men and women who set eyes on
you are solemnly bound to love you. So don't blame me
for loving you so much!

I rarely saw Muhammad without a book or magazine in
his hand. They were seldom connected with his studies, but
more likely to be poetry and stories. In our household the
only books were school textbooks for my nephews, along
with the Quran, of course, which occupied its special place
on a small piece of furniture we called the washbasin because
it had a slab of marble on the top. I questioned Muhammad
about every book he was reading, and, in turn, he told me
stories about the Caliph Harun al-Rashid,[10] Baghdad and
slave girls, and about people who had lived hundreds of years
before us.

When Fatme asked me what we'd been talking about, I
repeated everything he'd told me.

'So it's a history lesson you're getting, is it?' she
remarked.

When I was with Muhammad, I was like a cat wrapping
itself around the feet of someone who'd given it a bit of meat
or a slice of bread; or rubbing its body against a warm wall
when it was cold.

One day Muhammad asked me to go with him to see *The
White Rose*. Even though I wanted to say yes, I found myself
saying I couldn't, because I would be late to pick up my
two nephews from school. It didn't occur to me that he was
talking about going in the evening.

---

10 The fifth Abbasid Caliph. He was a great patron of art and
learning, and is best known for the unsurpassed splendour of his court
in Baghdad. Some of the stories of *The Thousand and One Nights*
were inspired by his opulent lifestyle, and King Shahryar (whose wife
Scheherazade tells the tales) may have been based on Harun himself.

'Do you want my brother to kill me?' I asked in amazement.
'Fatme will come with us,' he said.

'Listen,' I told him, 'even if Fatima, the Prophet's own daughter, were to go with us, he'd still kill me!'

Muhammad laughed and we agreed we'd go on Friday, the school holiday.

And that is how it was. He gave Fatme a pack of cigarettes with the two tickets hidden inside. We went into the dark cinema and Fatme sat beside me. Muhammad arrived a few moments later and sat next to her. He leaned across to explain this or that scene to me while Fatme wiped her eyes and sighed. Once or twice she touched her hand to his head.

Suddenly I found I could follow the Egyptian dialect; it was as though Raja, the film's heroine, had lifted me out of my seat, put her dress on me, and taken me with her to see the gardens. I was with her as she picked the white rose; with her as the car drove into the countryside. I became her, my heart exulting as Abdal-Wahhab sang to me. What else could I do but sing along with him, whom I loved and who was mine?

I longed for a gramophone and vases full of flowers. I wanted to wear a pleated skirt and a necklace. Why couldn't I be like Raja in the film, someone who was loved and spoilt by everyone, instead of just a stone-bearing donkey? Why was it that, whenever I looked up at the stars, Mother told me off? She was afraid warts would grow on my face. But Abdal-Wahhab could stare at the heavens and sing, 'I spent the long nights without sleep, without sleep as I counted the stars.'

When the film finished, Fatme dragged me out of my seat. I didn't want to leave, but we had to be out before the cinema lights came up, in case someone in the audience saw us with Muhammad.

Talk became rife in Fatme's household that Muhammad was sweet on me, but Fatme told me, 'The so-and-so's spreading a rumour that he's in love with you, so no one will suspect it's really me. Muhammad doesn't want to ruin my reputation for nothing. Good God, just see what love can do!'

I repeated to Fatme the very words used by Raja's father when he refused to allow his daughter to marry the singer: ' "I'm a father. How can I marry off my daughter to a mere singer? I leave it to your own conscience to decide. Just consider my role as a father. God help me!" ' To which I added, 'Yes, and Muhammad's family will say, "How can you possibly marry a mere seamstress when we're high-life people; we own horses and our father is village mayor?" '

'You sweet little scamp, you!' said Fatme, laughing. 'What a joker you are. Muhammad doesn't have two pennies to rub together. He's still at school. He can't get married and rent a house of his own.'

Then Muhammad stopped coming to visit Fatme. I decided that his family must have had something to do with it, although Fatme insisted he was just busy studying for his exams. Now I understood the true meaning of the word 'longing'. It was the feeling I had when I passed the fountain and he wasn't there; or when I saw his pen and inkwell on the bureau. I was bereft.

Three whole weeks passed before he appeared at the fountain again. Overcome with joy, I ran to him. He greeted me coldly. Was it, I wondered, because my bra had snapped and I wasn't wearing one? He ignored me and kept on reading the book in his hand.

'Is it a historical tale?' I asked.

'No,' he replied curtly. 'It's poetry.'

'What's it called?'

'*The Swinging of the Moon.*'

'So even the moon has a swing,' I said with a laugh.

He didn't laugh back. His severe expression reminded me of Ibrahim. I turned to leave, utterly perplexed.

'So you're engaged.' I turned back to him and he glared at me accusingly. 'And you kept it from me!'

The only thing I could think of was the vendor who had tried to get a kiss from me in return for some extra lard. Could I have become engaged to him without realising it?

'Come on, Kamila,' Muhammad said, raising his voice. 'Let's cut out all the deceit and hypocrisy. You're engaged to your dead sister's husband and you've been hiding it from me.'

'Me, engaged to that old man? By God's own life, by the Prophet and Imam Ali, I am not engaged to anyone.'

'Congratulations!' he said.

I began to cry. Here we were, the hero and heroine together, standing by the fountain. The hero was hurling accusations at the heroine, with her pale complexion and thick black hair. She fluttered around him in tears, protesting her innocence and trying to defend herself. I felt like throwing myself at his chest and weeping, 'No, no, you must believe me. You have to believe me.'

Muhammad called across the courtyard to Fatme's uncle, who was busy repairing a primus stove. He walked over.

'That family of yours are a load of criminals, by God! The same goes for the sheikh who drew up your engagement contract. I've heard the whole story from one of the witnesses. He didn't want to witness the engagement of an eleven-year-old girl. But eventually he gave in.'

I remembered the turbaned sheikh sitting in my nephews' room two years earlier. It suddenly struck me what those fateful words, 'You are hereby my witness,' had meant. And it explained what the turbaned sheikh and all those men were doing in our house. By this time Fatme was standing next to me, swaying from side to side, clucking in sympathy. I ran home to ask Mother whether it was true.

'The engagement,' Mother lied to me, 'was nothing more than a mock marriage for religious purposes. We did it so that God would not punish you if your brother-in-law saw you without a headscarf.'

I ran straight back to Fatme's.

'Too late!' Fatme told me. Muhammad had already left for his school in Sidon, swearing he'd never return to Beirut.

My heart sank, but Fatme hugged me and told me that Muhammad was deeply in love with me. She said he had simply melted in the face of my beauty and sense of fun; in fact, he had been in love with me ever since I asked him for his jacket to send to Abdal-Wahhab.

Her words made me sob. Was it possible that I was loved? I wept even more because Muhammad had gone away and might never come back to hear what I had to tell him.

He didn't stick to his resolution, though, and the day came when I found him waiting for me by the fountain again. The sight of him – standing in the sunlight, watching the dragonflies playing on the water – made me realise how much I loved him. But I felt shy and afraid he'd reject me.

'OK,' I told him. 'I did say the words, "You are hereby my witness," but it was a mock marriage, so if Abu-Hussein saw my hair I wouldn't enter hell. That's it and not for *tirrr*.'

Muhammad looked at me strangely and asked me what that last word was. I repeated it for him: '*Tirrr*.' When he asked what I meant by it, I hid my face, embarrassed, mortified, and unable to answer. I'd no idea where the word had come from, nor if it was a real word or I'd invented it to describe what happened between men and women. Was *tirrr* marriage? Kisses? Having babies?

A Single Drop of Blood

MUHAMMAD BECAME AS important to me as eating bread. When he gave me a bunch of violets, my mind went aflutter and my heart pounded. Was the bunch of violets really for me? I'd ask, and he'd reply that it was. I began to pirouette like a butterfly.

Then the day arrived when a single drop of blood on my underwear sent me crying in a panic to Fatme, convinced I was about to die.

It would seem that, when I spotted blood on my underwear and assumed it meant I was going to die, I was not too far off. It was as if that single drop of blood was an alarm bell, one that could cancel time – by days, months and years.

My family tricked me into letting someone take my measurements, by pretending I was the same size as Khadija's cousin, who couldn't be there for a fitting. But then I found, quite by chance, a white wedding dress and realised I was about to be married. I burst into tears and began to tear at my hair, holding my hands up to Mother and Khadija to show them I really had pulled out a clump of it.

'Don't do this to me,' I screamed, beating my chest. 'God have pity, God have pity!'

I ran to Fatme to tell her what was happening. She confessed that my brother-in-law had only let me learn how to sew so I could become a carbon copy of his former wife Manifa.

'Even you, Fatme,' I sobbed. 'Why didn't you warn me, why didn't you scream at my brother-in-law and shame him?'

How on earth could I have believed that my family wanted me to learn to sew so I'd have a profession?

'How could you do this to me?' I asked Mother through my tears.

She cried too and so did Khadija. But they had tricked me and now they were trying to talk me into the marriage. The hearts of three children lay in my hands, I was told. If I married their father, they would be able to bounce back and live normal lives. If I refused, then a cruel stepmother would let their hearts slowly fade and eventually cease beating.

Everything about my nephews made people sad. If they laughed, people began to cry because their mother would never get to hear their laughter. Even their religious names were a source of grief: Hussein was named after the Prophet's grandson, who was martyred and beheaded; his brother Hasan was poisoned; and Imam Ali, the Prophet's son-in-law, was murdered before his two sons.

I went to see my music-loving, easy-going brother Hasan, who had by now married the woman he loved. In tears I begged him to come to my rescue. Mother and Ibrahim were forcing me into marriage when I was only thirteen years old.

'Aren't you the eldest brother?' I asked. 'He's younger than you. He has to listen to you.'

'Be patient,' he replied, stroking my shoulder.

I dried my eyes and blew my nose and waited for him to finish his sentence. But as soon as I'd calmed down a bit, he seized his lute and asked if I'd like to hear him sing 'Oh rose of purest love'.

'Keep them on the run,' was Fatme's suggestion. In other words: make a series of impossible requests in return for agreeing to be married. 'That'll win you more time,' she said, 'especially since Abu-Hussein's such a skinflint!'

Back in Nabatiyeh, I had heard fairy tales in which this type of bargaining was crucial. I remembered the story of Clever Hasan: 'I want a peck of wheat from the stomach of a sparrow, but only if the bird has a blue feather in its wing. The right wing, never the left.' I also remembered the tale of the tall black genie who appeared from the magic bottle and said, 'Hey ho! Greetings. I'm here to do your bidding!' The hag said, 'Put me on your back and fly me to a land where there are shoes that can talk, stamp and clap.'

It always worked in the stories, so I decided to try. My first demand was for roast chicken, but it had to be from a restaurant. Otherwise I knew they'd bring me a chicken, keep it in the bathroom for several days, fatten it up a bit and then slaughter it and cook it for the entire family. I was convinced that no one in our household would set foot in a restaurant; such places were for rich, sophisticated people. To my great disappointment, the roast chicken duly arrived, purchased reluctantly by my brother-in-law. I pounced on it voraciously and began to swallow the flesh in chunks, sucking on the bones, even crunching on some of them, ignoring Ibrahim's disapproving glare.

Two days after getting the chicken, I let it be known that I still had no wish to marry my brother-in-law. Although we were living in the same apartment, I made myself scarce. When I heard him, I'd disappear. When they asked me why I was so scared of him (in fact, he made my skin crawl) I shouted at them that I was too young to be married.

When my aunt arrived from Nabatiyeh for a consultation about the snake in her stomach, she listened to my protests and then joined my family's campaign. She scolded me for being so selfish and not thinking about my sister's three children.

My next demand was that Mother and my aunt take me to the cinema.

Mother let out a shriek and asked for God's forgiveness.

'Good grief!' she said. 'I've lost two daughters in their prime, withering like basil leaves on the stem, and you expect me to go to the cinema?'

I reassured her that the film I had in mind was a comedy, without love scenes or singing.

'So you want to make me laugh, is that it? Why do you think I need to laugh?'

My aunt, however, urged her to take me so I'd agree to get married.

'Now tell me,' Mother asked. 'Will you agree to marry your brother-in-law, or are you just playing games with us, you genie of the fields?'

I swore by the Prophet, Imam Ali and the memory of my two dead sisters that this time I wouldn't change my mind. I went straight over to the mirror to fix my hair, feeling overjoyed that, for the first time ever, I could go to the cinema without feeling guilty or afraid that Ibrahim might catch me.

On our way there we passed a striptease cabaret. My heart was in my mouth for fear Mother would look up and her eyes fall on the scandalous pictures posted outside. To my relief I saw she was lowering her headscarf over her eyes, which were weak in any case.

But then the cabaret man at the door shouted, 'Just a quarter, that's all! A quarter-lira! Dancing, shimmying, jiggling breasts, arse-swaying, all for a quarter!'

Mother heard every word.

'Get away, you son of a bitch!' she screeched at him.

I seized her by the hand and dragged her away. We went into the cinema and found our seats. I watched again as the rays of light and dust hit the screen.

But the lights had only just gone down when people in the back seats started to shout, 'Tell that tall one to move further back. Get her to sit in the back row.'

I realised my aunt was perched on the top of her seat.

'Just stand up a moment and I'll adjust your seat,' I offered, but she shouted back, 'May God bury the people alive who turned off the lights. We are in Beirut, aren't we? There is no need to economise! Tell them to put the lights on so I can see what's in front of me.'

First we watched a newsreel about the war in Europe. I'd learnt the faces of the leaders from stickers that were sold everywhere in Beirut: an Italian with a square head; a German with a trimmed moustache, who was extremely upset and annoyed; and a fat Englishman with an equally fat black cigarette in his hand. I thought he held a black cigarette because he was in mourning for the start of war. There were scenes of tanks racing each other across the countryside. A tank approached the camera and its image filled the screen, bringing my aunt to her feet once more.

'Where on earth have you brought us?' she yelled.

I tugged my aunt's hand, trying to get her to sit down, to the accompaniment of jeers and catcalls. The newsreel came to an end and the film began. It was Laurel and Hardy, who reminded me of Abu-Hussein and Ibrahim. Laurel, the thin, short one with little to say, was my brother-in-law; Hardy, who was fat and big with a tiny moustache and a short temper, was gloomy Ibrahim. I was soon laughing so hard I had to keep slapping my cheeks.

Mother fidgeted in her seat.

'In the name of heaven,' she shouted finally, jumping up. 'Enough's enough. Tell them to calm down and stop making such a fuss! They keep running back and forth like the shuttle on a sewing machine. My eyes can't take it any more!'

'Oh for pity's sake, why don't you just sit down?' a man shouted at Mother.

With that, my aunt turned round.

'Pipe down, you good-for-nothings!' she yelled. 'How dare you talk to us without even being introduced.'

Proud of myself and my tactics, I went to Fatme's house to tell her how I was stalling the marriage with my demands.

'What makes you think you're such a hot shot,' she said, 'asking for roast chicken and a trip to the cinema? It's a gold watch and coiled gold bracelets you should be asking for.'

So I went home straight away and asked for the things Fatme had suggested. That night I slept well; I was confident that that sort of money would never leave my brother-in-law's pocket. He scolded us if the tap was left dripping. When the soap was as thin as a piece of peel, he attached it to a fresh bar. And once, when the cat stole the meat he'd brought home, he stood there aghast, holding the empty wrapping, turning it over in disbelief, and then began to weep. I quickly put the remaining piece of fat on a plate next to his prayer mat as he prayed, hoping that perhaps God would hear him and change that piece of fat back into a piece of meat.

But this time the only miracle was that my brother-in-law did not refuse my requests. Instead he bought me everything I asked for. When I saw the gold in Mother's and Khadija's hands, I fainted.

The next thing I heard was, 'Bring some rose water, quickly, bring rose water!'

The scent must have loosened my tongue because I began begging the two of them.

'He's old,' I kept repeating, while still only half-conscious. 'He's an adult and I'm still young, only a child.' I echoed all that I'd heard Fatme, her uncle, and Muhammad say.

At Fatme's house early the next morning I found Muhammad waiting for me by the garden gate. Before I could say a word he asked me to get my family to delay things for six months. By then he'd have graduated from his training to become a member of the government and found a job with the Sécurité Générale, the government interior ministry. As we walked into the garden, again I felt as if we were in a film.

Muhammad placed his hand over his heart and grasped me by the shoulders.

'Don't give in, no matter how much they pressure you,' he said. 'Just six months, and we'll be engaged. Don't be afraid.' He took a small photograph of himself out of his coat and handed it to me. I put it in my bra with a sigh. 'Promise me you won't get married, whatever happens.'

'I promise,' I repeated after him. 'I won't get married.'

I decided I'd promise the family to get married in six months' time, when I was fourteen. I would use the extra time to persuade Mother to stand by me and then put pressure on Ibrahim to release me from the engagement. But that night when I heard Abu-Hussein's footsteps on the stairs and Ibrahim shouting at one of his daughters, I changed my mind. I decided to escape to the south and ask Father to save me and let me stay with him for six months.

Should I set out on foot? No, that was a bad idea. They might catch up with me. Should I make use of the muleteers who travelled south in the early mornings? Or should I creep out at dawn and stow away in the bus for the south, before the driver arrived?

Escape into a Trap

EARLY IN THE morning I crept out, after stealing some cash from Abu-Hussein's jacket pocket. Before leaving I stood over Kamil, longing to kiss him. He looked so peaceful and young. How I wished he wasn't dependent upon my brother-in-law and this house; then he could have defended me. I made my way to Burj Square and caught the bus to the south. When the bus passed through Sidon I wanted to scream, 'Stop! Stop!' so that I could get out and run to Muhammad's school. But I swallowed my grief and stayed where I was.

I stepped off the bus at Nabatiyeh an hour and a half later, confident that nobody would follow me from Beirut. But although I felt relief, I also felt sad and alone. I didn't dare go to see Father and his wife, or my aunt with the snake in her stomach. So I made my way to my uncle the cobbler's stall and told him why I was back. He didn't even take the nails out of his mouth or put down his hammer. It was clear he had no intention of helping me.

Next I went to call on my rich older cousin Mira, who divided her time between Nabatiyeh and West Africa, where her husband owned a business. She welcomed me warmly and listened to my sad tale, shaking her head all the while, obviously moved. But she couldn't come up with a solution, though she thought hard about it; instead she offered me a huge meal of grilled meat and spinach pastries. We sat in the garden and enjoyed the scent of the orange trees. She tried to get me to stay with her, but I decided I couldn't wait any longer, so I set off for Father's house in the neighbouring village. As soon as I saw him I would say, 'Baba, I want to live with you and your wife. I don't want to live in Beirut any more.' If his wife reminded me of how Kamil and I had run away from their home, I'd ask them to forgive me and say that I'd been very young.

I made my way towards Father's house, thinking of Mother with each step. The red earth reminded me of our days together in the fields. How I longed to be back in those days, when I ran off with my brother, the hot lentils in his djellabah, I was terrified of meeting Ali Atrash. I knew now that there were worse things to fear than him. I averted my eyes from the road to our old home, so I wouldn't picture Mother waiting for us at the end. How could she marry me off to a man old enough to be my father? I remembered my friend Apple and started to cry. I wanted to see her, but I couldn't bear the thought of her playing without me. So I kept on running towards Father's village.

My chest heaved with sobs as I told Father how Mother and Ibrahim planned to marry me off to my brother-in-law. I pleaded with him to intervene and to let me live with him. Father didn't insist I must get married, or argue with me. He didn't even pat my shoulder or invite me inside and offer me something to eat. Instead he said absolutely nothing. He must still be angry, I told myself, because Kamil and I ran away and went back to Mother all those years ago. He left me outside, so I hung about on the porch between the house and the shed where his wife baked bread. When night fell, he still didn't offer me a place to sleep. I huddled in the shed, shivering with fright at the distant baying of wolves and jackals. Would they smell my scent, burst into the shed, and rip me apart? It was the hyenas I feared most.

Next morning Father didn't come looking for me, and no one offered me breakfast. I was too proud to go and ask for food. As soon as his wife finished her baking and spread out the loaves to cool, piling them up before going back inside the house, I lunged at the discarded burnt crusts. Then I scouted around the back of the house as Mother had done, searching for wild vegetables, endive, perhaps tomato shoots, maybe even some chickpeas or bean husks. But all I could find were thorns; and all I could feel was the sun beating down, and the occasional gust of wind.

On the second day I awoke to find that my period was with me again. I remembered that Mother had sometimes used an old piece of cloth. I had only my undershirt, which I tore into strips, burying the soiled pieces under the rocks in the field. I was worried the chickens might peck at them and become ill. One chicken had started to follow me whenever I went to the latrine to crouch; it waited for me, and then followed me back. Its companionship was a great source of comfort; it was almost as though it understood my condition. I swore a solemn oath never to eat chicken again.

Hunger reduced my energy but did nothing to weaken my resolve. I endured, remembering Mother's favourite saying: 'By God, I will be so patient, until patience itself understands just how patient I am!' Every time I felt hungry and weak, walking around the pasture, in the shed, or camping out on the porch, I remembered those words. I was so relieved not to be in Beirut; for me the city had come to embody my brother-in-law.

I only realised how tired and hungry I was when, on the third day, a neighbour of Father's spied me wandering aimlessly. She asked me why I was out on my own in the blistering sun.

I fell to me knees, crying.

'I'm hungry,' I kept repeating, 'so hungry.'

The woman took me by the hand and led me to her house. I told her I had run away from Beirut because I was to be married. The woman didn't cease cursing Father's cruel heart until she had me seated at her table and was bringing me a plate of string beans cooked in oil and a huge loaf of bread. To this very day I remember how wonderful that food tasted.

Once my stomach was full I could take in what the woman was saying.

'So this heartless clown was deliberately starving you. I'll cut my arm if he hasn't already agreed to your being married off to your brother-in-law. Shame on your stepmother, Hind[11] the liver eater.'

After I left the kind woman's home, I ran to find my aunt with the snake in her stomach. She was frying two eggs in the most expensive animal fat, so that the snake would smell the eggs when she opened her mouth wide and come out. I forgot my misery and sat down, desperate to eat the delicious eggs.

When nothing came out of my aunt's mouth, she yelled, 'Of course you don't want to come out, you wretched snake! Why come out when you can eat and drink all you want inside my stomach? I am going to show you. I am going to starve you!'

Then we sat down and ate the eggs before I headed to my cousin Mira's.

I hid at Mira's house for a month. My father would come to the house and ask for me, trying to charm Mira's helper into betraying me, but she would tell him over and over again that I had already left for Beirut, while I hid under Mira's bed. But then one day, while Mira was in the bathroom, Father caught me in the garden on my own. He cornered

---

11 Hind bint Ataba, who chewed upon the liver of the Prophet's uncle, Hamza, to quench her anger at the death of her father and brother who were killed on the battlefield of Uhud.

me and gave me a terrible beating when I tried to run away. Then he took me by the hand and didn't let go until I was back in the sitting room in Beirut. Later, I discovered that Father had been promised ten gold coins if my marriage to Abu-Hussein took place.

I managed to sneak out of the house and run to Fatme, to ask her about Muhammad. She told me he was still studying for his government position with the Sécurité Générale, and couldn't leave before he had graduated in three months' time.

I asked her to send him a message, but she shrugged and said, 'How can he help you now from so far away? It is impossible for him to leave his studies.'

Although I had abandoned all hope that my family would give up on the idea of marrying me off, I made a plan. I decided I would kill my brother-in-law and Ibrahim slowly and so I began to add salt to the cod liver oil they took each day. I was convinced that salt was a deadly poison; I'd seen slugs shrivel up and die when we put salt on their tails as they crawled between the kitchen and the back door. Day by day I increased the dose of salt and watched the two of them close their eyes and purse their lips to swallow the oil. I was certain that I was on the path to my final escape.

Meanwhile the dresses kept piling up on the table, tempting me to try them on. I kept telling myself not to do so. I contemplated stealing them and hiding them at Fatme's house; that way, when I married Muhammad, they'd all be mine. In the end my resolve was broken when I heard a particular song I loved on the radio. I selected a loose-fitting silk dress and spun around, watching the dress move with me, just like a plant or a sunflower. I gazed at myself in the mirror and remembered my forced marriage. Suddenly I was in a scene from a film: I was gripping the black wrought iron on the window and shaking it as if trying to break open the bars of a prison. I twisted and turned, shouting in a mix of classical Arabic and Egyptian dialect, 'Save me, ye people, save me!' And then quietly I pleaded, 'Muhammad, where are you? I need you.'

Unfortunately the salt failed to have the same effect on the two men as it had on the slugs; they didn't shrivel up and burst. One morning I awoke to find the white wedding dress with an artificial rose tiara laid out for me. I ran to our neighbour Umm Fawzi and begged her to keep me hidden in her attic and bring me food and drink. She wept along with me, well aware she could do nothing to help.

'I feel so sorry for you,' she kept saying. 'You're just like the fly running away from the spider, not knowing it's already doomed.'

' "I don't want him. Please help me!" ' These were Raja's words to her father in *The White Rose*. They came rushing back to me: ' "I don't love him. Please help me. I don't love him!" '

In the film, Raja's father says, 'I made a promise, and that's it.' My brother Ibrahim's only response was to beat me. I don't know how many hands it took to get me into that white dress, which was made of Atlas material – soft, shiny satin – and yet it scratched like pins and needles. But I do remember how I managed to slip from the clutches of those hands, run to the kerosene primus and smear black soot all over my face. Next I got the saucepans and smeared even more soot over my neck, exactly as I'd seen a mother do in Nabatiyeh when she lost a child. I tore at the dress and wrenched it off. I hurled myself at a pile of sacking we used to wipe the floor and wrapped myself in a sack, screaming and weeping. I rolled around on the floor, and then leapt for the kitchen window, but they pulled me back. All I could do was scream and cry as Ibrahim dragged me towards the room where Abu-Hussein was waiting. I shook him off and

ran to Mother's mattress, clinging to her and weeping. In a
rage, Abu-Hussein gathered all my beautiful dresses and tried
to set them on fire. I heard Mother and Khadija promising
him, as they snatched the dresses back, that they would make
me behave.

On the third night I capitulated. I stood still, like a tree, as
they forced me into the repaired wedding dress. But as soon
as they'd brought me back to the room and I set eyes on my
brother-in-law, I began screaming and pushing him away.

'Bring me some rose water!' I yelled. 'Bring me some rose
water before I pass out!'

This time Ibrahim was waiting for me by the door as I
tried to escape.

'Cut it out,' he said, 'or people will be saying that cousin
of the seamstress has been playing around with your mind, or
has done something worse to you!'

I didn't understand what he meant, but I was scared that
he might know about my friendship with Muhammad, or
have discovered that I kept his photograph in my bra; that
I'd gone to the cinema with him; that he'd urged me not to
get married; that he'd asked me to wait six months for him.
I was terrified they might harm Muhammad in some way
and so I went back into the room. When I saw Abu-Hussein
sitting on the mattress in the middle of his bedroom, waiting
for me, I let out a wail and tried to open the door again. But
it was locked from the outside.

'I beg you, bring me some rose water. I'm fainting.'

No one answered and the door remained locked. My
brother-in-law stood up and walked towards me. I screamed
as I shoved him away. I struck myself, I cursed him, and hit
myself harder. Then I held my breath, clutching my dress, as,
undeterred, he lifted it up.

I felt an intense pain in my throat and between my thighs
at the same time. I sank my teeth into my arm so deep that I

struck bone. When it was over, I saw blood between my legs. I pushed Abu-Hussein away and rushed back to the door and began pounding on it. To my amazement it opened.

I ran to Mother's bed, where I found her sobbing. I huddled close to her, wrapping my dress around me, weeping and moaning as she wept and moaned with me. I made no effort to avoid staining her nightgown with blood. Nor did I say, 'I want to kiss you before I die,' the words I'd used once when I'd smashed a jar of quince jam, cutting my arm and causing Ibrahim to mutter under his breath that he wished I were dead. This time, when I emerged from Abu-Hussein's room, I was truly slaughtered and the blood on the white dress was the proof.

How I Came to be Married to Mr Watch-out-or-else

AND THAT WAS how I came to be married to Abu-Hussein, a man eighteen years older than me, who had criticised Mother for still nursing me when I was more than one year old. I used to think of him as Mr Watch-out-or-else. Every time I ran or jumped or burst into fits of laughter, the other adults would warn me. 'Watch out or else,' they'd say.

The man I married loved cleanliness and would repeat over and over, 'Cleanliness is born out of faith.' I would lift up the carpet and shove the dirt gathered by the broom underneath, rather than collecting it with the dustpan. He'd summon me and show me how to search for bedbugs in the mattress, squashing them between two fingers to demonstrate how it should be done. Seeing the blood oozing, I would defy him and turn away, holding my nose.

He searched for cockroaches in drawers and cupboards, in the kitchen or under the sink. He'd ferret out their brown-coloured eggs, which looked like bean kernels. Sometimes I thought of taking some and putting them in a box to see if a cockroach emerged with its body first or its moustache. I was convinced they knew he was their number one enemy and that they hid until they knew it was safe to come out. They concealed themselves from him everywhere, even in the pottery water pitcher. 'Good grief!' Mother screamed when the pitcher broke. The tiny baby cockroaches hadn't even drowned; they simply scurried away and hid somewhere else.

I was married to a man who watched over me while I did the washing, demanding that I take extra care to scrub the three children's clothing. He rubbed his fingers on the outside of the pots to make sure there was no trace of fat or oil left on them. Nor was he satisfied with that alone; no, he also had to put his nose to them and sniff them. But all that paled next to the way he would conduct an inspection of my feet before he went to sleep. I still shared a mattress on the floor with Mother, but he'd lift the coverlet, look at my feet, and spit on them if he thought they weren't clean enough. 'Ugh!' I'd hear him say, after he spat. I neither moved nor tried to wipe off the spittle; instead I pretended to be asleep.

All his efforts to teach me how to clean and be a responsible housewife came to nothing. I would sweep the bedroom half-heartedly with one foot on the floor cloth, pushing it wherever was convenient. My husband would check whether I'd swept the floor under the chair, under the settee, and gone into all the corners. He soon realised that I never did, so he would move the furniture around piece by piece and watch as I swept. When I put the blanket and coverlet back on his bed, I didn't bother to rearrange the sheets. If one of my dresses fell off its hanger, I left it lying at the bottom of the wardrobe. If I had to peel potatoes, I'd find myself peeling halfway to the centre. When I cooked, I'd burn the food. My husband could be under no illusion: I was cut from an entirely different bolt of cloth from the one that produced his first wife. I had none of her traits: patience, cleanliness, industriousness, composure and housekeeping skills. The reason I so lacked those virtues had nothing to do with my youth; it was because I was just like Father – at least, that was what everybody said. I'd inherited his comedian's temperament – 'A bird-brain, just like your father,' my husband used to tell me. As for my capacity for stubbornness, my husband had seen nothing yet.

He got an inkling of my iron will after a relative from the south brought him a pail of yoghurt. When he caught me pouring out a glass of it, he scolded me and called me greedy. In fact it wasn't simply greed that had made me want the yoghurt; it reminded me of Nabatiyeh, of our house, of the cows, of the fig trees and my friend Apple, whose mother had given me yoghurt to drink. Not content simply with scolding me in front of everyone, Abu-Hussein got up on a chair and put the pail of yoghurt on top of the cupboard.

'That yoghurt's only for cooking,' he said, wagging a finger at me. 'I forbid anyone to touch it for any other reason.'

I swallowed the insult, pretended I didn't care, and busied myself with something else. But as soon as he left the room, I got up on the chair, took down the pail, helped myself to another drink and poured it over my head so that it dripped down on my face and clothes. Then I rushed out into the lounge, licking my hand like a cat. Everyone in the family gathered around laughing. The sight of my husband's mournful expression as the yoghurt dripped off me on to the floor made me laugh so hard I almost wet myself.

He mumbled over and over again, 'There is no strength except in God.'

He looked so miserable that I felt guilty and promised myself not to make fun of him any more. And yet he didn't realise that I was taking revenge on him; instead he blamed himself for not making sure that the pail was out of reach.

Snake Pit

THE NUMBER OF people living with us grew by the day, until our house resembled a snake pit. Everyone was crammed in, head to tail; each person skulked in their own domain. Everyone foraged for food or went to war to gain access to the only toilet, or hunted for kerosene to light the primus stove and warm up some water so they might take a bath – after which they'd need to track down a towel. By this time Ibrahim had brought Raoufa's two daughters, Maryam and Inaam, to live with us. The two brothers stayed with their father the gambler, while the third, the one with the wooden leg, became estranged from the family. He developed a cocaine habit and started consorting with lowlifes.

Once he boarded the tram Ibrahim was driving and asked him for money.

His uncle pushed him away as though he were any other scrounger.

'Go on,' he said, 'get lost!'

When Mother heard what had happened, she burst into tears.

'Why didn't he give the poor boy even a piastre?' she demanded. 'A mere piastre won't buy you much!'

With the arrival of my two nieces, my life changed for the better. Maryam, the elder of the two, was just a couple of years younger than me, but much taller, fine-featured and extremely calm. She was so grateful to Abu-Hussein for giving them refuge that she obeyed him without question and worked hard: cooking, washing and ironing. My husband nicknamed her Sultana, or Princess, and she called him Uncle. I felt as though heaven had sent me an angel who would laugh alongside me; someone who would love me as I loved her.

With so many mouths to feed, my husband brought home a large black box in which to keep provisions. It looked just like the Kaaba[12] in Mecca. He locked it with a large key and opened it twice a day. Before he went to work he would take out enough sugar, soap, oil, rice and lard to last us for the day. In the evening he would stand before the box again and, reciting the phrase, 'In the name of God,' he would call each of us by name and hand out dates, dried apricots, biscuits, Turkish delight, and occasionally baklava.

Sometimes I would take my rations and then go to the back of the queue as though I were lining up for the first time. When my husband insisted that he had already given me baklava, I would deny it vehemently. I wanted him to see that I was, after all, his wife and not just another member of the household. I demanded this privilege, but I would not allow intimacy between us. Respect and fear; that is what I had in my heart for my husband.

If he called for me in the night, I recoiled in disgust at the very thought of going near him. I would stay huddled on the mattress next to Mother, curled up like a frightened worm. I tried to forget what had happened on my wedding night and even managed to convince myself that the nightmare was over and would never return. Things between us were better during the day, although we seldom went out together. He didn't leave the house on Sundays, his one day off; he didn't like strolling like everyone else along the seafront or in the

12 A sacred black stone at the centre of the holiest place of worship in Islam.

Beirut pine forest. When I watched him pray, stretching his hands up to God, eyes closed, I was sure that his prayers would immediately reach his creator and that God would guarantee his wishes. But no matter how many times I told myself I must not tease him or I might incur the wrath of God, I couldn't help myself. I was especially bad when we went to Damascus.

Because we so seldom travelled, I was utterly astonished when Abu-Hussein agreed that we could go to Damascus. He did so because he saw it as a religious pilgrimage. I didn't mind this; I was simply delighted to be leaving Beirut. The plan was to visit the shrine of Sitt Zaynab,[13] the sister of Imam al-Hussein and the granddaughter of the Prophet.

Abu-Hussein, who never even rode in a tram, bus or car, took us on a train away from his daily routine of house, shop and the mosque. We were accompanied by his female cousins and one of their husbands. In the women's carriage of the train I told Abu-Hussein's cousins the story of *The White Rose*. I was the heroine, riding the train as it raced against the wind. I leaned my arms and head out of the window and, when the train lunged into a tunnel and everything went dark, I cried out to scare the women. They laughed among themselves, whispering, 'She's still a child, a mere girl.'

At the shrine to Sitt Zaynab we had to push our way through the crowd. I went straight to the shrine itself. I wanted to beseech Sitt Zaynab to intercede on Mother's behalf and

13 Known for her lasting sorrow after her brother al-Hussein, her two sons and all the men in her family were massacred at the Battle of Karbala. She took charge of all the women and children when they were in captivity, defying the enemy with fury and courage. She then devoted her life to the memory of Imam al-Hussein and became the narrator of the tragedy of Karbala.

ensure she wouldn't have to face any more disasters after the deaths of my two sisters. But what took my breath away, and made me gaze in wonder, was the gleam of the jewellery and bracelets thrown into the golden shrine as offerings. Would she arise one day, I asked myself, and put on all these jewels? I closed my eyes and prayed to Sitt Zaynab, weeping as I told her how Mother, Father, and Ibrahim had married me off to Abu-Hussein; she would understand, I thought, as she had experienced great tragedy in her lifetime. Drying my eyes, I opened my purse and took out the coin our neighbour had given me to make my devotion to Sitt Zaynab. But just as I was about to throw it in, I hesitated.

'Forgive me, Sitt Zaynab,' I entreated her. 'You've so many jewels here. Let me keep this coin. Let's pretend I've put the coin inside the enclosure.'

After leaving the shrine we headed to a nearby park to eat lunch. On the way we passed through the famous Hamidiyya Market. I desperately wanted a gold bracelet in the form of a snake, its head encrusted with two diamonds for the eyes. I begged Abu-Hussein to buy it for me, but he only quickened his pace. So I asked him instead for a golden Quran, dangling from a gold chain, thinking he might buy me something connected with religion. Running behind him, I promised I would say all the obligatory prayers, but he only walked faster. And then the gold market was behind us.

Before the sheer disappointment of it all could hit me, we reached another market, where everything gleamed and glistened: embroidered scarves, black silk fabric printed with silver polka dots, colourful clogs, nightdresses of smooth pink, blue or ivory silk.

'Good heavens,' I cried, 'look how gorgeous they are! Oh please buy me one.'

But he refused, saying he could buy one in Beirut from a fellow merchant for half the price.

'But,' I protested, crying, 'the merchant might not have exactly the same.'

My husband stared at the ground. As we came to the end of the market I redoubled my efforts.

'Please, please!' I begged, though by now I'd almost forgotten what I was begging him for.

I kept it up until he turned and shouted, 'What's the matter with you? I wish something would freeze the tongue in your head!'

We passed a little beggar boy, who stretched out his hand and asked us to spare a coin. Realising I was no different from him, I burst into tears.

Finally we reached the famous park near the shrine. People were picnicking on the grass under the trees, barbecuing meat and *Kafta*.[14] The wonderful smell lessened my misery a little, until I remembered that all we had to eat was boiled eggs and potatoes that my husband had brought along in a bag. We stood under the trees opposite the stream with its waterwheel, while I longed to sit down like all the other people who were smoking hookahs, cracking jokes and singing.

By now I was used to the way my husband would say, 'Oh God, Your prayers be upon the Prophet Muhammad and his family,' if he smelled something really nice. If ever I expressed delight at a bar of scented soap, he scolded me and made me repeat the correct invocation.

Now, looking at the stream and the waterwheel, I exclaimed, 'God, see how beautiful it is – just like the River Litani!'

He rounded on me, telling me I must say instead, 'God is powerful over all things. He is the Creator of the heavens and the earth.' I was angry. Now I couldn't even remark on the beauty of something without being told off.

---

14 Meatballs made from minced beef, lamb or veal and onion, garlic, herbs and spices.

Abu-Hussein huddled with his cousin's husband, 'consulting the prayer beads' to determine whether we women might sit down beside the waterwheel, or whether we'd have to move further away from the stream where no one could see or hear us. I was bitter and resentful when the bead consultation came to an end. 'Ask for God's will' indeed! It worked out very nicely for the men, who got to sit close to the waterwheel, while we women had to retreat to the very edge of the park and eat our dreary lunch of boiled eggs and potatoes.

The coin I hadn't thrown into Sitt Zaynab's shrine was still in my pocket and I considered running away. But the idea of revenge was sweeter, so instead I ran up to Abu-Hussein's cousin's husband and asked him to consult the beads 'for God's will' on something I had in mind.

'Of course, right away!' he replied, closing his eyes. When he opened his eyes and saw the bead indicating good luck, he smiled. 'The result is fine!' he declared.

With that I pushed him into the stream. The abrupt movement caught him off balance and he fell into the water. When he stepped back on to dry land his trousers were dripping wet. The women laughed behind their black veils.

'The girl's a menace!' my husband exclaimed.

'So whose idea was it to bring children along?' the man muttered.

'I made a secret vow to push you and God answered my prayer,' I said. 'You wouldn't want me to offend God, would you?'

On the train back to Beirut, Abu-Hussein's cousin and I laughed over the trick I'd played on her husband. I began to sing for her. Just then a tall, handsome army officer walked through our carriage and stopped to stare at me.

I pretended not to notice him as he addressed my companion.

'Is this your daughter?' he asked her.

'Yes, she is,' she replied, enjoying the joke. 'She's the apple of my eye!'

'You've a really pretty daughter!' he said with disarming candour. 'My intentions are honourable and I'd like to propose.' He asked her for our address so he could call and seek my hand.

As she hesitated, I plunged straight in and told him my name and our address. I also give Abu-Hussein's name as my father. The officer bade us farewell, placing his hand on his heart, and smiled at me. How I wished that my husband really was my father and this officer was someone who could come to seek my hand! I thought of Muhammad. The six months had passed and he must have graduated and heard that I'd got married. I imagined he hated me for not waiting for him as I had promised. I wondered if he would forgive me if he knew what had happened to me after he'd left.

The officer took us at our word. The following evening there was a knock at the door and there he stood with his father. In a moment the entire household, old and young, men and women, had gathered around the prospective groom. Maryam and I hid behind the kitchen door, listening. Abu-Hussein and Ibrahim greeted the visitors. Everyone assumed the officer must have come to ask for Maryam's hand, but then he gave my name.

Abu-Hussein briskly corrected the officer's mis-apprehension.

'Kamila's my wife,' he said. 'It must be her niece you have in mind.'

'So who was the girl in the train from Damascus yesterday?' the officer asked.

'God damn your treacherous heart!' my husband swore at him indignantly. 'That was my wife!'

I hurriedly locked the door and begged Mother to protect me, though she was trembling with fear too, at what Ibrahim might do. I didn't wait for a scolding, or even a beating, before I burst into tears. I wept because I would never be engaged to this handsome officer. I clung to the window bars and screamed. When I noticed the handsome boy next door watching me, I screamed even louder.

Fatima

SUDDENLY THE WORLD turned dark. I'd been skipping
with the neighbourhood girls when I began to feel sick.
I rubbed my eyes, but the world grew darker still. I collapsed
and, as so often when I was frightened, I cried out, 'Help,
please! Some rose water. I'm feeling faint.'

One of our neighbours guessed I was pregnant. She took
me by the hand and led me downstairs. Despite the fact that
she was a direct descendant of the Prophet Muhammad, her
curses and imprecations against our family came bursting out
in a steady stream.

'God damn the beard of the sheikh who married you off!'
she fumed. 'You're just a child. What a scandal!'

After that I had to be more careful. I sat and watched the
other girls skip. My stomach had not yet started to swell and
I found it hard to believe it ever would. As the woman had
said, I was still just a girl; surely God must realise it. But God
didn't help me. Instead my stomach grew rounder by the
day. I overheard passers-by say, 'So a mere baby's going to
have another baby!' It didn't help that I was so tiny myself.

At least my pregnancy meant I could sleep without fear.
I ate what I wanted and went out whenever I felt like it, so
long as I was back before dark. I got to watch every single film
that came on, and for a while I was accompanied by my rich
older cousin Mira, who was visiting Beirut from Nabatiyeh
while her husband was away in West Africa. In spite of the
age difference, our friendship soon deepened. She was like

the film stars we saw on the screen: the dresses she wore, the cigarette constantly in her hand, her crêpe-soled shoes and the crocodile-skin handbag that made a clicking sound when she opened it – all of these things made her seem from the world of the cinema. A wonderful scent of cologne would waft from that handbag and I'd glimpse the coins within. Her stay gave me the strength I needed to defy Ibrahim, who was still watching me, disapproving of every move I made.

Mira took me to see the film *Long Live Love!* When I found out that Abdal-Wahhab was playing the lead opposite a different actress from the one in *The White Rose*, I was upset. But as soon as I saw the new actress, I fell in love with her and forgot all about the other one. Mira and I also went to see *Layla, Daughter of the Desert*. In this one, Layla, a beautiful Bedouin girl, was in love with her brave cousin who came to rescue her from the Persian King Chosroes. After attacking the King's fortress, her cousin saved her, brought her back to her family, and married her. Until then I had been trying to shut Muhammad out of my mind. Now I wished he could have saved me!

As I watched the film, I began to see that love was the most important thing in the world – more important even than money and food. The heroine wasn't living in a palace, but in the desert in a Bedouin tent. Mira said she too longed for the Bedouin desert life, but as soon as we left the cinema we were back in the modern world, stopping at shop windows to look at clothes and buying ice cream and chocolate, forgetting all about desert existence.

When Mira was with me, I wasn't afraid at home. We would listen to the radio, and I would turn the volume up. Ibrahim was in awe of Mira's sophistication and confidence and so all he did was frown; he didn't dare insist that I turn it down. I whispered to my cousin that we were like butterflies, while Abu-Hussein and Ibrahim were hornets trying to sting us. But after Mira rejoined her husband in Africa, the hornets were back in control in no time.

At the first sign of my contractions, Khadija did as my husband asked and hurried me to the American University Hospital. The doctor measured my waist, stomach and feet as if I were a piece of cloth and he the tailor.

When he asked my age and was told I was fifteen, he could not disguise his contempt.

'Is it because your family cannot feed you,' he said scathingly, 'that they had to marry you off?'

The doctor asked where the baby's father was, and Khadija told him that my husband was afraid of hospitals. Abu-Hussein had only visited a hospital once and that was after Manifa had died. He had rushed to his dead wife's room so he could recite the Muslim statement of faith and turn her bed to face Mecca.

'I wish he was here,' replied the doctor with disgust. 'I'd like to give him a piece of my mind for marrying a child!'

My daughter stretched and yawned at our first meeting. Her arrival added to the power I'd gained while she was still in my womb. Because of her, I got to sleep in my husband's bed while he slept on a mattress on the floor. I stayed in bed, leaving it only to take a bath or use the toilet. And Abu-Hussein began to respond to my requests. He got me a nightgown of pink natural silk and I put a carnation of the same colour in my hair. Each morning I ate a chicken – not just a thin slice of meat but a whole chicken that had been slaughtered just for me. This went on for forty days, as the custom dictated, to provide my body with the nourishment it needed while I was nursing the baby. I would eat every bit of the chicken, both breast and thighs. I sucked on the bones like some fierce carnivore, making a huge noise. With the chicken disposed of, I would wait for the *meghlie*, the sweet

pudding of hazelnuts, walnuts and pine nuts that was offered
to visitors when a child was born.

My baby was the soft toy I'd never hugged or played with.
She was just like the dolls I'd seen in the Beirut shops, the
ones made of flesh-coloured porcelain that squeaked when
they were laid down to sleep. But the day arrived when I
got out of bed and gave my baby to the many hands ready to
help me look after her. In fact, they took over completely,
worried that I'd drop her or let her swallow some water
when washing her. Mother put her in a cradle, which she
moved from room to room. My husband insisted on calling
her Fatima, after the Prophet's daughter. I had wanted to
name her Raja or Samira after my favourite film stars, but I
didn't object for fear of making the Prophet angry.

For all the pampering and luxury I received after Fatima
was born, I couldn't forget how she had come to grow inside
my womb, on that night when my husband had straddled me
like I was a little donkey, and I'd bitten my own arm down
to the bone.

Nadia's Nightclub

ALTHOUGH I LOVED my daughter dearly, there were still times when I managed to forget her presence in my life, particularly when I was listening to songs on the radio. Even before the customary forty-day lying-in period was over, I was longing to get out of the house, go to the cinema, and enjoy the bustle of the city again.

Shortly after I left my bed, I was invited to my first coffee morning at the house of a neighbour's sister-in-law. There I met a group of ladies like me, who enjoyed singing and going to the cinema. They shared my sense of fun and love of beautiful clothes.

The idea was for each hostess to designate a day towards the end of the month when the other women would show up wearing their fanciest clothes. Then we'd sit chatting, drinking coffee, and eating bonbons and chocolates. My husband didn't like these social occasions and was especially opposed to drinking coffee and offering it to others. He associated it with time-wasting and tittle-tattle. But I soon plucked up the courage to hold coffee mornings of my own. I managed to persuade Abu-Hussein to bring me a particular type of chocolate and white bonbons filled with almonds. I preferred the pink and blue ones, but he wouldn't buy me those; in Abu-Hussein's mind, white sweets were less frivolous than the coloured ones.

On the days I held my coffee mornings, I'd secretly buy some flowers from a peddler, who would also surreptitiously

sell me coffee. As soon as our gathering was over, I'd distribute
the flowers among the neighbours so my husband wouldn't
see them. He would never buy flowers, believing it to be
wasteful to spend money on something that died so quickly.

One morning, my husband felt unwell and was late leaving
for work. I waited anxiously by the door, listening out for
the peddler's footsteps. When he knocked, I shut the door
in his face. The moment my husband went into the kitchen,
I rushed back to the window and asked the peddler to come
upstairs again. Then my husband appeared just as the peddler
knocked, so I closed it in his face again. As my husband went
into the lounge, I rushed to summon the peddler a third
time, but he merely shook his head in disbelief and went on
his way. I was sure that he'd tell everyone what a shame it
was I'd lost my mind while I was still so young.

At one of these coffee mornings, I met Fadila, who came
from a highly religious family of prominent merchants. She
was a few years older than me, and like me she loved to sing
and to watch films. She told me that her real ambition was to
become a singer in Nadia's famous nightclub and made me
promise I'd never tell a soul. She seized my hand and took
me into the kitchen, where she began singing in the style of
one of the famous female singers of the day:

> Liar, liar – they all say that about me:
> You're a liar.
> Never, never, never, no liar I.

I stood watching Fadila as she swayed, pranced and
gestured with her hands and fingers. I tried not to laugh. She
looked just like an ape who had eaten something sour. But I
promised I'd go with her to speak to Nadia at her nightclub.

So one morning Fadila and I went in search of Nadia,
flitting through Burj Square as quickly as we could, lest

Ibrahim spot us from his tram. I tried to give my new friend some advice, suggesting it might be a good idea to try singing somewhere other than Nadia's, especially when I saw she carried a bundle, like a peasant. In it, she had everything she owned: dresses, underwear, scarves, as well as a small mirror and eyebrow tweezers. But she wouldn't listen.

We saw a man hovering at a door to the club with a cigarette in his mouth, his hair slicked down with brilliantine. We were sure this must be the entrance to the famous nightclub, which was talked about by everyone who loved entertainment and singing, especially my brother Hasan. I felt a pang of jealousy at Fadila's absolute conviction that she would be a singer even though her family would disown her on the spot if she succeeded.

I felt as if, by entering the club, we were crossing a line from which there could be no return. Even a man would risk his reputation by entering: 'That guy's no good, going from one dive to the next!' people would say. I pictured drunken men standing in front of us, making rude gestures with beer bottles and then forcing the contents down our gullets. Then I imagined Nadia rushing up to me and seizing me by the hand, filled with sheer delight at having finally discovered me, just as the prince of poets, Ahmad Shawqi,[15] had discovered the Egyptian singer Abdal-Wahhab.

We had to convince a woman cleaning the floor that we urgently needed to talk to Nadia. Then we waited for half an hour until she showed up. Around us there were many chairs and wooden tables, just like the ones we had at home. Suspended from the ceiling was the notorious swing on which Nadia would perch to sing, swooping backwards and forwards.

15 One of Egypt's most celebrated poets and one of the leaders of the modern Arabic literary movement.

Finally Nadia appeared. A famous singer she may have been, but she looked just like an ordinary woman to me, wearing a dressing gown rather than the floor-length dress I'd imagined. Fadila rushed up to her and told her how she wished to become a singer, but without even hearing her sing or giving me a single glance Nadia chucked us out.

'Go away!' she said. 'Go home! Please, I don't want any trouble. Please go home before your tribe comes up from the south to close my place down.'

Obviously she'd recognised Fadila's southern accent. Although Fadila was disappointed at being treated so rudely, we couldn't help giggling at the phrase she'd used – 'tribe from the south' – as if she was referring to people living in the deepest jungle.

Despite the brush-off from Nadia, I found myself longing to visit the nightclub again and started dreaming up ways to make it happen. Then I had a truly wicked idea. If it worked, I'd be in seventh heaven; if it failed, I'd be doomed. When my husband's devout women cousins arrived from the south to visit, I told everyone in the house that we'd been invited to the home of a woman from a very pious family. But I took them to the club instead, telling them that it was a secret and that I was taking them to see some wonders. When they refused to take off their sheer black veils I realised they hadn't understood what I meant by Nadia's nightclub. They hadn't a clue what a comedy sketch was and they'd never even heard of Umar al-Zooni, the king of comedy.

We took our box seats just as the music began and all of a sudden one of the women lifted her veil. The other women followed suit, laughing and shrieking at the clown as he went into his comic routine on stage. 'Wow, this is great!' they yelled. They'd never known how singing and dancing, music and comedy could be such a tonic; or how time could pass so quickly in such a happy atmosphere.

We watched a dancer. Then Nadia came floating down on her swing, clinging to its ropes that were decorated with jasmine flowers. She scattered petals on the people below, and the singer Fouad Zaydan, a friend of my brother Hasan, appeared on stage wearing a wonderful jacket with white and brown checks, his brilliantine-caked hair gleaming in the lights.

'The ship has left the shore of my heart, where has it gone?' he sang. 'The ship has vanished with my loved ones.'

This was 1943, when there was a compulsory blackout each night on Burj Square. All the windows of the nightclub were painted black. No one was allowed out on the streets without a club or cinema ticket. We left the club, terrified that we'd be arrested. But no policeman bothered us; in fact we were in luck because, although it was almost eleven o'clock at night, the trams were still running. The women kept swaying to the rhythm of the songs they'd heard, swimming their way through a world they'd never known existed. For my part I was relaxed: Ibrahim only drove his tram during the day.

Once we got home, they were starving. How was I going to feed them when we were supposed to have filled our stomachs at the house where we'd supposedly been invited? I sneaked into the kitchen in the dark, stole some bread and meat, and warned the women to chew silently. They followed my instructions so well they looked almost like film stars, eating their food with their mouths clamped firmly shut.

'I declare,' one said, 'this sandwich tastes better than a whole lamb.'

'Now I understand,' said another, 'why someone in love can't eat anything; why they get as thin as a needle. I'm in love, but I don't know who with. Tonight I've fallen in love, God forgive me!'

The rest of the night passed without incident, though I had a moment of panic when the one who'd declared she'd fallen in love started talking in her sleep.

'Bring the fire, boy!' she shouted, meaning a red-hot coal for the hookah. Then she made gurgling noises like the pipe she'd seen being used at the nightclub.

Funnily enough, Fadila did eventually get to sing to Nadia, although it was from a distance, while English fighter planes screamed overhead. We had been on the roof watching the Allied planes drop leaflets announcing independence for Syria and Lebanon when we heard music, which was heralding the arrival of Allied soldiers on motorbikes in Burj Square. I ran there as fast as I could with Fadila, as well as all my nieces and nephews. It wasn't the Allies we were hoping to see, like everybody else, but the singers and actors we guessed would be watching from the balconies of the clubs and cabarets. When we saw Nadia on the balcony of her club, Fadila burst into her song, ' "Liar liar, no I'm not a liar." ' But of course Nadia couldn't hear her above the noise.

'Good God … You could Sew a Dress for a Flea'

A T ONE OF my coffee mornings, I noticed one of the women wearing a wonderful pair of stockings. They were softer and smoother than silk, just like the foam from soap. They were made from something called nylon. I explained what I wanted to Abu-Hussein and borrowed a pair to show him.

'Devil take it!' he said. 'For shame! You want to display your flesh in public? For shame. What's wrong with the best-quality cotton I've always provided?'

Mother said, 'Good God, even a snail would leave a thicker trace than that nylon stuff!'

I took my time putting my feet into the borrowed stockings, as though I was handling eggs, though I'd been told that they were 'ladder-resistant'. I fastened the garters and walked around in the stockings, absolutely determined to buy some, no matter what they cost. I'd already spent all my savings on my third coffee morning and the visit to Nadia's nightclub, so as usual I needed to come up with a plan. I went to see our neighbour and begged her to confront Abu-Hussein with a false claim for a debt when he left for work the next morning.

'A pox on you!' she exclaimed, as she handed over the ill-gotten gains. 'You'll have me sent straight to hell. And a pox on the person who married you off when you were still a child.'

She had to fast for a whole week and say extra prayers to atone for the deliberate lie she'd told. Meanwhile I rushed out and bought the magic stockings. I put them on and danced around, singing a song from Nadia's nightclub: ' "Now everything's in the open; all the girls are ladder-resistant!" '

I was desperate to buy all the shoes and dresses I'd seen in films. I wanted brilliantine to make my hair look glossy; I also wanted hairgrips and perfumed soap instead of the institutional-smelling Lifebuoy. But what I hankered for most was a handbag and real lacy silk underwear, not nasty cotton bloomers that reached down to my knees. I wanted lace petticoats too, not flannel shirts that hung below my waist. And shoes. More than anything I wanted a pair of new shoes, not the old white pair Abu-Hussein had bought for me, which he dyed black or brown for winter, and which left me with stained feet when it rained. I decided to slash the shoes with a razor blade so that he'd finally buy me some new ones. But my husband wasn't having any of it.

When I protested, he reminded me that my dead sister had never had a penny of her own, even when she'd worked so hard for his business. I was the very opposite of Ibrahim's wife Khadija, too, who put every single penny she earned aside for her children.

But I continued to steal money from Abu-Hussein whenever he left the room, or went to do his ablutions before prayers, or when he slept. Ibrahim brought home a piece of leather to mend Khadija's and his children's shoes and I cut off a piece and sold it. I even pinched a pair of shoes from a female relative, who'd hung around our house for a whole week, and sold them to a friend.

Then one day, as I watched Abu-Hussein unlock the black box and take out our day's provisions, a truly devilish scheme occurred to me. I waited until he was fast asleep that night and stole the key from his pocket. Then I went to a shop in another neighbourhood and had an exact copy made.

Now I was able to take advantage of Khadija's absences from the kitchen. I could open the box, scoop out some of the provisions, put them in containers, and take them to the homes of friends and neighbours and sell them at half-price. Sometimes I even sent Ibrahim's daughter in my place. All went well until my husband came home early from work and ran into one of Ibrahim's daughters hastily hiding a paper bag behind her back. He grabbed her and found some of the household lard inside.

My husband complained to Ibrahim about my pilfering. Then he went to see our neighbour, a highly respected judge, and asked him to have a word with me. Embarrassed and indignant, I went straight to see the judge myself. My husband was a skinflint, I explained, who considered even coffee beans to be an expendable luxury. I told the judge the only thing my husband thought about me was that I was lazy; I described how he checked my feet when I was asleep to see if I'd washed them. I was still young, I said, not old like him. When the judge tried to point out that Abu-Hussein bought me new dresses, obviously having been told as much by my husband, I posed a question.

'Look at me, your honour. Tell me, how much fabric do I need to make a dress?' By that I meant that, since I was short, it only took two yards of nice, expensive fabric to make me a dress.

Beaten into submission, all the judge could say was, 'God is almighty and He alone has the power and the might!'

This did nothing to stop Ibrahim from yelling and screaming at me.

'You don't have a single drop of shame in your entire body! Good God, you're so cunning, you could sew a dress for a flea. Now everyone will spread the word that you're a nasty little thief.'

With disgust oozing out of his nostrils, Ibrahim raised a hand and struck me. I was overcome by my hatred and my powerlessness. Frustrated beyond endurance, I ran to the primus stove, doused myself in Kerosene, and grabbed a box of matches. But Ibrahim leapt over and snatched them from my hand. I began to cry and couldn't stop. I stood there panting, looking around at the world, relieved I hadn't actually burnt myself alive, and glad that I'd managed to scare Ibrahim. But my skin had started to sting and by the next morning I was covered in a terrible rash.

In spite of my feelings of desperation and fear, when I got caught stealing, I was totally unrepentant. After all, I needed money. The list of wonderful things I wanted — the clothes and hair ribbons — got longer, and the films on Burj Square kept changing. I sold my wristwatch and said it had fallen into a ditch full of rainwater. My husband spent hours bent double with a sieve, sifting through the water and mud in the hope of finding it.

I watched Abu-Hussein's trousers like a hawk, but to no avail. He even started taking his clothes with him into the bathroom. So one day I knocked on the bathroom door and asked if he'd like me to rub his back with a loofah, just like a normal wife would do. My husband was happy; normally I wouldn't let him touch me or even come near me. I rubbed his back and put soapsuds all over his head, then scrubbed his back again and put even more soap on his head. I poured some water to make the suds froth right up until they were dripping down his forehead and into his eyes.

'You're making my eyes sting,' he grumbled.

I gasped, pretending to be surprised, and then scooped up some water. But I didn't pour it over him until I'd reached out and removed some coins from his pocket. Only then did I pour the water over his head. The soapsuds must have hurt a lot because he began swearing at me and calling me a pimp's daughter.

When I'd spent the money and told all the women in the house and my female neighbours about my little plan, they burst out laughing. Word spread about my exploits, but people tolerated me because I was young and funny. And anyway, the entire quarter knew how generous I was to the poor, giving out both food and undergarments when they came to the house. Soon my husband pinned a notice to the front door: 'No begging at this house.'

But the beggars couldn't read or write, so the notice stayed up a day or two before Ibrahim ripped it down.

The Gallant of the Night

TWO YEARS PASSED before I discovered that a bouquet of flowers sent to me after Fatima's birth had been from Muhammad. It had never occurred to me that they might have been from him because, a year after I'd got married, he'd sent me a message through Fatme:

> You're married? You've betrayed me! I'm the biggest fool in the world for surrendering my heart to a little girl. I hope I never set eyes on you again!

After the boy at the grocer's delivered the bouquet, Ibrahim had been determined to learn who'd sent it. He persisted for months, quizzing the boy on the subject. The boy changed his story each time, eventually insisting that it was from one of the ladies who came to my coffee mornings. I was certain the boy next door had sent the bouquet, until quite by chance I bumped into Fatme and Muhammad's sister Miskiah. She told me Muhammad had sent the flowers; and that, even though he'd sworn he'd never love anyone again or get married, he was still in love with me. She went on to tell me that he'd become a detective in the Sécurité Générale and had recently transferred to Beirut. In fact he was living with her and his other brothers, no more than five minutes away from our house.

My heart began to pound with sheer joy. Every word he'd ever said to me or I to him, every gesture we'd exchanged came flooding back. I began falling in love with him all over again. And then, as if in response to my reawakened feelings, one morning I awoke early and saw a blue silk handkerchief on my windowsill. The next day there was a red carnation, the next day a frangipani flower, then a sprig of basil. As I lay in bed at night, I listened for the sound of his footsteps until I fell asleep. Then, I'd dream of footsteps to the sound of our neighbour's cistern, water falling drop by drop.

With the arrival of winter, the wooden shutters were kept tightly closed and so Muhammad sent me a rose via the boy at the grocer. Then one day I saw a dead rose placed carefully on the building's electricity box. I clutched it to my heart and hurried to the grocer's.

'What's the significance of a dead rose?' I asked. 'Do you think that the man who gave me this rose is sick?'

'Yes,' he replied, with a dramatic look. 'Very sick!'

'Did he tell you,' I asked, 'that this was the last time he'd be sending a rose?'

'Yes, he said this was the last time he would send you a rose.'

I hurried straight over to Fatme's house and told her about the dead rose and asked after Muhammad's health. It was as if my visit to Fatme gave him the green light. The next day, on my way to a coffee morning, I spotted him in the distance, reading a newspaper.

He walked up to me.

'Look at you, married under all that finery,' he said, gesturing to my golden bracelets, earrings and necklace. 'So the gold shone so bright that you forgot about me.'

Tears slid down my cheeks and I wanted to explain everything to him. Instead, I let him hold my hand, oblivious to the passers-by.

From then on I saw him almost whenever I left the house, like a rock in the middle of the road. I'd forgotten

how attractive and wonderful he was. Whenever I saw him,
I'd think: Muhammad's even better-looking than Abdal-
Wahhab!

He began to follow me everywhere. Mira came to stay
again and we went to the cinema. As we watched the film,
I heard a whistle each time the hero proclaimed his love for
the heroine. When I looked around at the end, there was my
hero, sitting in the back row. Sometimes Mira would take
me along with a group of women to the Fawwar Antelis
Park to pick cyclamen. I'd sit there happily, jingling my gold
bracelets. Then I'd stand up and do an impersonation of my
friend Fadila singing 'Liar, liar!' or describe the plot of the
very latest film I'd seen. And often I'd spot Muhammad,
alone or with a friend, sitting right opposite our table and
staring straight at me; if I brought a cup up to my mouth,
I'd see him take a drink too. I'd smile, and so would he; I'd
put my hand on my cheek and he'd imitate me exactly. He'd
point to the brooch of cherries I'd pinned to my chest and
indicate I should move them to the left. When I stood to
wash my hands, he'd start plucking a flower and scattering its
petals on the ground.

Every time I set eyes on him, my heart began to pound.
Places became intimate and beautiful; I was happy and smiled
all the time. Someone loved me and understood me. I was
content to make do with the language of signs and pounding
hearts. I was a married woman; I could not go beyond certain
limits. But all he seemed to ask was to follow me wherever I
went. It seemed that he just wanted to be near me.

Each morning, my niece Maryam would find a bloom
waiting when she got up to knead the bread. She'd hide it in
her dress pocket for me.

'Just look what the gallant of the night has left!' she'd
whisper, watching me clutch the rose to my heart. 'Be
careful, Auntie,' she would warn me. 'Take good care. Please

remember, we're all dependent on Abu-Hussein. If you put a finger too far into the water, the current may carry you away!'

She was right, of course, but whenever I saw Muhammad, my mind would detach itself and run towards him.

Once a thief managed to get into our house early one morning. Maryam, as she was kneading the bread, spied him hiding behind the door. She pushed against the door as hard as she could, trying to squash him. All of a sudden she stopped pushing.

'For my sake,' she said, 'I hope you're not Muhammad.'

'No,' the thief replied. 'My name's Mustapha.'

Clang, Clang, Clang ... Gotcha, Gotcha, Gotcha!

BY NOW I was thinking so much about Muhammad that I couldn't stand being in our house. Even if I was on my own outside, I felt closer to him. Making matters worse, there was the huge and ever-widening rift between me and Ibrahim, and between me and Mother too. There was trouble every time I wanted to go out. The noose seemed to be tightening around me and Maryam. If we even laughed, we'd hear my husband say, 'The Devil's with us,' or Ibrahim would bellow, 'Bitch's daughter!'

If we plucked our eyebrows, we'd stay out of sight till the redness disappeared. Maryam hid herself away when she bleached her black hair with peroxide, keeping it concealed for several days under a scarf. But the thing we feared most was Ibrahim catching us on our way to the cinema in Burj Square. We became so paranoid that we believed he might cut us off by this corner or that bend in the road, even far away from the tram line. Clang, clang, clang – he'd lean his foot on the warning bell of the tram and the noise would echo all around. Clang, clang, clang ... gotcha, gotcha, gotcha!

Then Ibrahim was suspended from driving the tram for two months after he hit a pedestrian. He ran away to the south, lest the family of the injured man retaliate. And suddenly, for two months, I was free. Free to appreciate how wide Burj Square actually was, and how beautiful! I noticed the shops and the lovely things on display by the doors and in the shop windows. Though I feared that the other tram drivers were in league with Ibrahim, I began riding the tram in the middle of the day.

Of course Ibrahim's desperately controlling behaviour towards the women in his family wasn't unusual. Most of my friends were scared of every man in their family – even distant relatives – and this included the rich and the grand, like my glamorous cousin Mira. In my eyes Mira was as strong and beautiful as al-Buraq[16] – until her brother spotted us coming out of the cinema one afternoon. Very late that night, he knocked on our door and insisted on searching for her in the sleeping household. He dragged her into the kitchen to hit her, oblivious to the fact he'd managed to wake us all. I listened, incredulous, as she began to cry. It was then that I realised that, for all her money and the gold flashing from her neck and wrists, she was as powerless as me. It made no difference that she was a married woman and a mother, with a crocodile-skin handbag that opened with a click.

This put an end to Mira's cinema visits for a time. I came up with one enticement after another, all to no avail – until *The Apple Seller* took Beirut by storm. Mira was desperate to see this film, about a simple apple seller and a rich young man who made a bet with his friend that he could transform her into an aristocratic girl. It was only towards the end, when she was attending a ball, that the girl discovered the young man was interested in her only because of a bet.

For this film Mira managed to overcome her fears. She devised a masterly scheme to get us all to the cinema: she invited my husband's business partner and his wife to come with us, thereby putting Ibrahim and my husband on the spot. They couldn't refuse, and so they agreed to come and to bring Khadija as well. We took our seats and were so entranced by the film that it wasn't until the lights came up

16 The splendid white steed on which the Prophet Muhammad rode into the seven heavens.

that I realised that my husband was sound asleep. Ibrahim frowned as usual and said nothing about the film.

After that night I thought of myself as the apple seller, while Muhammad was the aristocrat who taught me to read and write. I longed to sit with him by the fountain at Fatme's again and chat about films and film stars. I would tell him that the cinema had become my school, teaching me about life, history and geography. I learned about a continent called Europe and saw scenes from the war. The cinema taught me how to speak and dress. It took me inside splendid houses and hovels, and introduced me to the people who lived in them. I desperately wanted to live like some of them, but I also thanked God that my life was better than that of many others. On the screen I met people like me, others like Ibrahim, and still more like my husband.

Every time Ibrahim or Mother asked me where I was going, I thought of the Umar al-Zooni song:

> Where are we off to by night and day?
> You see the cinema next to the bar.
> You see the people in droves,
> Every type, every complexion,
> This way and that,
> In and out of view.
> They're all off to the cinema,
> This way and that,
> All of them off to the cinema.

Love's First Signs

JUST AS MARYAM had feared, a torrent of feelings for Muhammad swept me away. The time came when I really was with him: on a street corner; in a restaurant near al-Rawche, the famous rock on Beirut's seafront from which jilted lovers leapt to their deaths; or in a park outside Beirut, where we'd gone by taxi. We held hands, afraid we'd be separated. When we met and strolled together, I wasn't afraid; I would convince myself that Ibrahim and Abu-Hussein were at work. In any case, neither of them knew of the out-of-the-way places where we spent time. But the moment I stepped back across the threshold of the house, I'd be overcome with fear. Was Ibrahim angrier than usual? Was he spying on me? Did he know I was meeting Muhammad – were my brother and my husband planning to catch me out?

However great these fears, they didn't stop me from seeing Muhammad. My happiest moments occurred when I was with him. I wanted nothing more. It was again as if Muhammad were the teacher and I the pupil. He took a piece of paper out of his pocket and held my hand, reading what he had written while he was waiting for me:

As she came close to me, her face appeared through her flimsy veil like the face of the very moon shrouded in a squadron of clouds. My heart pounded as she came towards me with measured steps, walking with all the grace of an antelope. On her lovely face was an innocent smile, repeated on exquisite pink lips crafted to perfection by the Lord of All. Her pearly teeth, perfectly set, gave due glory to their Creator – how wonderful they were! I took in the rays from her languid eyes that were so filled with sweet delight and temptation. My beloved did not speak. Instead two tears fluttered on her cheeks and fell into my heart like a thunderbolt, two little tears of gold rolling down over the purest silver. With my voice a tissue of sobs and shudders, I asked her, 'How is it that my beloved is in tears, while my own heart cries too?'

I was amazed to find I understood every single word of his classical Arabic and fought back the urge to cry. Could I possibly be so important, someone who engendered such feelings in Muhammad? I found myself agreeing to meet him in his room.

The very next day, I entered the front door to the house that he shared with his family and took a few steps towards his bedroom. The room contained only a table, his bed, papers and books. I stood there, hand to my heart. I didn't want to sit on his bed. He came over to me and touched my hand. I was happy just to look at him. I listened as his whispers grew louder, but could hear nothing he said. I glanced at his face and then threw myself into his arms. He hugged me as hard as he could, just like we were in one of the films I loved, and said my name over and over: 'Kamila, Kamila, Kamila.'

'Muhammad, Muhammad, Muhammad,' I replied. How I loved his name – the Prophet's own! In that name, my love found its blessing – though inside, I had to suppress a laugh since Muhammad was also my husband's name.[17]

---

17 In the Arab world the father takes on the name of his eldest son, so Muhammad became Abu-(father of)Hussein after the birth of his firstborn.

I began to meet him almost every day, as soon as he returned from work at about one o'clock. I came to love his tiny room; there was nowhere else I wanted to be. It was like being in the cinema, far removed from the sounds of our house – from the voices of the old, the young and even babies, from chatter about rancid oil and weevils in the rice sack.

Each day, after we'd eaten, Muhammad would kiss me. Gradually I surrendered to his kisses. He would embrace me and try to touch my breasts, but I would push him away. I wanted to keep our love unconsummated. But soon I relaxed, surrendering my lips to him and releasing my hands from my chest. I'd never told him how the events of my wedding night made me dislike the sight of my body and how, even though I was utterly devoted to my baby daughter, I still couldn't believe I'd actually carried her inside me or experienced the contractions to deliver her. I remembered the pain of the birth with utter horror.

Then Muhammad had to leave Beirut for several weeks because of his job. He sent me a letter via his sister Miskiah, which a friend read aloud:

The further apart we are, the more I feel my life is an arid desert. Just two days ago we were living so close to each other, almost inseparable. Now you are so far away. What are you doing? I've started counting the minutes that keep us apart, the ones already passed and the ones that remain.

Impetuously I ripped a piece of paper out of my nephew's notebook. With a pencil I drew a picture of two little birds perched on two flowers, inhaling the scent. I drew the leaves in heart shapes, then a sun and moon. Next I drew a nest for the two little birds. I kept my drawing and gave it to him when he returned.

He looked at it and gave me a passionate kiss. Then we seemed to rise and hover above the room. When we returned to his familiar small room, we both began to cry. We wept because I'd allowed another man to lie on top of me and rob me of my virginity. We cried because Muhammad, such a decent and honourable man, was in love with a married woman and I was betraying my husband. I sobbed because I found it unbearable that I must return to a house in which I felt I didn't belong, to a man I didn't care for.

Back at home, I watched my husband eat, bending over his plate so as not to let a single crumb fall on to the table. I wanted to scream, 'Divorce me!' When he opened the black box, I wanted to shout, 'Divorce me!' When I looked at Ibrahim, I wanted to scream, 'What did I ever do to make you torture me so?' And I wanted to yell at Mother too. 'Why have you wronged me like this? Am I not your flesh and blood?'

Muhammad always calmed me down. He breathed gently on my face as if he was soothing a deep wound. And then one day I realised what we had done. I began to fear that I might be carrying Muhammad's baby. A new baby with hair as smooth as Muhammad's and honey-coloured eyes that were almost green.

That evening, when Abu-Hussein went to bed, I climbed into his bed and moved closer to him for the first time in three years. He couldn't believe his luck. He clung to me for a few moments and, when I didn't scream, he mounted me, while I bit my arm in an attempt to stay calm.

'You Cry so you can go to the Cinema, and then you Come Home Crying!'

I STEPPED OUT OF the cinema, totally devastated. Nawal, the heroine of *Tears of Love*, was dead. I was furious with her lover. After her husband died, she had gone back to him.

'Forgive me!' she had begged him. 'Forgive me. Please accept my submission and forgive me.'

'I forgive you,' replied Abdal-Wahhab. 'I forgive you!'

'You're my life,' she told him. 'I have no life other than with you.'

But then he accused her of hypocrisy and deceit as she used the very words she'd spoken to her husband on her wedding night. Abdal-Wahhab rejected her, so she ran out and threw herself into the canal.

I burst into tears. It was as though the floodgates had opened and the waters were flowing down my face.

Yet again a film had spoken to me. It felt like a reflection of my own life. Just like Nawal, I'd been forced into marriage. Like her, I'd found true love, but my hands were tied because of my marriage, my child and the new baby inside my womb.

On my way home I passed the studio of Narcissus, an Armenian photographer, and went inside.

'I want you to take my photograph,' I told him, before he could say a word.

He offered various backdrops: you could be pictured riding in a plane, sitting on a white wooden crescent, standing next to a table decorated with a bouquet of flowers. He suggested I hold a rose as though I was smelling it.

'I want a picture of my face,' I told him, holding a black scarf, just as Nawal did in the film when she returned to her lover's house.

'What's distressing you, madam?' the photographer asked as he prepared his equipment. I told him I'd been to see the film *Tears of Love* and that I was in mourning because the heroine had thrown herself in the canal.

'But it's only a movie,' he replied with a chuckle. 'You don't believe everything you see on the screen, do you?'

I explained what Nawal had endured, but he kept trying to make me laugh.

'Come on, madam,' he said, 'smile! It was just a film! They only made it for the money!'

I leapt up in a fury.

'Do you suppose for a single second,' I shouted, 'that the man who sings over his beloved's grave, "Oh you who sleep eternally beneath the soil, I have come to weep over the passion of lovers. Ye clouds, ye stars, I am true to my love!" is thinking only of money?'

'It's all about money,' he said, hiding his face under the camera cloth. Then he shouted, '*Mona Lisa*! That's who you are. If she were in the next room she'd be following you with those eyes of hers!'

I'd no idea what he was talking about. I'd become Nawal. She was dead after suffering terribly; I was suffering every moment too. The very thought of returning home made me ill.

The photographer took my picture.

'You *are* just like the *Mona Lisa*,' he said. 'Are you from Beirut?' I told him I was from Nabatiyeh.

'Good heavens,' he replied. 'A *Mona Lisa* from Nabatiyeh, not from Italy! You're the first woman to come in here without her mother or father.' He sounded impressed.

Of course, I realised, I was alone with the photographer. He might tilt my head this way and that, and then ask me to untie my hair or put on lipstick or kohl – all these intimacies with a stranger could not be allowed.

But I didn't care that I was alone with him. I found myself opening my heart to him.

'Photographs aren't allowed in our house,' I told him. 'That's why I want to have my picture taken.'

I removed my headscarf and asked him to take another picture without it.

He let out a whistle, just like a bird.

'You're so young!' he said. 'One day soon you'll marry somebody very high up.' Then he held up his hand.

I began to cry. I found myself telling him the story of my life, how cruel my family was to me.

'I want to be rid of this life,' I told him, 'just like Nawal ...'

The photographer interrupted me.

'No, no,' he said. 'Why do you want to be like Nawal? She's crazy, committing suicide. She's like a silver ring that's tarnished. You have to rub your sorrows away, and then the silver will shine through like a diamond again.'

Back home, sobbing and weeping, I told the story of the film to Khadija, Mother and Maryam.

'You cry so you can go to the cinema,' Mother remarked, 'and then you come home crying! And it costs a lot of money. Why don't you just stay here?'

I went on crying. Why had Nawal committed suicide? Why hadn't she pleaded with her beloved? Why hadn't she raised hell? I imagined rubbing a tarnished ring until it shone with light. I promised myself I'd stay strong and not let despair get the better of me.

The Camel Howdah

I WAS PRACTICALLY LIVING with Muhammad. In my mind, it was as if his house and mine were one, despite the other buildings, shops, cars and pedestrians that stood between. I took his washing home and Maryam and I washed it in secret. Then she would iron his things so I could take them back the next day and put them in his wardrobe.

As I moved around his tiny room, I felt as if it were my own, as if I had not a care in the world, as if I didn't need to hold my breath when passing his neighbours, or even the walls, in case they revealed my secret. His room looked out on to a side alley. I'd invented numerous ways of attracting his attention to let him know I was outside waiting for him. I would knock on his window or put a pile of sand or a matchstick on the sill.

Sometimes I called in on his sister when Muhammad was at work. When I got up to go, I'd beg her not to accompany me to the door. Then I'd sneak into his room and close the door behind me. Sometimes he left me alone inside his room when his work required him to go out for an hour. He would lock the door behind him and leave me with a jerrycan to pee in.

Once when he was gone I had a terrible need to poo. I hunted for newspapers and sheets of paper, piled them up and then crouched down with my eyes shut, praying that they weren't important documents. I wrapped up the piles of paper, put them inside a paper bag, opened the window and looked out to make sure no one was in the side alley. Then I threw the bag outside and closed the window again, leaving the shutters ajar so I could keep an eye on the bag. The doctor's son, who lived in the same building, spotted it and circled around it before deciding to open it up. Disgusted, he began to curse and swear, looking around for the malicious person who'd played this dirty trick on him. My heart pounded. Had anyone seen me open the window and throw out the bag?

I started to shiver with fear, terrified of a scandal. It was as if I was watching myself, calmly observing from a distance. It reminded me that I was married. My house was not this room – my home was where my husband and daughter, Ibrahim and Mother all lived, together with the rest of the extended family and all of the endless visitors. I raised my eyes to the ceiling and prayed to God to rescue me just this once. I promised that, whatever happened, I'd never set foot in this room again.

But as soon as the doctor's son gave up on the mystery bag and went on his way, I found that I wasn't putting on my shoes and going home. Instead, I looked around the room, imagining that it was an old-fashioned camel howdah like I'd seen in films: a tent that sat on top of a camel, concealing the women and protecting them from the raging sands. I remained there, waiting for Muhammad, as though I was too ill to move and awaited a doctor.

In a way, Muhammad did play the role of my doctor. He seemed to have antennae that allowed him to sense my most trivial thoughts, even before they were fully formed. Although he had little money, he would bring me luxurious food: things like pistachios, grilled chicken, or dried beef as tender as asparagus tips. I would hide his gifts under the bed at home and take them out only when the house was asleep. I'd share them with Maryam and we'd eat in the dark before settling down again. Muhammad really does love me, I would tell myself. He's spending all his money, depriving himself of these things so I can enjoy them. Then I chided myself for being so greedy and tried to appreciate my lover's true generosity.

When Muhammad returned, I told him his room was like a camel howdah. The simile delighted him. He promised he'd teach me how to read and write as soon as possible. As we sat together, he read me a letter he'd received from his brother. The language, more formal, was so different. His brother used expressions and words like 'damask rose', 'jasmine', or 'Syrian apples'. He ended with a blessing: 'Peace be with you along with the chirping of sparrows, the roar of waves, the cooing of doves, the ripple of waters, the rustle of leaves, the waft of scent and the flash of brilliance.'

Before long, without a thought, I felt that I'd become a part of Muhammad's circle of family and friends, whose letters he read to me so often. I loved the way they wrote to each other. As he read, I would think of my own family and shudder.

We went to see another film called *Dananir*, starring the famous singer Umm Kulthum as a Bedouin girl named Dananir. One day the vizier Jafar – who came from the Barmakid family, known for its generosity – heard her singing and offered to take her to his palace to school her in the art of singing. Dananir was thrilled by the offer, which would enable her to live in Baghdad. But the Caliph, Harun al-Rashid, heard about her lovely voice and asked Jafar for Dananir, so she could sing in his palace. Jafar turned down the Caliph's request, because he had fallen in love with Dananir. The Caliph had Jafar killed, imagining that Dananir would then obey his wishes and sing for him, but she defied him and refused, even when he ordered her imprisonment.

But eventually he took pity on her and released her. Dananir, free to sing for her dead beloved, promised to remain true to him till death.

I was so moved by the love scenes between Dananir and Jafar that I began to despair. It was the fifth film I'd seen in which the consequence of true love was death. The family always opposed the union and someone would cruelly expose their love.

The next day I visited Muhammad. He took my hand and read out what he had written that night when he'd been unable to sleep:

Weep for the Barmakid family, massacred at the hands of Caliph Harun al-Rashid! Woe for Jafar and his catastrophic love for Dananir, that woman whose loyalty and devotion was like the purest water poured into the heart. She kept her pledge to her beloved Jafar, when he was alive and after he'd been murdered. That was true loyalty. Oh God, please let our union last in life and death.

Gazing into my eyes, he asked if I'd be as loyal as Dananir. I couldn't think why he asked such a question when he was my whole life. But he was insistent: had I been unfaithful to my husband with anyone but him? The question shocked me. I laughed it off, but inside I was nervous. Did Muhammad know about the boy next door, who had first noticed me when I ran screaming from the house at the sight of my white wedding dress? From that moment he'd watched me intently, indicating that he wanted to meet, though I kept things to an exchange of glances, flirting with him on my own terms.

When I left the house the following day, heading for Muhammad's room, crowds blocked the entrance to our alleyway and the street beyond, stemming from the front of the Prime Minister's home. Riyad al-Solh, who'd recently taken up residence, had caused much controversy. There had been demonstrations throughout Beirut, with several people killed or wounded. This violence followed the arrest, by the French mandate authorities, of the President of the Republic, Bishara al-Khoury, along with the Prime Minister and other ministers. It was the final stage of the struggle by the Lebanese national forces against the French before the country won total independence.

I had to push through in order to reach Muhammad's door. When I didn't find him at home, I was worried that he'd been put on duty with the rest of the Lebanese guards. But as I turned for home again, he appeared and signalled to me to follow him inside. Not even bothering to kiss me, he told me we were seeing history in the making – independence for Lebanon, an end to the French mandate and a provisional government at Bashamun!

I asked God to ensure the demonstrations continued, so I could use them as an excuse for being late home. But Muhammad told me I must leave immediately, because he wanted to check on relatives working as guards near the HQ of the British general.[18] He'd heard rumours of people being wounded and wanted to go to Burj Square to see what was happening. I begged him to take me with him, but he refused. At that moment, I decided that he didn't love me the way I loved him. I was distraught. I even considered agreeing to meet the boy next door in revenge, but I didn't have the heart for it.

18 General Spears, head of the mandate authority.

How I Came to Call my Second Baby Hanan

I T WASN'T THE nausea that made me refuse to sleep with Muhammad again. It was my fear that the baby would look half like Muhammad and half like my husband.

I didn't want to tell him I was pregnant. So I rejected being intimate with him – I kept saying I wasn't feeling well, that there wasn't enough time or that someone might hear us. Finally Muhammad lost patience and told me Ibn al-Mutazz would never have accepted my excuses. Nervously I asked who Ibn al-Mutazz was. A famous Arab poet, he replied, who wrote, 'Enjoy your beloved every day, for you never know when distance will separate you.'

When he recited this line, I felt as though my hand was being amputated! How could he possibly imagine we'd ever be separated?

'But you don't belong to me,' he said. 'Now or ever. You're a married woman.'

My heart collapsed. In my mind, I was on a ship taking me to a land called Muhammad, far away from fear and trouble, from Ibrahim and my husband. But now suddenly the ship had capsized and I was drowning.

Muhammad tried to comfort me.

Holding me tightly, he vowed, 'Death before I'd ever abandon you.'

He took a piece of paper out of his pocket and read what he'd written on it:

I love the path you walk on and the bed you sleep in. I love
the pillow, the sheets, the house, the roof and the walls.
If only I could be an invisible breeze which entered your
house through the window at dawn and played ... I love the
brilliant moon in the night sky because its light resembles
you. I love the clear sky because it's like your eyes.

He began to caress me again, but I shoved him away. He
dashed to the table drawer and took out a revolver, pointing
it first at my head, then at his own. Terrified, I forced a
smile, trying to lighten the mood, and then I told him I was
pregnant. Muhammad hurled the revolver on to the bed, put
his head between his hands and began to cry – he actually
burst into floods of tears. I picked up the heavy revolver, and
walked out of his bedroom, along the corridor to the kitchen,
as if to announce to the occupants of the entire house that I
was a human being, not a genie or a sprite. There was no one
indoors, but his elder brother – who had not acknowledged
me until this moment – was in the garden. I handed him the
revolver without a word. He took it, also without speaking,
shaking his head. I went back inside and held Muhammad's
head against me as we both wept. I assumed we cried for the
same reason: I was going to give birth to a baby that was half
his, in my husband's house.

But then he turned on me, shouting, 'How on earth could
you have let your husband have sex with you?'

I explained about the half-baby and the reason I'd slept
with Abu-Hussein. He stared at me in disbelief, suddenly
calm. He had been very careful, he said, so I wouldn't get
pregnant. And now I'd managed to betray him with my own
husband. Realising my obvious confusion, and though I was
already pregnant with my second daughter, my lover told me
the facts of life.

★   ★   ★

When it came time for me to deliver the baby and the contractions grew really bad, Maryam took me to the hospital. It was the same obstetrician as before.

'You know, I remember you from last time,' he exclaimed. 'I gave a lecture later in which I told the students how I'd delivered a baby to a fifteen-year-old girl.'

That doctor was extremely well known, one of the most famous in Lebanon. Muhammad told me he'd written books on childbirth and motherhood.

As the doctor held up my second daughter, he smiled and said, 'Well, I've brought you a lovely girl. Your husband's going to think you can only produce girls. Maybe now he'll leave you alone! What are you going to call her?'

'My husband's away on the pilgrimage to Mecca,' I replied. 'He instructed me before he left that, if I gave birth to a boy, I was to call him Mustapha, or if to a girl, Zaynab. I love Sitt Zaynab, of course, but I don't want my daughter to have a religious name. It's enough that he made me call my first daughter Fatima. This new baby's as lovely as the moon! I want to call her Zulfa.'

The doctor laughed, correcting my pronunciation. 'It's Zalfa, not Zulfa, which means a beautiful woman with a tiny nose! But listen, you should give her a name you can pronounce!'

The nurse brought me a bouquet of roses that had just been delivered, saying they were from a relative who came by every day to ask how I was. Clutching the bouquet to my breast, I closed my eyes. Until then, no one had brought me a single rose, and I realised I'd had no visitors apart from Maryam.

A couple of days after the birth, when I saw how kind the doctor was being, I asked if it would be possible for me to go to the cinema. I'd only be out a couple of hours to see the new film *Hanan*. When I went home, I told him, my family would insist on the custom of not letting me leave my bed for forty days. Then I wouldn't get to see the film.

The doctor laughed out loud.

'Hanan! Call your daughter Hanan. It's a pretty name.'

'You're right,' I replied. 'Hanan's a wonderful name.' And that was how I came to call my daughter Hanan.

He didn't say yes to the cinema, but he didn't say no, although he did tell the nurses about our conversation. They started to tease me, especially after I told them I wanted to get my daughter's name registered as soon as possible and confront my husband with a fait accompli. When they suggested he might object and give her another name – one he liked – I assured them he was so miserly that he'd never willingly pay the registration fee twice.

In the end, I did indeed go out. I met Muhammad and we went to the film *Hanan*. I sat next to him, praying to God not to let my milk start flowing.

But when Muhammad kissed my hand and said, 'Thank God you are well!' the milk began to drip from my breasts.

As the film started, he pointed to the screen to show me the word 'Hanan', assuring me it was a lovely name that had many meanings. But unfortunately the film itself wasn't very good; it was about betrayal between two business partners. I hardly remember it.

Abu-Hussein did not return to Beirut with the rest of the pilgrims, but stayed on to perform even more prayers and get his fill of the holy Mecca. To outdo the other pilgrims, he slept by the noble Kaaba in Saudi Arabia, touched the Prophet's tomb and visited the city of Medina. Two months later he arrived home without warning. I dashed to place my new baby girl next to Ibrahim's new daughter, who'd also been born during his absence.

'Which is your daughter?' I asked, and he pointed to Hanan at once. She looked exactly like him. I smiled and treated him tenderly, fearful he might decide to change her name. I showed him all the respect he deserved as a haji, a returning pilgrim. Then I waited to see the things I'd asked him to bring me back from the pilgrimage: silk fabrics and pieces of turquoise and gold, as pilgrims usually do when they return from visiting the holy places. First he gave me some blessed water from the Zemzem well, some prayer mats from Mount Arafat and a string of black prayer beads. I ignored them and instead attacked a wrapped package. Excited and happy, I ripped the paper off, and found myself holding a piece of coarse white cloth. It was a blessed funeral shroud. I laughed as I wrapped myself in this shroud. I went out into the sitting room and lay down on the floor, dead, while everybody pinched me to make me giggle.

We began calling my husband the Haji. When I felt like teasing him I'd say, 'Hajuj!' Everyone laughed. He'd been extremely religious before the pilgrimage, but now he was even more devout. He announced prayer times in a loud voice, just like a crier going around the villages announcing deaths and marriages. He encouraged everyone, old and young, to perform their ablutions and to pray; and he urged all the women, from Maryam and my nieces to our female neighbours, to keep their heads covered.

Each night he'd recite the shahada, a statement of faith, in case he died in his sleep, and he expected everyone else in the house to do the same. He was always bent double on his prayer mat. It aggravated me because he took up most of the floor space in our bedroom and he wouldn't answer my questions when he was praying. There was always something I wanted to ask, and so I would only leave him to his devotions when he'd nodded or shaken his head to answer me.

I don't know why, but sometimes, when he was crouching before God like a tiny lamb, I had the urge to make him laugh. 'I'm going to get the Sphinx to laugh,' I'd say, 'in spite of himself.' Once I pinned a long strip of cloth to the back of his pyjama bottoms so that, each time he stood and then kneeled again and prostrated himself, it moved with him, like a tail. I began to laugh loudly, attracting the attention of the family. Fatima pointed to her father's tail and laughed. Finally, he laughed too.

The Lady and Ibrahim

W AS IT GOD who came to rescue me and made Ibrahim fall in love? He became like all lovers, seeing and hearing nothing except his own beating heart. The lady next door – who lived by herself in a room overlooking the garden and shared a kitchen and bathroom with our neighbours – had started making eyes at him. I saw this as a blessing, even though I was very fond of his wife Khadija. All I wanted was for him to mind his own business and ignore my various exploits and the obvious fact that I was in love.

We called this neighbour the Lady, assuming she was a spinster and still a virgin. Later, when Ibrahim started seeing a lot of her, we changed her nickname to Two-rooms-sitting-room-and-kitchen, because she'd tell him repeatedly that she owned an apartment consisting of 'two rooms: sitting room and kitchen'. I eavesdropped on the two of them, having never for a second imagined that Ibrahim, of all people, would resort to such a dalliance. I assumed their relationship would never progress beyond greetings and conversation. But then the day came when Khadija knocked at the Lady's door.

'Tell him his dinner's ready,' she said. 'If he's hungry, that is.'

The Lady had never tried to hide from Khadija that Ibrahim had been calling a lot and she'd made it clear that she would have no objection to becoming his second wife.

But Ibrahim was chastened. He returned to his home to eat dinner, and never visited the Lady again. Khadija, now pregnant with their seventh child, never broached the topic of the Lady. She just carried on with her household chores as though nothing had happened. Every woman in the neighbourhood saluted Khadija for her wit and cunning; she'd made it seem as though he was free to do what he wanted and that she was just a submissive wife who cared only about her husband's well-being. But in reality, she had put an end to their love affair.

We learned later that the Lady had once worked on the farm of a rich Beiruti who had bought up large tracts of land in the Bekaa Valley. The man — who was handsome, high class, and a smooth talker — visited the farm every so often and noticed the Lady. She pleased him and bore him a child. The delivery was helped along by the local midwife, who wrapped the screaming newborn boy in a towel and disappeared with him, only to return in tears to tell the woman the baby had died. The Lady believed her, trusting that God had taken pity on her and her child by ending its life.

This did not stop her from becoming pregnant a second time, again by the rich man. She gave birth to a second son, and again the midwife took the baby away, only to return in tears, saying that this baby was dead too. 'God alone knows,' she said, 'why your babies die.' Then the rich man's sister-in-law intervened and told the Lady she must prepare to leave the farm for good and go to Beirut to live. They'd bought her an apartment in the city consisting of 'two rooms: sitting room and kitchen'. The Lady decided to let out this property and rent a small room instead. As time rolled on and she grew older, she began to search for her two children, certain that they hadn't died, as she'd been told. But I don't believe she ever found them.

The Walnut Tree Knows Everything

ONCE HIS VISITS to the Lady had stopped, Ibrahim began to watch me again. I came up with a brilliant solution: going with the family for the summer months to a resort. I couldn't stand the suffocating heat of Beirut any longer, or the sky, which hurled down hot droplets of water that only increased the humidity. After insistent pleading, the Haji gave in and rented us a summer place in Bhamdoun, a well-known mountain resort. The fact that we could rent a place in the mountains was a clear sign of our new status as middle-class people. We were inundated with visitors – Bhamdoun was known as the bride of summer locations.

Each morning Abu-Hussein and Kamil (who was still living at home with us) went twenty kilometres down to work in Beirut and did not return until evening. I started to wander the open fields, just as I had in Nabatiyeh, feeling young and free once more. From the window, I looked out on valleys and houses with red-tiled roofs, instead of the prying eyes of the neighbours. I almost forgot Ibrahim existed, though I missed Khadija and her family. But Maryam was with us, and she and I spent all our time together.

Muhammad began to take the bus to see me. Alighting in the centre of Bhamdoun with only a couple of hours to spare, he'd pray to God that he'd find me somewhere. First he'd do the rounds of the places Maryam and I frequented. If we weren't at any of them, he'd stand opposite our house until one of us looked out of the window. (It was bound to

happen, since we were always watching out for him.) Then
I'd run outside, barefoot, to see him. We'd head for a walnut
tree that had managed to grow, in defiance of nature, on its
own rocky patch amid yellow fern and red-coloured stone.
Muhammad carved on the tree the date our love began, with
my name and his, just like in the film *Tears of Love*. Each
time, he'd add another groove with the date of our latest
meeting.

Once we met at night, with Maryam as our chaperone as
usual. I'd told everyone that I'd lost my gold bracelet among
the vines, and that Maryam and I were going out with a lamp
to search for it. We strolled through the vines.

'You're not one of the daughters of Eve,' he told me.

'Why not?' I asked. 'Is it because I'm too short?'

'No,' he replied. 'Eve was cunning and full of guile.'

But hadn't I been cunning too? I'd come up with a way
of stealing out of the house to be with him. We walked in
the moonlight amid the vines; they rose like giants that had
fallen asleep standing up and been covered with foliage. It
was silent, except for his voice and the sound of the wind,
which scared me. A dog chased after us, barking. I clung
tightly to Muhammad. As soon as the dog lost interest, I
relaxed and asked the retreating animal if the Haji had sent
it to follow us. The thought made the three of us laugh and
then I asked Muhammad to place a hand on my heart, which
was beating wildly.

'Your heart cannot endure fear and love at the same time,'
he told me.

Later he wrote about our night-time excursion and read
it aloud to me:

It's as though I hear that heart, your heart, which holds me
fast, pound fiercely. Ah, the joy of listening to its rhythm
as the shivers of love pulse in my veins. If only this night

would never end and this moon would never rise again so
I could stay for ever at your side ...

Here I was, living a pleasant life twice over, just as God had
decreed for me: once when I met Muhammad in person,
in flesh and blood; and then when he wrote about our
encounters so that we could meet again, on paper. We started
writing to each other – not from Cairo to Beirut, as in the
film *Tears of Love*, but from Bhamdoun to Beirut. Gathering
all my courage, I confided in our landlord's daughter, who
was my age. She agreed to write to him for me, and to read
me his letters. Every time Maryam went down to Beirut for
the day to see her family, she would return with a letter from
Muhammad. In one of his first letters, he told me to check
the walnut tree. So I would return to the walnut tree each
day to look for a sign: a stone placed in a special way, an
ivory bead, or a wilted rose. I'd picture him carefully leaving
these things for me to find.

As the summers passed, I grew more and more careless about
hiding our outings in Bhamdoun. I was confident that no
one would find out about my relationship with Muhammad.
I even let Maryam take photos with Muhammad's camera
as he lifted me in his arms. In one picture I am trying to
hold down my skirt for fear of exposing my thighs, and my
slippers are falling off my feet. In another, we are shaking
hands, as if an invisible third party is introducing us.

I didn't dare keep any of the pictures for myself, in case
they fell into the wrong hands. Instead, I left them with
Muhammad, although I would borrow them to show Fadila.
The pictures did not hide how in love we were. I looked so
happy in them, so unafraid, because our new home lay in
the midst of nature. Its walls were trees and rocks. My two
daughters were our cover. If native Bhamdounis came across

us gazing lovingly at each other, they saw a mother and father still very much in love, their two daughters playing around them. Those photographs made me ask myself: Can our love be a reality if it exists only in secret?

Four Years or Four Seconds

FOR FOUR WHOLE years, Muhammad and I allowed no one to get in the way of our affair. But Muhammad was increasingly under pressure from his family. My lover's elder brother tried to persuade him to end the relationship and wrote him a letter:

> I don't deny you're in love with the woman, or that she's equally worthy of your love, but you know better than anyone the right thing to do. From the bottom of my heart, I've wanted to be the one man who could bring your desires to fruition, even at the cost of life itself. You also know I am no hypocrite and will do anything to preserve my brother Muhammad's honour. So, I beg you, pause to take stock and consult your heart. As God and His angels will witness, I don't like having to talk to you like this, but at the same time I'd much prefer it if you distanced yourself from the unattainable, something that may well cost us all dear.

Muhammad read the letter to me, then folded it and put it away without saying a word. Shortly after he received this letter, his mother – who had regularly visited him and his brothers and sisters for long periods – left Beirut and went home to their village.

'She's run away from me and you,' Muhammad told me, broken-hearted. He took my hand and kissed it.

I had an instant image of Ibrahim yelling at me: 'I've known you all my life. I can read you like the back of my hand!' To banish the thought, I shrugged and imagined Muhammad with his head on my breast as I sang to him.

His family were desperate for him to marry. His sister Miskiah was my informer. Once she showed me photos of young girls of marriageable age; some of the women in his family hoped he might choose one. I snatched them and drew beards and moustaches on their faces. But this didn't deter Miskiah from confiding in me that his family had chosen a bride for him. She told me when the young woman and her mother would be paying a visit to the house, and so I hid in his room. As I heard them approach the house, I moved a ring from my right to my left hand so it looked exactly like an engagement ring. I opened the window and, with my hand visible, began to sing.

Later I heard from Miskiah that, when the mother and daughter heard my singing from Muhammad's window and saw my hand with its engagement ring, they'd turned back the way they'd come. The mother later sent a strongly worded reproof to Muhammad's family.

During those four years, Muhammad became more and more desperate. He took to creeping up the stairs to my house at midnight or daybreak, not to leave me a flower or a tip of basil, but to spy into my bedroom to make sure I wasn't sharing the bed with my husband.

His suspicion rubbed off on me. I'd sneak to his room half an hour before we were due to meet so I could go through his pockets. I'd sniff his clothes for traces of a new scent. I'd search for a strand of hair different in colour and texture to mine. When he told me that he'd been assigned a new job at the port, issuing visas for tourists from the big ocean liners, I became convinced that he would fall in love with some blonde – a tourist or a girl who worked in a nightclub.

I talked Fadila into coming with me to the port to keep an eye on him. As soon as we got there and heard the din and saw all the customs officers, we realised we'd never catch him flirting. But Fadila couldn't resist stopping one of the porters and asking him which vessel had brought in all these foreign women.

'Why, are you offering to be their pimp?' the porter asked.

She let fly with curses on him and all the generations of his family, and we scurried off. I was sorry to go; the port was a lovely place, with the snow-covered mountains behind it and the ships looking like houses anchored in the sea.

After we left Fadila started crying, saying, 'You see, that man guessed I wasn't a married woman or a mother. Why am I still without a man? Everyone who shows an interest in me runs away as soon as he hears me speak. I don't understand it.'

Though I didn't find any proof that Muhammad was planning to take a wife, I became more and more jealous with every breath I took. Once I even hid inside his wardrobe two hours before we were due to meet. I sat in the dark, determined to catch him with another woman. I must have dozed off, because the next thing I heard was the sound of his footsteps pacing the room.

Then the bed squeaked and I heard him sigh, followed by the sound of the window opening.

'My Kamila must have been held up somehow,' he said.

'I'm here in the wardrobe,' I said, without thinking.

I came out, laughing, and confessed to what I'd been doing. He laughed and hugged me to him until my bones were almost cracking.

'How on earth could I bring a woman to my room,' he exclaimed, 'when your photo's hanging in a gold frame above the mosquito net?'

He took my hand and kissed it.

'You're scared I'm going to get married, aren't you?' he asked – and he was right.

Love had abandoned us in a desert. Whenever we savoured the sweet waters of its happiness, our thirst for each other only intensified. I scolded him, as he did me; I held him to account, as he did me; and all because we could not become one. Reality stood in our way.

I was terrified of not being able to visit him. If I was ill and had to stay in bed, how would I see him? His fears were different: How can she love me when she's living with another man? How can I possibly go on showering her with so much love and then returning to my room alone at night?

But all of Muhammad's jealousy and anger paled in the face of what one of Muhammad's brothers did to me when he fell in love with Maryam and she rejected him. She didn't care for the way he looked or the way he talked. 'If only he were like Muhammad,' she said. 'You'd never dream they were brothers!'

In fact none of Muhammad's four brothers resembled him, in appearance, personality or intelligence. Though Muhammad wasn't the first-born son, he behaved as though he was the eldest. Everyone turned to Muhammad for advice, but he carried the responsibility lightly. 'We're all of the same flesh and blood,' he would say.

This did nothing to stop Maryam's rejected suitor going to Abu-Hussein's shop and telling him about my relationship with Muhammad.

He began by saying, 'Did you know your wife Kamila is always at our house visiting my brother in his room?

Sorry, but the husband's always the very last person to find out.'

The Haji's world spun upside down. But that evening, he waited until his normal homecoming time to take me aside and ask for my explanation.

'Lies, treachery!' I yelled. 'Bring me the Quran so I can swear on it.'

He brought over the Quran, clutching his head and saying it was about to burst.

I held the Quran and closed my eyes. Please, God, I whispered in my heart, I'm going to tell a lie. I beg you, listen to what I have to say. Please remember how they married me off against my will. Then I swore in a loud voice that I did not have a relationship with Muhammad, and insisted that Muhammad's sister was one of my closest friends.

I didn't go to see Muhammad at his house the next day. Usually I ate lunch with him and then we'd nap. As we lay together like this I could almost believe we were married. An hour later I'd get up so that I'd be home when Fatima returned from school. But that day, I went straight to Muhammad's office and waited in the street until he came out. As soon as he saw me, he realised what had happened. It took him quite a while to calm me down. Then he made me panic by asking if I wanted to divorce my husband and marry him. Everything could be settled, he explained.

'What are you suggesting? I might as well throw myself under the next car!' I shouted.

By asking for a divorce, I would have confirmed to the Haji, to Ibrahim, and to everyone, that I was a fraud – that I had lied when I swore on the Quran that I was not having an affair with Muhammad. This would have had grave consequences.

Again he calmed me down and promised he'd send his

oldest brother over to see my husband and assure him that the rumours he'd heard weren't true. Sure enough, the eldest brother hurried round to my husband's shop to assert my innocence. He accused his feckless younger brother of lying, blaming it on his unhappiness after Maryam's rejection. He assured my husband I was like a daughter to them all; that in their house my status was equal to his own sister's.

This did nothing to make me feel safe. They couldn't protect me from Ibrahim; I knew he would do everything to prove I was lying, and I was right. Until now I had been like a gazelle, camouflaging itself next to a stone or a tree every time it sensed the lion − Ibrahim − was watching. Now there was no escape. I came out of the bathroom, which was at the rear of the kitchen, and there was Ibrahim waiting for me. I prayed that someone would appear, even one of the children. But no one came to rescue me.

Ibrahim snarled at me.

'You have no shame and if you thought I was fooled you're mistaken. I have always been aware of your relationship with that bastard; did he think he could get away with it because of his job? He has no honour … no respect, not for you, not for us, but above all not for himself.'

In desperation, I begged him.

'I swear by God that everything you've heard was fabrication and lies,' I said.

But I realised immediately that I'd poured petrol on the already thirsty flames of his fury. His moustache seemed bushier, and his hand struck me again and again, like a meat tenderiser, as he shouted curses with every blow. Finally my howls and cries attracted some members of the family, but only his wife had the courage to pull me away from his anger and hate.

Humiliated and desperate, I withdrew, like a dove that had had its wings clipped. My sobs eventually subsided but my heart was broken at the realisation that I would no longer be able to see Muhammad.

Abu-Hussein and Ibrahim now decreed that I could only leave the house with Khadija. But I continued to sneak out alone, fully aware that in doing so I was returning to the heart of danger. Muhammad would wait around the corner. He'd grown thinner. He would urge me to forget about what had happened, saying his brother was full of remorse, and insisting that we resume our relationship as before. Quivering from head to toe, I'd remind him about the Haji and Ibrahim's new rule and tell him that it was impossible for us to see each other for the time being.

Out of self-preservation I hung around the house like a ghost, making sure when I did go out that everyone knew I was with Khadija. But despite my protestations, I had the strong impression that no one was fooled. Walking past a shop, I overheard the owner tell his assistant, 'No one can hide love, pregnancy, or riding on a camel.' I nearly turned and cursed both men, recalling how I'd seen a woman paraded in Nabatiyeh because she had had an adulterous affair and become pregnant. They'd brought a saddleless donkey and put her on it, with her head facing backwards and her back towards the front. Humiliated, she'd cursed at the onlookers in anger. Instead I held my tongue and continued walking as if I had heard nothing, thanking God I was in Beirut and not in Nabatiyeh.

While my circumstances were different from that woman in Nabatiyeh, I could not ignore the fact that my day of reckoning was at hand. I decided that the only way I could divert my husband's attention was to let him sleep with me. I told him jokingly one morning that I had dreamed I gave birth to a baby boy and we called him Mustapha. That night I made it clear, with great effort and disgust, that the Haji could get into my bed. I tried to push him away from me at the right moment, so I wouldn't get pregnant. My husband didn't have a clue what I was doing. He was unaware of these methods and tricks. I was relieved when it was over, and went to the kitchen to boil some water on the kerosene primus. This was my way of announcing to Ibrahim that I had slept with my husband and everything between us was normal – boiling water at night was always an indication that intercourse had taken place.

Climbing back into bed, I cried at the thought of Muhammad, murmuring, 'Forgive me, what I did was only for our love.'

Muhammad, despairing that things might never return to the way they'd been, wrote me a letter. I had insisted that all letters be delivered by hand. I could no longer trust any of his old strategies – leaving a letter under a stone or in the bottom of a bag of bananas – so he handed it to the boy at the grocer's, who gave it to Maryam. Since I could not easily leave the house, the letter slept safe for a few days in my bra next to my heart, until it was read to me by Fatme:

So, have we really forgotten the wonderful past, only to live in a miserable present? You're mine, whether you like it or not. Your life is part of mine. Every day we spend apart is a loss without recompense. Come to me, Kamila, and I'll ignore my family. Think only of the one who loves you, who worships you. I pledge myself to live for your sake. Come to me, Kamila. Life is short, our lifespan is not for ever. Your being so far away from me is a loss; your living at such a distance is like a void.

Fulfil my wish, Kamila, and we will go to a world where
no other human beings live, where we are alone, where
flowers and shrubs beguile us, where there are swallows
and nightingales ...

'You Lead Her this Way and that … Do You Expect Me to Resole her Shoes Every Day?'

A T THE END of the month I waited for my period, and waited. When there was no sign of it I became paralysed with fear: Muhammad would accuse me of disloyalty and leave me, and aside from that I did not want to have a third child with my husband. Had God heard me when I'd lied to the Haji about my dream of baby Mustapha?

But although it was unwelcome, my pregnancy gave me the strength and courage to deal with Ibrahim. I came up with a variety of ruses to escape from the house without Khadija. I'd take Mother with me, leave her with a relative and then make my way to Muhammad. Sometimes I'd send a message to my brother Hasan's wife, asking her to stop by and take me to the dentist; but as soon as I was in the street I would abandon her and run to Muhammad. I even managed to take Khadija along with me to the cinema, where Muhammad was to meet us.

Khadija agreed despite her best instincts. She sat there in a panic, weighed down by the thought of the domestic duties she'd abandoned, especially since Ibrahim was so demanding and unpredictable that she lived in fear of his temper.

Once inside the cinema, I left a seat vacant beside me and Muhammad came and sat nervously in it. All I wanted was to go back to the ease of our past meetings. I couldn't rejoice that I was sitting in the cinema next to Muhammad; I felt only weary and dejected. It was as though what had happened was merely the first breath of wind in what would soon become a cyclone. I panicked, lifting my hand to draw Muhammad's head to mine, but found myself touching my headscarf instead.

Afterwards Khadija didn't want to talk about the film. We had to speed home because she was terrified Ibrahim would arrive before us. And she was right to be afraid.

When he came home he grabbed her shoes and inspected them. He blamed me for their dishevelled state.

'You lead her this way and that,' he shouted at me, 'just like the shuttle on a sewing machine. Do you expect me to resole her shoes every day?'

His Indifference Sucks up my Desires; His Desires Suck up my very Blood

I CONTINUED TO MEET Muhammad, although never in his room, but then he sent me a message that I could not ignore:

> I am very miserable and feel a great longing for everything. It's as though I can feel my own end approaching. So at least come and say goodbye.

This time, gaining reassurance and strength from Hanan's tiny hand, I took my daughter along with me to Muhammad's room, telling her that we were visiting the doctor.

We couldn't live out our love in the way Muhammad had hoped, as he expressed in that letter: 'You're mine, whether you like it or not ...' He had no idea of the realities of my life – that I had been pregnant, that I had aborted the baby, Mustapha.

I hadn't, like other desperate pregnant women who wanted to get rid of their babies, asked someone else to hit me on my back, nor had I been injected with quinine, two guaranteed methods of aborting. Instead, I jumped secretly from my bed to the floor until I nearly fainted, and yet still I didn't stop. Then I drank some boiled parsley, all the while asking the baby inside me for forgiveness.

Finally one morning I was wrenched from sleep by agonising cramps and, drenched in blood, I saw Mustapha, no bigger than my finger. I screamed and soon everybody came running to help me. I don't know who put the foetus in a soup bowl full of water, but he was displayed for one day, pink and tiny with a slender thread trailing from him. All the children in our house and the neighbours had a peek before we buried him in the garden.

I prayed and asked for God's forgiveness, believing that Mustapha had wanted to be aborted and I had simply helped him. What else could it be, when so many women tried to get rid of their pregnancy and failed? I was upset by this loss. But to my relief, in a few days I began to feel strong again, just like the *malu-malu* – the touch-me-not plant, which folds and droops its sensitive leaves when touched, but quickly revives itself. But I pretended that I was still raw and vulnerable so Ibrahim would leave me alone.

Muhammad was living in another reality: he was stressed and unhappy, and his family was putting even greater pressure on him to leave me. His older brother even wrote to me, sending the letter via his wife. I repeated it to Fatme, our neighbour, reciting, ' "If you really love Muhammad, you should leave him. He's ruining his chances in life for your sake. By concentrating on the here and now he's neglecting his own future." '

I couldn't understand what he meant. Muhammad worked for the government and, though he often complained about his miserable salary, he'd managed to buy himself a suit of the very finest material, costing 140 lira. His shirts were extremely elegant, as were his socks, shoes, handkerchiefs and ties. Everything about him was fashionable. He bought himself some sunglasses too. No one in my family had ever worn sunglasses; dark glasses were only for the blind. For the first time ever, I tried on a pair and saw the mountains and trees in a romantic orange glow. Muhammad also owned a pair of binoculars to watch birds and eagles; he patronised restaurants and cafés and went to the movies. The only people I'd heard about who lived this way were film stars and the rich.

I decided that, for all their sophistication, his family were the same as Ibrahim and my husband: people who didn't believe in love.

When I criticised his brother for writing to me, Muhammad defended him. I was flabbergasted. Suddenly he had become critical of me, just like my husband or Ibrahim. He started blaming me for the most trivial things, which left me feeling he couldn't stand me any more.

I tried to ignore his depression, even when he began to curse his luck. But then he accused me of only being capable of flirting. It was true that I sang to him, but only as a way of showing my love for him. Gradually I realised that what he really wanted was a wife. I had noticed that, when he saw me taking his freshly washed and ironed clothes out of a small bag, his eyes would glisten and he'd sigh deeply. I asked him if this was what he really wanted, and he confessed that he was desperate for a wife who'd do those things for him.

'But don't I wash your laundry for you?' I asked.

'Well, not really,' he answered.

I resolved to leave and not return till he started behaving as he used to, comforting myself with the proverb that said that every beginning must have its end. Testing the water, I asked him if his mother still disapproved of our relationship.

'Yes, she wants me to marry and have children,' he replied. 'Poor Mother, I can't go on upsetting her when her health's the way it is.'

And so I suggested, pinching my thigh all the while, that we should separate.

He snapped back, 'How can we? You follow me about like a shadow – how can I meet anyone else?'

I wanted to scream at him, but I swallowed my words, blaming him for not appreciating the danger I put myself in each time I visited him. I left, putting his keys on the table and swearing by the Prophet and all the Shia Imams that I'd never set foot in his room again – and comforting myself that it would be for my own sanity. I'd had enough of plots and lies and deceits, enough of dragging people with me as chaperones in order to meet him without being caught. I'd even used my own two daughters. I'd had enough of entering his room like a fugitive. Enough of racing home before Ibrahim and my husband returned from work.

Maryam did her best to console me, to help me understand Muhammad's attitude, but I could only wait for the next day to dawn, to find out if he really wanted it to be over.

I went to his room as usual, this time with my brother Kamil – who knew all about my relationship with Muhammad – bitterly regretting having dumped my keys the day before. I made a small heap of sand on the windowsill to signal I was there, but no response followed. Kamil left me and I wandered around the streets for some time before returning in the afternoon and piling more sand until there were veritable little pyramids of it along his windowsill. All to no effect.

That evening I thanked God for having created darkness, exhaustion, drowsiness and drooping eyelids. I fell asleep in bed between my daughters, thanking God once again for the two of them. But as soon as the clock showed one o'clock the next day, there I was again, hanging around outside Muhammad's room. Yesterday's pile of sand had disappeared, so I placed another on the windowsill. I returned an hour later to find it still there. Either he wasn't at home, or he didn't want to see me. A little girl watching from a balcony across the street asked if I was building a house with the sand. I ignored her and then someone began calling to her. Without even turning round, I knew the looks I felt burning into my back were her mother's. Then I heard a loud slap. The mother had hit the little girl because she was talking to me. I was, in her opinion, a fallen woman.

At that moment, Muhammad opened his door. Sheer delight overwhelmed me and, when I stepped inside, my anxieties gone, I joked that neither of us could stand being apart for even a single day. He didn't laugh with me, and I sensed he was very low on energy. A strange feeling of sorrow came over me, because I was imposing myself on him yet again.

He broke the news that his name was on a list of people being sent by the government to the Bekaa Valley to eradicate hashish production. Once again my heart sank; he really was leaving me. I demanded to know where our love had gone.

Before he had the chance to reply, I spoke to him in classical Arabic, which I'd learnt from listening to the radio and from films so that I would sound literate.

'The day of reckoning is at hand, that day when the lover loses patience; the day when the lover stands with open arms and says, "Either my beloved will come at this moment, take my arm and hug me to her as I hug her, or else I will uproot her from my life. She is that molar without which I cannot eat, but which causes me pain, day and night." '

Muhammad wept when he heard me use these words, because he could see how much I loved him. He pleaded with me to divorce my husband and marry him. But I blocked both my ears and my heart.

As I leaned over to kiss him, he pushed me away.

'Kisses are a soothing balm for pain,' he said, 'but only for a little while. Their effect soon wears thin.'

I tried to tell him that we would be free to marry one day, because my husband would die. For just a moment, it was as if Muhammad had discovered the meaning of life. Why, he asked, had I never told him that my husband was suffering from a terminal illness? No, I said, he would die sometime because he was older than us. Muhammad let out a derisory laugh and so I told him instead that we could marry when my daughters were older.

'And how long will that be?' he asked.

'Ten years,' I replied.

He turned my face towards him, forcing me to look him straight in the eye. We were not acting out parts in a film, he insisted. Our love must lead to marriage; we must stop telling lies. Spending a couple of hours together here and there was no real life. I was deceiving myself, just as I'd done when I used a razor blade to scratch my two daughters out of the photograph of me and Muhammad under the walnut tree. Left in their places were two blank patches, like passing clouds, so no one would know I had taken them along with me.

Muhammad demanded an answer. Did I want to be his wife? If I said yes, he would seek a divorce from my husband. If I said no, he'd know I was wasting his time.

Divorce my husband and abandon my daughters? I could see Ibrahim nodding his head. He'd been correct all along about me: I was a flighty woman without dignity or scruples, and a liar completely lacking in character. All I could think of was Abu-Hussein, seemingly unaware of my deceit, complacent in his piety.

I remained silent, and so Muhammad answered for me.

'I get it,' he said. 'You're just frittering away time with me, no more, no less! Well, now I know.'

I went home on my own, without trying to find someone to chaperone me. As our house loomed in the distance, I felt as if it had two arms reaching out to grab me by the neck and strangle me. I could see only darkness ahead of me.

Ibrahim was waiting. I knew I was late, but I hadn't realised how late. He slapped me hard, then shook me, demanding to know where I'd been. In the end my husband came to my rescue. In despair I hit my head on the wall with all my might and went to bed alone, while my two daughters clung to Maryam.

Next morning I got up and headed for al-Rawche, the suicide rock for jilted lovers. I thought of Umm Fawzi and finally understood how she could have ended her life three years ago without giving a thought to her daughters.

Umm Fawzi was the neighbour whom I had asked to hide me in the attic so I could avoid getting married; the one who had unwillingly conned the Haji into giving her money so I could buy stockings. She was my friend, but since she rarely left the house, I would visit her and tell her the stories of films I'd seen.

She was Abu-Fawzi's second wife; his first wife had died and left him with a daughter. The girl lived with Abu-Fawzi and Umm Fawzi for a short while, but then Umm Fawzi's brother fell in love with her and married her. Years went by. But the girl regularly fought with her mother-in-law – Umm Fawzi's mother – and once, when her own husband lifted his arm to strike her, she doused herself with kerosene. Her husband tried to save her, but she died in the flames.

Abu-Fawzi blamed his son-in-law and his wife's family for his daughter's death.

'By the right of the Prophet Muhammad,' he cursed them, 'may their daughters be consumed by fire in this world and the next!'

He had forgotten that his own wife was one of their daughters. From the moment he uttered that prayer, his wife began threatening to kill herself. It happened whenever they had an argument, however trivial. Her husband ignored her threats; after all, they liked each other and had three children together, all paragons of beauty and good manners.

I went into Umm Fawzi's house just a few minutes before she doused herself in kerosene. Her door was wide open; nobody in our neighbourhood closed their door. I saw her stretched out on the sofa, her face turned to the wall. Assuming she was sound asleep, I crept back out. I was halfway up our stairs when I heard her screams. The neighbours tried to put out the flames with blankets, coverlets and water from the pond.

I stood there, in the middle of her sitting room, shrieking. I blamed myself.

'God strike me down!' I cried. 'Why didn't I speak to you? Burn me instead. Please, God, do it to me!'

How could Umm Fawzi do this to herself when she had three children, when she knew how much I loved her? How could she? For days afterwards she battled on with her painful burns.

It frightened me that her husband's prayer had been granted, just one year after he'd uttered those dreadful words, 'May their daughters be consumed by fire in this world and the next!' Umm Fawzi lay dying, like shining tar on the ground. I collected the scattered remnants of her singed hair, weeping as I gathered the strands into a clump, vowing to take them to Sitt Zaynab's shrine in Damascus.

Were people's prayers really answered in this way? Was someone out there praying that Muhammad would leave me, or that God would make me die?

Frustration and despair had taken control of me. They were my left foot and my right foot, giving me resolve, and providing me with the necessary logic and desire to kill myself. I left the road and walked until I reached a small cliff overlooking the sea. I would not self-immolate like Umm Fawzi and so many other women in Lebanon at that time. I did not want to die from my burns or, if I survived, live with the scars of my failure. My hope was that, through suicide, I'd cause a huge scandal, something to make people point their fingers at Ibrahim and hold him responsible. He'd slapped me, hadn't he? I wanted to die so I'd be free. It would be a death that brought shame on my family. Therein lay the source of my strength, just as Umm Fawzi had taken revenge on her own husband by committing suicide.

And what of Muhammad? He'd realise I'd finally given up. All my energy had been exhausted: energy for living with or without him, with or without my daughters. The love I felt for him could never stagnate; it was like a tempest, a hurricane, something I couldn't contain.

I looked down at the surging roar of the waves and stared hard into them. It was as if the sea was calling out to me. Just then a hand reached out and pulled me back. Still speechless, hearing only the roar of the sea, drowning in my sweat, I turned. A young man had been watching me. He pulled me away from the rocks and then insisted on accompanying me home, even though I told him I'd changed my mind and had no intention of killing myself. Despite my protestations, he remained unconvinced. I swore by God and the Prophet, but to no avail. Eventually I confessed to him that I was really more scared of my brother finding out I'd tried to commit suicide than I was of death itself. Hurriedly I fixed my hair under its black scarf and checked my clothes. I started to run, as if I were shouting out, 'Let me show you how beautiful life is.' I raised my head to the skies. I thanked God that I was in Beirut, the city of Yagog and Magog, and that no one knew about my foolishness.

Silk Valley

S OON I LEARNED from Miskiah, Muhammad's sister, that
he was engaged. The films I'd seen helped me understand
his reason for marrying: he had given up hope that I would ever
become his wife, and was eager now to build his own future,
to have children. This logic calmed me briefly; then anger and
jealousy took hold and I became determined to see his fiancée.
Miskiah told me a time when I might glimpse her walking past
Muhammad's house. As soon as I saw her, I prayed silently,
'Thank you, God, for helping me in my struggle!' The fiancée
was nowhere near as pretty or fashionable as me. I could tell
that she never went to films, wouldn't sing and certainly never
flirted. Another thought occurred to me: Muhammad didn't
deserve me. If he did, how could he possibly contemplate
having such a woman as his wife?

Before he left to take up his new post in Silk Valley, a
remote region close to the Syrian border full of smugglers,
Muhammad and I met one final time. He handed me five
addressed envelopes with postage stamps stuck on them. I had
to promise to send him letters so he'd know how I was. I
was to put them in the letter box in the street opposite our
house where an army commandant lived; that way, the letters
would be sure to reach him quickly. When he gave me those
envelopes I knew that he wanted to keep in contact with me.

Yet again, we regretted not having been more serious
about his promise to teach me to read and write. We shared
the blame for squandering our time together.

Less than a week after he'd gone, I dictated my first letter to Fatme. I told him I thought of him every time I saw damask roses in bloom or passed his house. How I longed to see his window half-open so I could rush in to him! I closed with the words of the song, 'You're on my mind, and I can't stand being apart from you.'

A letter came back from Muhammad via Miskiah, and Fatme read it to me. He'd written out Umm Kulthum's song 'Write to me, write to me':

> Write to me and explain to me
> About a heart and its fixations,
> About your absence; for how long?
> Enough of suffering, the result of your being
> Far distant, and of your own choice.
> Write to me of a time when we may meet,
> Write to me morning and evening.

I asked what the other words were on the page, and Fatme read, 'Lyrics by Bayram al-Tunisi and music by Zakariyya Ahmad.' I was more touched by that than by the song itself: he was treating me as his peer, someone who would want to know a literary source.

I had noticed how much Fatme enjoyed reading out Muhammad's letters. She relished the atmosphere of conspiracy, as we drank coffee and took surreptitious puffs on cigarettes. Tears would well in her eyes as she read.

'I'm telling you this without the slightest bit of jealousy,' she once said, tapping the wooden table for good luck. 'If you travelled the entire inhabited globe in quest of another man, you'd never find one like him.' I expected her to add, 'A person who worships you the way he does.' But instead she said, 'Someone who's a decent person, not a thug or a womaniser.'

I knew what she meant. I was married with two daughters, and married women inevitably attracted men who wanted to spend time with them for only one reason. All of that was utterly different from the love that Muhammad and I felt for each other.

Fatme couldn't write back to Muhammad for me on that particular day. It had grown dark, and she was scared that her brother, who was visiting her from the south, would arrive home and find her writing a love letter. I had to resort to taking my own daughter Fatima into the bathroom with me, with paper and pencil hidden in my dress pocket. I sat Fatima down and dictated the letter, watching her sound out the words as the pencil moved under her childish fingers.

Kamila, what are you doing, asking your eight-year-old daughter to write your lover a letter? I asked myself.

But Fatima adored Muhammad. She would watch for him to appear at the top of the alley, where he'd wait for me, and when he saw her he'd give her a little pink rubber doll or a wooden figurine of a gazelle. She was used to seeing Muhammad around in the neighbourhood or at Bhamdoun. When we went for strolls, Fatima listened as we sang songs to each other. She was well aware that he was the 'big secret'. She kept it to herself, out of her love for me, though she was also devoted to her father. As Fatima wrote my letter, I was aware of her pride and sense of achievement at being able to do such a thing. Once it was done, I folded it and put it in my bra.

This is what it said:

My dear Muhammad,

I love you so much! I shall follow you wherever you go. Love of my soul, all I want is to please you. I'm longing to see you and afraid for you. What am I to do with this love of mine? I want you here, close to me; it is torture when you're so far away! Your kisses tell me you love me, so why did you leave me? When you are near, my dearly beloved, you can console me. Come back to me here! Oh letter, winging your way to him, promise me, by the Prophet himself, to say hello to him. Oh letter, how lucky you are, winging your way to him; soon you'll be in my lover's hands.

I grew very bored, especially during the middle of the day, when I would have been with Muhammad. But, determined not to make Ibrahim suspicious, I set off out when my various women chaperones came by as usual to get me. Since Muhammad had gone away I had nowhere to go, so I would walk around aimlessly before coming back home. I was tempted to get on a bus and visit Muhammad for the day, but I didn't, because Ibrahim had given me lots of leeway recently and I didn't want to test it.

The months sped by. Muhammad returned to Beirut for a holiday and confided in me that he planned to break off his engagement. His fiancée was protesting at the way he neglected her and had accused him of being in love with me. I had expected this to happen: engagement, marriage and children could be mere formalities with some people, but never for a man like Muhammad. I thanked God that our relationship was strong once more, and I promised that I would fast and pray twice as often to compensate for my lies and deceit.

There's No More Money in My Husband's Drawer

F IVE MONTHS HAD passed since Muhammad's return from Silk Valley. Separation had only strengthened our love.

One morning Ibrahim shook his head at me in sheer derision.

'It's as though you don't begin to realise how bad things are,' he said. 'You sit there chewing gum and ask to go out!'

I'd heard from Khadija that Abu-Hussein's shop had been losing money, but had paid little attention. After all, there'd been no changes at home. The Haji still provided meat, vegetables, rice and white bread. The house continued to teem with relatives and friends. In any case, when I asked the Haji about it, he wouldn't confide in me. We were not like other married couples. We were simply two people who happened to live in the same house, each leading separate lives.

Before long the situation became clear. My husband's business partner claimed that he had bought shares on the stock exchange with some of the profits from the business, but without telling the Haji. Then the share price dropped alarmingly. They'd invested in a lot of stock and could no longer meet the repayments and interest. The partner proposed selling some land to keep the business afloat, and wanted to know whether my husband had any land he could sell as well. The situation left my husband baffled: why wasn't his partner speaking to him face to face, instead of through a lawyer? Besides, he had no land to sell. Instead he agreed to sell most of our expensive Persian carpets, which he had bought not for their beauty but because they were very durable. He would keep only three rugs for himself. Then he had to sell our best furniture. In tears he asked me to give him my jewellery. I cried too as I handed it over. I wept for my armlets, each shaped like a snake; my bracelet which looked like *dababa* (army tank) tracks; and the bracelet hung with gold English sovereigns that we called 'Ottoman' lira. The entire family gathered round as I used soap to ease the ten bands off my wrists, as if they didn't want to leave me. I sobbed even more when I heard their clinking in the distance.

Hadn't I seen myself just like Nawal in the film *Tears of Love*? Now here I was, surrendering my jewels to my husband in the same way. The only difference was their use: while her husband took them to use at the gaming table and lost everything, mine needed them to keep his business afloat.

Whenever I'd seen my husband sitting behind the long wooden cutting table in his shop, holding a huge pair of scissors, it had struck me how unsuitable those shears were for someone with his tiny hands, beady eyes and slight stature. His was a figure that could virtually disappear inside the cavernous space of his storeroom, with its hundreds of bolts of English, French and Italian cloth. I'd see before me the orphan boy who'd arrived in Beirut, treading a straight and narrow path, just as he'd been taught to do by the religious scholar who'd raised him. He'd lived his life in the city, like a horse with blinkers, so shy that all he ever saw of Beirut was the ground beneath his feet.

My husband's business partner was, in contrast, a larger man who laughed a lot and had a very loud voice, one joke following the next. In fact, when I saw his empty coffee cups and the cigarette butts piled in his ashtray, I wished my husband could approach life with the same abandon.

Several weeks passed before the partner's lawyer got in touch with the Haji again, telling him that his contribution to retain his half of the shop wasn't enough. The lawyer claimed that the partner had saved the shop by selling all his land. Now he needed Abu-Hussein to sign the transfer papers. I asked my husband why he'd agreed to assign his shares to the partner if they weren't giving back the furniture, the Persian carpets and my jewellery, but he wouldn't talk to me about it. It was as if I had no right to ask.

The news hit the streets. As the vendors hawked their wares – 'Now friends, we've got some fantastic perfume here,' or, 'How about some al-Sudan's soap?' – they'd add, 'Have you heard the latest? The Haji al-Shaykh has been swallowed whole by the lion!' (Lion was the family name of his partner.)

In fact the Haji had been swallowed gradually, without realising it. A couple of years earlier, my brother Kamil had discovered a stash of money hidden in the shop. Suspicious, he'd handed it immediately to the Haji. But instead of suspecting his partner, my husband just handed the cash over to him without question. This was my husband: habitually interfering in every single aspect of our lives, however trivial; and yet investing, without question, blind trust in his dishonest business partner.

A renowned lawyer approached my husband, offering his legal services, but the Haji turned him down.

'God is the only lawyer,' he asserted.

He sat on his prayer mat, praying and glorifying God. By the time he'd finished praying and weeping, his eyes had become red blobs, like tomatoes, and his forehead was a patchwork of deep trenches.

I wept for him too, but inside I seethed. Instead of

accepting the lawyer's offer to defend him, he fell forward on to his prayer mat and did nothing.

I tried in vain to urge him to take action, going so far as to call him a chicken. And though I went on behaving as if I was still married to the owner of a shop in Souq Sursouq, the news of our downfall gradually spread through Beirut, to the families from the south, and finally to Muhammad.

He reproached me for having kept him in the dark about the situation. He took me in his arms and gave me a hug.

'You realise, don't you,' he said, 'that this is God's way of ensuring you can get a divorce and we can marry.'

I couldn't believe how opportunistic he was being and I told him so. But, he said, it was unfair to accuse him of thinking that way. Circumstances had suddenly turned in our favour, nothing more or less. I didn't want to hear him tell me again how I'd been destroying his future hopes, that it felt as if the eleven years we'd spent together had just been a way of passing the hours and keeping ourselves amused. Instead, I asked him for more time to think the whole thing over.

A general aura of sorrow took over the house. My husband's relatives who'd been living with us went their own ways. Apart from three prayer mats, the floors were bare. The dire situation tightened around us like a vice: thoughts of coffee mornings, gold bracelets clinking on my arm and summers at Bhamdoun vanished in a trice.

My nephews' lives were transformed overnight. The Haji bought two small wooden stalls for them and they began selling thread and sewing materials in the market. If Hussein the Ideologue, at age eighteen, ever saw a pupil or friend from his school on the horizon, he'd abandon his stall and hide. By this time, he had joined the Popular Party of Greater Syria,[19]

---

19 The PPS, founded by Antun Saadeh, which advocated a greater Syrian state, to be known as the Fertile Crescent, encompassing Syria, Lebanon, Jordan and Palestine/Israel.

and hung the founder's portrait and the party's emblem in our home. Muhammad urged me to get him to resign his membership at once, since the government was opposed to its leader and what the party stood for.

The ex-partner returned and reopened the shop under a new name, in partnership with one of his brothers. The Haji asked for a job on a monthly salary to support us. I could not understand how the Haji could maintain his dignity and avoid humiliation. The ex-partner agreed, and my husband stuck with it until he could no longer stand the lack of respect with which the owner's brother treated him. One day he snatched the tape measure from around his neck, threw it at the brother and left the shop for the last time.

He then purchased a stand only a few metres from his former shop. Each morning he would walk past the old premises, greeting his ex-partner as if nothing had happened, and praising God for everything. The stand was pitched right by the entrance to a large shop belonging to a merchant who was aware that my husband was honest and had been a successful businessman, and so he allowed the Haji to be there. The very sight of him attending his modest little stand – selling cotton underwear, socks and other items, with no tape measure around his neck and no large pair of scissors in his tiny hand – aroused sorrow and regret in the hearts of all his former acquaintances.

Summer arrived. Instead of going to Bhamdoun for the season, we moved the mattresses, sheets and mosquito nets up on to the roof. There we slept in the open, trying as best we could to escape Beirut's stifling heat. We named our new summer abode Roof Bhamdoun.

The family disaster had its benefits. Everyone, young and old, was preoccupied by our misfortune. This meant they paid less attention to me and I was often free to be with

Muhammad. But with our relationship back as it had been, he started to fuss again. He was always happy to see me and forget his frustrations (a word I'd learned from him), but when the time came to part the grumbling would begin. I was not able to counter his black moods, nor could I defend myself when he blamed me for them. They would flare up for the silliest reasons, such as when we'd see a film with a happy ending. We went to see *Rabihah*, a film about a Bedouin woman who met a man from the city who was taking part in a hunt with a prince and his attendants. The young man's horse threw him to the ground, but no one else in the hunting party noticed. Rabihah ran to his aid. They fell in love but, when her family discovered he was from the city, the head of the tribe ordered them to be separated and the woman married to a cousin. On her wedding night, Rabihah ran away to the city to be with the young man.

Throughout the film, Muhammad groaned, sighed and wriggled. He whispered in my ear that this film was our guiding light. When he told me there was something he must do and refused to ride on the tram home with me, I thought: He's finally decided to leave me. I'd guessed correctly: Muhammad didn't meet me in his room the next day or for days afterwards. Instead he sent me a letter via Maryam. I could tell it was an angry letter from its length and his handwriting: the words seemed rushed and bigger than usual. I raced to Fatme's house, and when I couldn't find her I went out into the garden, where a young male cousin of hers sat studying by the fountain, exactly where I had met Muhammad. I stood on the spot where we had been so happy, holding an angry letter from him. Without hesitation I asked the young man to read the letter to me, and was mortified by what I heard:

How I long to be swallowed up by hell and leave this unsettling world. For every beautiful memory, every happy moment I've spent with you, there are as many painful memories that erase from my life all that is beautiful. Time and again I've thought of leaving you, but I've utterly failed. Now I've reached the point where I can stand this bitter life no longer. I intend to leave you, whatever the cost. Death seems an easier fate than this torture. So here I am, writing this letter to bid you farewell. Be patient and remember you are not mine; you belong to the owner of that house to deal with as he pleases. You share his food and his life. I can only see myself being kept at a distance, separated from you by any number of impassable barriers. How can you expect me to sleep soundly or lead a happy life? It makes me happy to know you are so near, yet the thought of the future pains me, tortures me, and deprives me of all life's pleasures, especially the pleasure of having you close by. Love is pointless when I am continually burned by the fires of accursed jealousy. You are the only thing I ever think about; all the time my mind is preoccupied by my love for you. Even worse, I am incapable of escaping from this utterly pointless love …

'Forgive me' – 'God is the Forgiver'; 'Forgive me' – 'I have Forgiven you'

MUHAMMAD AVOIDED ME for an entire ten days. When I lost hope of bumping into him I became determined to find out what was going on, and so I went to his office. When he saw me his jaw dropped and a deep flush stained his cheeks. He asked me if I wanted a drink, as though getting me a drink was more important than talking to me. Then he insisted that I went home, promising to discuss matters with me later. But I wouldn't budge. A colleague entered the room, and Muhammad, embarrassed, busied himself dealing with his enquiry and ignored me completely. I nearly screamed, 'Could it be possible that our relationship has come to this?'

Instead I stood up, muttering something like, 'Oh! Did you really think you were such a big deal!' and stormed out.

Another week passed and I avoided everyone, unable even to face myself in the mirror because I felt so humiliated. Then, quite by chance, Muhammad saw me in the street with one of my daughters and gave me a look that meant he wanted to meet again. When we did meet, he told me he'd decided to take things into his own hands. He'd been to see my father in the south, and my brother Hasan, and had asked for their help in getting my husband to agree to a divorce. Although I had been terrified of a divorce and the scandal it would involve, in the end I was relieved that he had finally talked to them on my behalf. Unbeknown to me, Hasan – rather than discussing things with my husband – came straight to the house and took Ibrahim aside. When Ibrahim heard the news, he fainted.

As if the last pieces of a complicated jigsaw had been fitted into place, everything afterwards seemed to happen easily. In no time I found myself sitting with Abu-Hussein before a sheikh in the shariah court. I renounced any claims I might have had to my daughters and made the traditional request for my husband's forgiveness: 'Forgive me.'

He replied, with tears in his eyes, 'God is the forgiver.'

He then asked me to forgive him, and with tears in my eyes I pronounced the traditional phrase, 'I have forgiven you.'

Could it really be true that I was sitting in front of a sheikh as he signed our divorce papers?

Afterwards, Father arrived and took me away to the south. I wondered whether Muhammad had promised my father cash, like Abu-Hussein, who had once paid my father gold coins to force me into marrying him.

As I climbed aboard the bus headed for the south, I burst into tears. It was taking me far away from my neighbourhood and my two daughters, Mother and Maryam, Khadija, my nephews and nieces, the neighbours. I remembered the day Mother and I arrived in Beirut, completely empty-handed. Now here I was with a small suitcase on my lap containing all my clothes. But the further we moved from Beirut, the less sad and the more relaxed I began to feel.

We didn't go back to Nabatiyeh itself, but to the region of al-Qulayeh, where Father leased fig trees during the summer. I helped Father and his wife and my half-brother to keep the birds off the figs until they had ripened and could be laid out in the sun to dry.

After a few days, Hasan's wife arrived with my daughters. I'd been dying to see them. I'd been reassured to know

they were being cared for by Maryam, Mother, Khadija
and their father, but I felt even happier to have them at
my side.

On our first evening together, the girls announced they'd
take turns dancing. Fatima was the first to get to her feet; she
danced while my half-brother blew on a flute. We circled
about her, clapping our hands – me, Father and his wife.
Then it was Hanan's turn. She danced and danced before
going back to sit beside her sister. I began to sing, expressing
the most heartfelt desire to live like this for the rest of my
life, in a cabin amid the fig trees, grape vines and bees, far
from the hubbub of Beirut and our crowded house. I raised
a call for freedom, just like Layla in the film *Daughter of the
Desert*. Now I could sleep between my two daughters as my
own mother had. The beautiful colour of the flesh of the fig
entered my daughters' cheeks as the mountain air made them
bloom with health.

After another two weeks, Muhammad arrived in a smart
suit. Seeing him from afar, my heart left my body and rushed
towards him. My daughter Fatima was delighted, but Hanan
hung back shyly. After a few awkward moments, a small
fly went up his nose. As he bent over, trying to eject it, it
seemed the fly had arrived at just the right moment to break
the tension.

Two days later, Hasan's wife returned to take my daughters
back to their father in Beirut. I told myself that I'd be seeing
them again in a couple of weeks, as soon as I'd returned
to the city, when at least we'd be living in the same
neighbourhood. Yet my heart sank as I watched them taking
my sister-in-law by the hand. Both girls turned to look back
at me, as if seeking confirmation that I really was prepared
to let them go. I stood rooted to the spot. The bus halted
and they climbed aboard. Their little eyes watched me as the

bus pulled away, as if warning me this was my last chance if I wanted us to stay together. The din of the bus penetrated my ears. I bit my finger. For the first time I realised exactly what I'd done.

The Persian Carpet

A S MUHAMMAD AND I got out of the car that brought us back to Beirut from the south, I could hardly believe we were together and that I'd become his wife so soon after my divorce. When Father tried to insist we should wait for the three-month canonical menstruation period before I remarried, Muhammad took his revolver out of his holster and pointed it at Father's head. Now, here I was entering my old howdah with pride, instead of sneaking in like a thief. I felt like passing on the good news to the cupboard, the mirror, the bed, the table and the chair: We're married and things have changed! For the very first time we could open the door leading out to a bench overlooking the small garden. But, though we didn't double-lock ourselves inside any longer, it was hard to stop acting like a criminal. I soon discovered my divorce was the neighbourhood scandal and that Muhammad's family accepted my presence only very reluctantly. Because I was the one who'd divorced my husband, the blame lay with me. And I'd abandoned my daughters, the elder aged ten and the younger seven, all because I didn't dare to fight for them. I'd known when I sought a divorce that the sheikh wouldn't consider me a good mother, since I had committed adultery.

I begged Muhammad to let my girls know I was back in town. We laughed when he returned, saying he'd asked his go-between, the boy at the grocer's, to tell them. Terrified that my daughters wouldn't be allowed to see me, I started pacing the room like a caged beast. When the doorbell rang I rushed to open it. There they stood! I gave them a big hug and showered them with a million kisses before asking if anyone at home knew they were here. I looked at their plaits, which I was so used to braiding myself, and just managed to hold back the tears.

Then Hanan spied the Persian carpet I'd laid down.

'Hey,' she yelled, 'there's the stolen carpet!'

I winked at Fatima, as she'd been the one who'd helped me sneak it over to Muhammad's. It was the smallest of our carpets, and at the beginning of each summer the Haji would take them to the roof, lay them out, brush them down, then leave them for one day under the sun before brushing them once again. Then he'd roll them up with mothballs and place them on top of the cupboard until the beginning of winter. When he found only two carpets up there he went insane, accusing everyone of stealing. In spite of all the commotion and fuss, Fatima had proved to be a rock and never revealed the secret to a soul. But Hanan soon ensured that everyone in the house and neighbourhood knew where the stolen carpet had been discovered. Furious, my ex-husband and his son, Hussein the Ideologue, tried to ban my daughters from visiting me. Yet the girls still managed to sneak out when they were supposed to be playing. I visited the female principal of their school, explaining about my divorce and asking her permission to see them there. She congratulated me for what I'd done and said I was very courageous.

That word she used, 'courageous', became a source of great pleasure to me. It was better than 'selfish' and 'frivolous', the two epithets most regularly used to describe me before I divorced Abu-Hussein and married Muhammad. My ex-husband had gone as far as calling me 'tarred' (as in 'tarred and feathered'). The school principal, who wore sleeveless blouses, gold sandals and dyed her hair, laughed as she told me she was the daughter of a renowned religious Imam. She was a graduate of the American University, yet this had not stopped her brother from tracking her from one beach to the next, to check whether she was wearing the bathing suit she kept hidden inside a towel. She managed to maintain her deception, claiming she only wore the bathing suit when she was in the bath. When her mother confronted her over traces of sand found inside it, she'd shrugged her shoulders and said she'd brought the sand home on purpose to add to her bath, so she could feel she was really swimming in the sea. 'A pinch of salt as well,' she'd added defiantly, 'and just a sprig of seaweed to go with it!'

That word 'courageous' was an ointment to salve my wounds. Muhammad and I had both been 'brazen'; we'd challenged society. Everyone was whispering about our scandal and my divorce, though no one had stopped for a second to consider the scandal of forcing a fourteen-year-old girl to marry her widowed brother-in-law. On the contrary, practically the entire family sided with my husband and felt sorry for my two daughters. I was ostracised. No one contacted me, except for my brother Hasan, his wife, and Kamil, who was now happily married. Mother loathed Muhammad, the cause of my divorce. Maryam had to stay inside the house, terrified that Abu-Hussein and Ibrahim would accuse her of collusion.

My coffee-morning friends cut me dead, as did the neighbours. I fought back with the only weapon I had: my love for Muhammad. I thought about the sheer misery of those women I'd once known so well, women who, unlike me, had never tasted the sweet pleasures of love and passion. Their spouses never watched films the way Muhammad and I did; they didn't understand songs or fall under their spell; they never recorded their thoughts, wrote down proverbs, memorised poetry and recited it by heart. I decided

Muhammad was enough for me and rejected the rest of them as they had rejected me. I pictured myself floating in a river, passing trees and rocks, leaving them behind. But I still couldn't forget them.

I was singled out, vilified, because I had divorced my husband and married the man I loved. But across the neighbourhood, they were all at it behind closed doors. One of our neighbours was having an affair with a married man next door. Their houses were connected by a locked door with a cupboard pushed against it. In the summer, when her lover's family left for the south, she moved the cupboard aside. Wherever you looked there were countless tales of illicit love affairs that flourished so long as they were kept secret. I had to bite my tongue not to scream, 'People in glass houses shouldn't throw stones!'

It choked me to think of poor Maryam stuck in that house. But knowing that she was about to be married comforted me, and in any case, I was certain the Haji would marry somebody else soon to look after the housekeeping.

I was haunted by the old house and neighbourhood. When I awoke from my siesta, my heart would begin to pound. I'd look around for my shoes, so I could tear back to the old house, scared to death I might be late. But as soon as I saw the coloured scarf I'd begun wearing in place of my black one, and the loafers instead of my old shoes, I calmed down.

I didn't really regain any of my old spirit till Maryam got married. It was as though we'd been two parts of a magnet that had been separated, and finally brought back together again – especially since she too had married the man she loved, the Prime Minister's bodyguard. When Maryam and I sat down with our husbands, the common denominator between the four of us was love. We'd fallen in love in secret, and, in the case of us two women, endured a miserable, almost terrifying childhood. We shared a good laugh when I told her that the Haji was still sending beggars round to knock on our door. Muhammad was so fed up with it that he'd tell them in French, '*Complet!*' He was also getting fed up with my relatives from the south, who were forever asking for official favours: 'Please, Muhammad, help me, I need an eye operation,' or, 'Help, Muhammad, we need new irrigation in the tobacco field.'

Then Maryam described how, after she became pregnant, my daughter Hanan kept crying because she wanted to go and visit her. So from time to time the Haji brought her over and she got to sleep in the bed Maryam had prepared for the baby. The news made me smile, but inside my heart was breaking for my youngest, who must have needed affection, especially with the departure of Maryam. As I'd known he would, Abu-Hussein had married again. She was a barren woman from the south, a woman who was mean, abrupt, and unkind to my daughters and nephews. I'd heard that she would hurry to the kitchen when she heard the fridge door open, even in the dead of night, just to catch the culprit.

'I'm a Member of the Family Suffering this Misfortune'

ONE MORNING, MUHAMMAD shook me awake to tell me that my nephew Hussein the Ideologue had tried to assassinate a senior judge.[20]

Muhammad was assigned as one of the investigating officers to ransack our family home in search of the young man. They'd be interrogating family members one by one. Muhammad refused his superior's orders, explaining the personal reasons why he was unable to do such a thing. How could be possibly go into his wife's old home, revolver in hand, after he had divorced her from her family, and was banned from entering it?

I didn't want Muhammad to go to his office the following morning. I was afraid my family would think he was joining the search for my nephew. I too was forbidden to visit the family house, and so I longed to turn myself into a cat, so I could sit with the women to support them.

It was an enormous disaster for the entire family. The Haji and my other two nephews were taken in for questioning. The Haji either refused to answer questions or responded with a single sentence, 'Only God knows.' Finally, the chief detective lost patience and slapped him in the face. But the Haji only continued to respond with his single sentence; he neither changed his tone, nor met his interrogator's eyes.

---

20 He made an attempt on the life of a senior judge of the court that had condemned Antun Saadeh, leader of the PPS, to death.

Muhammad kept me informed of what was happening. My middle nephew had been put in prison for three months in order to force the family to tell the authorities where the Ideologue was hiding.

When Muhammad explained why he could not enter our house along with the other detectives, his boss had told him he understood. But he also made it clear to Muhammad that a promotion was waiting for him if he could somehow sniff out the whereabouts of the fugitive boy.

'I'm well aware of the proverb, "One man's disaster is another's gain," ' Muhammad told his boss. 'But the problem is that I'm a member of the family suffering this misfortune.'

I was delighted by these words. I sent a message to my family through Hasan's wife, passing on Muhammad's advice not to talk to the press.

When the Ideologue had been missing a whole week, Muhammad heaved a deep sigh of relief and whispered to me, 'OK, he's got away. God be with him!'

I sighed too. It seemed I was the only person who understood why my hot-headed nephew had done such a thing: he felt the need to act against a perceived injustice, because his father had been so humiliated.

As with most crises, there was one positive outcome: the flight of the Ideologue meant my two daughters were able to visit me more often without shaking in their boots on the way home.

Monkey Shit

I TRIED EVERY JOKE and funny trick in my repertoire to make my transition from my old house to Muhammad's go smoothly, but without success. Our old howdah no longer lifted me up; it no longer served as our love nest, a place to rock and comfort me. My old house still felt like home. It had been full of fear, but it was also full of the din of family and neighbours, who called to each other from windows, balconies and rooftops. How I wished I could have been standing on the roof with Maryam when they brought home the corpse of our neighbour, the Prime Minister, after he was assassinated in Amman! I could no longer crane my neck along with the other members of the family to see what gifts and letters Ibrahim's son had sent back from America, where he was studying. When he didn't send me greetings I was so upset; it meant I'd become the undesirable aunt.

I thought I'd manage to win over Muhammad's family and that the wall of ice betwen us would finally melt. When Muhammad was assigned a two-week posting to the provinces, I fondly imagined that during those two weeks his family members would soften. With Muhammad away, they wouldn't even be wondering about the scenes of love and passion going on behind our door.

But I remained a prisoner. To avoid gossip, Muhammad asked me only to go out with his sister or sister-in-law, a request that made me very angry, although I agreed. I had no desire to allow others an opportunity to gossip or suspect that I might fall in love with someone else: 'She's done it once already, so what's to stop her doing it again, or even a third time?'

When Muhammad returned after his fortnight away, he exclaimed, 'My God, you're so beautiful. Now I know why I'm dying of love for you. You're gorgeous!'

A few moments later, I headed barefoot for the kitchen to bring him some fruit I'd been preparing.

It was then that I overheard his sister-in-law complaining.

'OK,' she said to the others, 'so all the trouble we've gone to to get hold of some monkey shit has been for nothing!'

'Hurry up and get rid of it,' her husband replied, 'before the stench starts rising.'

I tiptoed to the front door and peered outside. In the corner, by the entrance, was a pile of black monkey shit. The next day, Miskiah told me that the idea had been to cast a spell so that, as soon as Muhammad set eyes on me, he'd find me as ugly as the pile of poo.

After the monkey-shit episode, Muhammad's eldest nephew was helping his mother plant their small garden, and threw her a knife. It grazed my daughter Fatima's leg as she stood watching. I had severe doubts about whether it was an accident. Muhammad thought my accusations completely ridiculous, but he promised he'd work on finding us our own house.

The feeling that someone was trying to do us harm only made our love intensify. When we went to the cinema, I was happy and proud to clasp his arm. And yet, when he decided to have a new dress made for me, I chose the seamstress who had made the trousseau for my first marriage. I didn't know how to reply when he asked, 'Why that seamstress and not another?' I managed to come up with the answer a few months later, when I realised that I'd chosen her because she was a major part of my past. In spite of my intense love for

Muhammad, I was still homesick for our old house, when it was OK that my household responsibilities were a tissue of chaos – burnt food, semi-clean clothes and unfinished housework.

Now I had no choice but to be a new kind of mistress of the house. I felt like a student who must complete her assignments as well as possible, or else her teacher would be annoyed. I had to prepare the food and put it on the table; we didn't eat standing up the way we used to in my old house, taking scoops from the saucepan. Now I had to lay out clean towels, look for buttons that had come off his shirts and sew them back on, make sure the iron wasn't too hot when I ironed his trousers, and sprinkle water on his collar and press it so it stood up straight. But these tasks didn't suit my impatient nature. Muhammad also asked me to remember everything I spent; by the end of the first week in the month I'd managed to get through his entire salary. Then he asked me to report to him each night on what I'd bought that day, so he could keep a record of our expenses. I started to feel the diary he kept was even more restrictive than the way the Haji had hidden money and bought everything himself. Muhammad discovered I didn't know how to count money, but simply held out a handful of cash so that vendors could take what they needed and then give me the change.

I began to ask myself whether I'd exchanged one kind of fear for another that was even more complicated. Once Hanan arrived during her midday break as I was pounding meat, getting lunch ready for Muhammad. She brought a piece of cloth for me to make her some gym shorts like her sister's for sports lessons. I said I'd do it after lunch and, if she came back tomorrow, they'd be ready. She began to cry, saying the teacher would beat her because the sports class was in two hours' time. In a total quandary, I looked around: should I leave the meat, hurry inside to the sewing machine and make the shorts for her? I could explain things to Muhammad later, though he'd be extremely hungry. Sensing my panic, my daughter suggested that she borrow her sister's pair, thinking this would make things easier for me. But that only made me feel worse. Why was I so scared of Muhammad? Why, if only for a single second, did I once think about returning to my old house, even to the Haji himself? Was it because life had suddenly become so serious, now that I was married to Muhammad? I could no longer laugh at everything; was I expected to turn a new page and change my very personality as well? 'Consider my status, Kamila,' I could hear him say. 'Consider my position.'

My Third Daughter Ahlam; My First Son Toufic

WHEN I WAS pregnant with my first child with Muhammad, he kissed my tummy day and night, and talked to his baby in the womb. It made me see exactly what had been missing when I had had my two daughters, and in my life with Abu-Hussein. After I gave birth to a daughter, Ahlam, Muhammad would talk to her while she was nursing, watching her carefully and explaining why he'd given her a name which meant 'dreams'. In his diary he recorded how she'd nursed, how she'd burped, the date when her first tooth broke through, and then her molars; he recorded when she stood for the first time, when she took her first faltering steps, how she wouldn't go to sleep unless she'd played with my hair first. We gave her a first-birthday party, just like in the films. I invited Fatima and Hanan, Kamil (who had become a cook at a famous restaurant in downtown Beirut), Hasan and his wife, Mother, and some of Muhammad's brothers and sisters. Muhammad made every effort to keep the atmosphere cordial on this happy occasion, but the shadow of my divorce and our subsequent marriage hung over the gathered company.

With great relief we moved to our own house. I loved it. Mother moved from Kamil's place to live with me when I found I was pregnant again. I didn't think Toufic, the new child, could win over Muhammad as Ahlam had. But poems, panegyrics and popular verses flooded in for Toufic, until the very walls seemed to echo in praise of the newborn, and all because he was a boy. Among the verses written for my new son were lines penned by a famous poet, entitled 'The Little King': 'If I'd been there the night he was born, I'd have dressed Night's body in Day's garb.'

And that was how the chapter on my divorce finally closed. I'd produced an heir apparent and proved I could be a worthy wife for Muhammad. I finally realised why Fatme had described Muhammad as being 'high-life' all those years ago. He had nobility. His family were descended from a tribe of noble origin, and there were recorded tales of their great deeds. His father was renowned for having fought against the Turks and for his great strength. It was said that the people from his village in the south were even scared of his horse.

Muhammad began to fuss over the new arrival. He blamed me if the baby caught a cold or had diarrhoea, always using the same reproach: 'You must have let him catch cold, then he got congested and started to cough. Kamila, you're supposed to be taking care of him, you know. Please do it for my sake!'

It frightened me. I knew that whether my baby lived or died depended more on me than on God's will or medical care. I reverted to my old role, the stone-bearing donkey, unloading one burden only to take up another, this time in my womb. I became pregnant for the fifth time and gave birth to a little daughter, Majida, with green eyes. After the delivery I lay there with milk oozing from my breasts, feeling just like one of our cows back in Nabatiyeh. I leaned over her to moo and clean her up with my tongue.

Mother hurried into the room, as if her spirit had been revived.

'By God, Kamila,' she said, 'I can hear cows mooing in Beirut. Is it possible, do you think? Let's go and find them!'

She took the afterbirth away in a bucket covered with a cloth. Accompanied by Fatima and Hanan, she walked some

distance till she came to a ditch. She dug a deep hole with her
bare hands and with a scoop tipped it all in before covering it
again. The three of them then stayed for an hour, watching
over the afterbirth till the smell dissipated to make sure it
didn't attract cats or dogs.

I had given birth at home aided by a professional midwife
since we couldn't spare the money for hospital fees any
more, nor for gold jewellery, pretty dresses or shoes. Money
ran through our fingers like water from a broken jug. I
would stand at the door in the morning as Muhammad left
for work, shouting to him in a voice loud enough for the
women neighbours to hear, 'Don't forget to drop by the
jeweller's and get me some nice armlets. And ask him if he's
repaired the pair of earrings!'

Mother stayed on with us to help me raise the children.
Then, when Muhammad was promoted, he hired a servant
girl. We were invited to his colleagues' birthday parties and
went out to restaurants with them. I'd talk to refined people,
but all the while my thoughts would be on the children left
at home with Mother, whose sight was getting worse. Once
we returned home to find her sound asleep, and the children
scattered like feral monkeys through the house.

Mother and I suffered from the same disease of indolence,
Muhammad remarked.

'Fine,' I replied, 'just bring me a kilo of meat and watch
how I spring up like fire. I'll pound the meat and make some
Kafta. Once I've eaten some of that, you'll see how quickly
I get my strength back.'

But this was bravado talk. I was exhausted. I was bleeding
constantly, and the babies, teething in succession, screamed.
I tried to be like Khadija, picking up the children's clothes
from the floor with her toes as she carried her baby around
on her hip. But before long I would collapse on the bed, too

tired even to whisper words of adoration to Muhammad. I
wanted to lie down to sleep rather than do housework or
deal with the children. Muhammad did not believe I was
exhausted – he believed I was lazy. Once, a bitter cold spell
hit the capital when he was away for two days on official
business. When he heard about it he took a taxi back to
Beirut, arriving home at midnight and rushing straight to
the children's bedroom to make sure they were properly
covered. He'd convinced himself I'd be sound asleep, warm
and cosy, while the poor children shivered in their beds.

Ra's al-Naqurah

MUHAMMAD'S JOB TOOK us to Ra's al-Naqurah, a remote army outpost on the Lebanese–Israeli border. As soldiers helped us with our belongings and officers greeted us, I thanked God for this luxury at last. I saw the lush garden, climbed the staircase, entered our bedroom and gazed out at the blue sea stretching before me. The only time I'd seen its colour matched was in washing powder, to which you added a cube of Nile whitener.

'Where are we?' I asked Muhammad, singing as I twirled around, just like Layla Murad in the film. 'Is it the Red Sea? Alexandria? Marsa Matruh?'

When he began to bring me fish every day, small or big, silver or coloured, I knew for sure I'd gone up several rungs on the social ladder. When fishermen were caught using dynamite to fish, the soldiers would confiscate the fish and issue a fine. The fish would then be distributed to us and the other officials. When I was a little girl and stood in doorways selling bibs, I'd often smell fish cooking. Oh, how I'd longed to taste some! But the Haji would never buy fish. 'What's the point,' he'd say, 'when there are so many of us? I'd be happy to get some, but with so many people in the house, a whole shoal of fish wouldn't be enough.'

Our new house was large, with five bedrooms around a courtyard, two large reception rooms on the first floor, as well as a kitchen and other rooms on the ground floor. As we sipped coffee on the balcony of our home, Muhammad would point out the Lebanese–Israeli border. I came to understand the importance of his post at Ra's al-Naqurah. He was responsible for such a vast area of land and sea. Looking along the shore at the rocks and the flat plains, I was reminded of Mufaddala, the daughter of my aunt who thought she had a snake in her stomach. Mufaddala had married a Palestinian and they'd moved to Palestine, but after 1948 and the creation of the State of Israel there'd been no more news of her. If only Mufaddala could be told I was now married to the director in charge of the frontier; if only I knew where she was so I could ask her to meet me and persuade Muhammad to let her cross the border back into Lebanon. If only that could happen, then my aunt would stop crying, and Mother too. They were so sad because Mufaddala seemed to be lost for ever.

Mother had told me how, after 1948, each morning my aunt would run towards the border, calling, 'Mufaddala, Mufaddala.' She kept trying in vain to cut the barbed wire with a sickle or with stones, and would pound her head with rocks. She'd only stop when her face was covered in blood. Then she'd go again to the border at night, hoping that her cries of 'Mufaddala, Mufaddala' had raised an echo in Palestine–Israel that would bring her daughter back.

While Muhammad was busy working, I spent my time taking the children on walks with the wives of other officials. I'd sing for them and tell them the stories of films I'd seen.

'You're not like a director's wife,' one said with a note of relief when they saw me picking endive, wild thyme and camomile. I smiled back and sighed. How would they react, I wondered, if I told them how I used to sneak into the wheat fields with Mother after the harvesters had left so we wouldn't starve?

Weeks went by, then months. Gradually we strayed further and further from the settlement on our walks. One day, we headed for a solitary palm tree I'd seen from our balcony. Suddenly a soldier began to shout and chase after us. We'd wandered into Israeli territory. The other wives began to tremble: one invoked the Virgin Mary, another Jesus and a third the Prophet Muhammad. I didn't invoke anyone. All I cared about was seeing something other than waves, white foam, large smooth pebbles and green grass.

I woke up one morning clutching my head.

'The roar of the sea is boring into my skull!' I complained to Muhammad. I had to block my ears to stop the noise of the crashing waves throbbing inside my brain.

Muhammad noticed my change of mood; even my love of telling jokes seemed to have abandoned me. I stopped hanging around with the officials and their wives and trying to be that wonderful woman, the director's wife. I no longer wanted to go to the beach with Muhammad and the children. The very sight of the sea made my heart pound. When the waves were rough, I wanted to grab hold of the children and run, in case the waves swallowed them up. When I stopped eating fish and could hardly stand, Muhammad called in a doctor who visited Ra's al-Naqurah every month to check on the officials in that wilderness. When he asked me how I was feeling, I told him about the roar of the waves and my urge to cry if the sea changed colour. He told me I was suffering from a kind of depression that affected people in remote places. In tears I told him about my aunt's daughter, and he nodded, confirming his diagnosis.

'Of course,' he said, 'worrying about this young woman only makes you feel worse.'

As the sea roared on the beach below the house, I didn't dare mention my two daughters in Beirut to the doctor. The fact was that I missed them terribly, and each heartbeat of the waves made me feel even further away.

But I snapped back to my old self when Muhammad brought home a woman who'd been apprehended for trying to cross over into Israel. She swore she was Lebanese and had relatives there. Though she spoke Arabic, Muhammad couldn't tell from her accent whether she was Lebanese or Palestinian. She began to cry, begging Muhammad to let her go, but he put her in a room on the ground floor and locked the door, saying that a detective would come next day to question her. I asked to speak with her. Muhammad refused. He wouldn't even let me go downstairs with him when he took her some food. I couldn't stop thinking about this woman locked up on the ground floor. I started calling her 'the prisoner'.

I decided what to do. I waited until Muhammad was in bed and sound asleep before reaching under his pillow where he kept his keys. I tiptoed downstairs and unlocked the door. The woman was still crying. I tried to talk to her, but she kept on weeping. The only thing I could make out was that she was in some kind of trouble; why else would she have exposed herself to such danger? I started to cry too. Why hadn't my cousin, Mufaddala, sneaked back across in this way?

I brought her some food in a bag, took her hand, and opened the door for her.

'Go on,' I told her, 'start running!'

She leaned forward to kiss my hand, but I withdrew it.

'Run quickly! Save yourself! Go on!'

Within seconds she was lost in the darkness.

I went back to bed and put the keys under Muhammad's pillow. I couldn't sleep. My depression had left the house, running out into the night with the woman. I lay listening to the roar of the waves, wondering if she had managed to sneak into Palestine or hide out somewhere in Lebanese territory. When morning came Muhammad dressed quickly, took the keys and disappeared.

Then he came back upstairs and into the bedroom and hugged me to him.

'Now what exactly am I supposed to tell the detective?' he whispered in my ear. 'That my wife stole the keys and let the woman go? For all you know she could have been a dangerous spy!'

Two Muhammads

OUR TIME IN Ra's al-Naqurah came to an end and we returned to the bustle and expense of Beirut. By now there were two Muhammads in my life. The first one wore houndstooth suits and crisply ironed shirts. He was the Muhammad with sleek brown hair, the one who was always reading a book with a piece of paper or a pen in his hand. He was forever reciting popular poetry he'd memorised, or verses composed by his friends. This was the Muhammad who made me feel insanely jealous as I watched him licking a lamb bone with relish. I was jealous because his wide hazel eyes showed his love for everything that was stylish and beautiful and I wanted him to love only me. This Muhammad was the one I thought about, recalling the smell of his body when he was away. He only had to look at me to gain complete control over my heart and soul.

The second Muhammad ensured that I was constantly pregnant, having miscarriages or giving birth to one baby after another. I was exhausted all the time. It seemed that I only had to smell Muhammad or be hugged by him to get pregnant, and I tried very hard to abort each pregnancy. I managed to miscarry twins after jumping off tables and taking lots of aspirin. Ahlam saw me doing this, and threatened to tell her father; at this point, she was only six years old.

My doctor never advised me about my pregnancies, the

miscarriages or the bleeding I suffered when I was pregnant. Nor did Muhammad and I agree to stop producing children until my body could recover and our financial situation improved. Muhammad wanted another boy and as many children as possible regardless of our lack of money and my fatigue. He would say, 'You go ahead and have the babies, I will look after them.'

This second Muhammad helped me raise the children with boundless energy. If he had a headache, he'd put a band around his head to relieve the pain, and carry on. He fussed over the children and the house, and even borrowed money so we could spend a summer in Bhamdoun. There, I thought often of the first Muhammad. Together we visited the local village, the spring and the chinaberry trees; we found our names and the dates we'd met carved into the walnut tree. We sat under the tree, trying to relive those earlier times when I had sung 'Oh sleepy love'. He asked me to sing to him again, and I did, though my stomach was distended with our fourth child and I felt so tired that I only wanted to sleep. I mustered up every flirtatious move I had left as I sang Shadiya's song:

> I catch up with you and you run away from me;
> I go after you but you escape.
> Who has changed you so?
> Who has made you hate me so?
> Why won't you tell me?

In spite of my best efforts, Muhammad shook his head.

'Your voice isn't what it was,' he said regretfully. 'It's almost as though it's been strangled by a rope.'

He meant that my love for him was diminishing because I couldn't sing as passionately as I had before.

His words made us both laugh. I said it was as though we each carried a thermometer, in order to test whether our love was still at its peak. The next morning I snuggled up to Muhammad as he opened the newspaper and read me the world's events. In the evening I hurried to him again as he opened his notebook.

On the day my identity card recorded as my birthday (we weren't sure it was my exact birthday), he read me a poem:

Birthday by Iliyya Abu Madi

What am I to give you, my angel, on your birthday,
When you already possess everything?
Bracelet, armlet of purest gold?
I do not like to see chains on your wrist.
Wine? There does not exist on this earth a wine
Like the one that pours from your glances.
Roses? For me the most beauteous rose
Is the one I have plucked from your cheeks.
Or carnelian perhaps, blazing red like my very life blood,
And the precious red carnelian in your luscious lips.
I have nothing to give you more dear than the soul itself,
And my own soul is a pawn in your hands.

I asked him to recite the poem again. Then I recited it almost word for word back to him. He hugged me, crying and blaming himself for never having taught me to read and write. I dried his eyes but then began crying too.

'A stick of wood with some lead in it; I'm through because of it!' I shouted, and then I turned the words into a song: 'Because of a stick of wood with some lead in it, I was through. Every time I began to learn to read and write, my belly grew!'

Inside my belly was a fifth little girl. When she was born, she looked just like Kadsuma, the heroine in the film *Sayonara*, and so that was her name.

The 1958 Revolution Happened Because of Me

I HAD ALWAYS BELIEVED that tension would regularly erupt between lovers, families and workmates, but would never escalate into situations beyond one's control. And yet this was what happened in Lebanon in the spring of 1958.[21] In our neighbourhood armed gangs and revolutionaries made death threats against government employees, particularly if they worked for the police, the army or the Sécurité Générale. When Muhammad was told he'd be killed if he didn't resign from his job, and the nearby residence of the Prime Minister was blown up by the insurgents while a crowd rejoiced as it burned, we knew it was time to escape to a Christian neighbourhood. I suggested to Muhammad that we take refuge at Ibrahim's house – after all, I was blood kin. Following his older son's return from America

---

21 Lebanon's 1958 sectarian clashes were brief and involved relatively few casualties, but represented the most serious rift between the Muslim and Christian Maronite sects since independence in 1943. The immediate reason for the situation was each sect's extreme sensitivity to competing regional interests. The Muslim and Druze communities were very keen to commit Lebanon to Egyptian President Gamal Abdel Nasser's request for Arab unity, while the Christian Maronites were resolutely pro-Western in their outlook. The US Sixth Fleet intervened to quell the disturbances, and the situation was defused by a deal that saw the departure of Maronite President Camille Chamoun, whose unconstitutional ambition for another six-year term was the trigger for the unrest, and the election of the supposedly reformist army general Fouad Chehab. But the confrontation exposed fundamental weaknesses in Lebanon's consociational democracy.

with an aeronautical degree, Ibrahim had moved from the house he shared with the Haji and into a house in a Christian neighbourhood.

The next day I bade farewell to our neighbours. We were terrified that the Nasserites would appear at any moment. I cried as I left the key with Leila, our neighbour who had become a good friend. We had often discussed the films we'd seen, and she would tell me the plots of novels she read, as the reader that I could never be.

When the taxi scheduled to take us to our new home didn't arrive, we felt sure the driver must be aligned with the revolutionaries planning to arrest Muhammad. So Muhammad decided to go downstairs and look for another taxi, rather than wait inside the house. Out on the street we found a taxi, but without its driver. I sat in the back with the four children, while Muhammad sat in the front. Was it all part of a plot? Had the driver betrayed us?

While Muhammad tried to figure out what to do next, the children and I became very anxious. The driver came out of Shorty's falafel shop, carrying an enormous falafel sandwich. That shop was always crammed with people — some of them buying, others simply hoping to be entertained by the proprietor, a dwarf who wore high-heeled wooden clogs, and his tall wife. When they argued, Shorty would stand on a chair to slap her.

Eventually we managed to get through the road blocks without trouble. But instead of feeling relieved to be out of danger, I began to panic as we neared Ibrahim's house. It wasn't the first time I'd seen him and his family since I'd married Muhammad; we'd bumped into them quite by chance when we were all at Maryam's house after she gave birth to her first child, and we had made peace with each other then.

When we finally arrived, Ibrahim and Khadija could not

have greeted us more warmly. The other big surprise was that we found Fatima and Hanan there too. The street fighting had prevented me from seeing my daughters for quite some time. They were on their way to Nabatiyeh to take refuge from the troubles, which had reached their neighbourhood.

Once my children were in bed, I pinched myself. Here I was in Ibrahim's house – the man who had arranged my forced marriage, the one who'd fainted clean away when Hasan broached the topic of my divorce, the one who'd urged Abu-Hussein to go ahead and divorce me. 'Muhammad is bound to leave her,' he'd told the Haji. 'He'll never marry her. She's already a wife and mother of two children.' He had wanted to see me humiliated, but now he was opening his house to give us shelter. I knew perfectly well, of course, that my current husband's sweet nature imposed its own kind of respect. And he also held a senior position in the Sécurité Générale. But I think that Ibrahim's change of heart was also due to the fact that by now I'd produced four more children by Muhammad. I'd passed the test. I could enjoy genuine married status. I had returned to the family, honoured and respected.

Before I dropped off to sleep, I asked Muhammad if dire circumstances make people more hard-hearted. It seemed as though success softened people's hard edges and made them more tolerant. Suddenly I admired Ibrahim, snatched from school and thrown straight into life's struggles. In spite of everything, he'd fought for his own children to have a good education by saving money, little by little. And now here he was, the owner of a house; or, more precisely, a villa.

Muhammad Kamal

THE 1958 REVOLUTION ended. Lebanon didn't unite with Egypt after all. The US Sixth Fleet intervened and General Fouad Chehab was elected President. I gave birth to another boy, the last in the litter. Muhammad insisted our son be named Muhammad Kamal, so I could call him Muhammad and he could call the boy Kamula. Our friends were troubled by our choice of name, since naming a child for his father with the father still alive seemed destined to bring us bad luck, especially since the baby had come after a number of miscarriages.

In fact Muhammad Kamal arrived at just the right moment, when our love had been flagging. I'd been constantly exhausted and plagued by feelings of jealousy. We were short of money. But the baby rekindled our love. Under President Chehab we began to enjoy the fruits of Muhammad's success. He was appointed bureau chief for the entire Bekaa Valley and we moved away from Beirut. Muhammad rented us a large house not far from his work. Two local girls came to help me with the housework, the childcare, and the cooking. We travelled sometimes with the children, at other times without them. Some evenings we would sit on the wide balcony, looking out at the mountains and trees. On the festival of the Prophet Muhammad's birth we celebrated with fireworks. The children whooped with delight as they watched the bright lights gleaming in the dark. One day Muhammad took them to a granary where they saw wheat being threshed. Muhammad tipped the worker and the children got to sit on the thresher while the cow dragged them around in circles.

He brought them a small truck filled with melons, and another filled with sand so they could play on the balcony after a neighbour yelled at them for playing in builder's sand left at the side of the house. I tried to calm myself, because I felt so optimistic amidst all this harmony and contentment. I'd never thought about death, in spite of all the bleeding and miscarriages I'd endured. Muhammad was never ill, but he feared death because he feared losing his good fortune.

One night he gathered all the children around him, holding Muhammad Kamal, not yet six months old, in his arms. He loaded his revolver and looked up at the sky.

'If you're really up there,' he yelled, 'then listen to me. Don't ever take them away from me. If you decide to kill me off, then you don't exist. Listen to me, I beg you: never take them away from me!'

With that he fired the revolver into the air, and all the doves and the other birds took off into the sky. Our neighbour came rushing out to see what was happening and all of a sudden the moon emerged from behind a cloud.

'You see,' said Muhammad, 'the moon's happy with me.'

The incident made me wonder whether his fear of death was somehow linked to the fact that he'd begun driving a car after only three weeks' instruction. Or was it that he'd suddenly become aware of the phases of human existence: birth, youth, old age and death? But I was still only thirty-four years old, and Muhammad thirty-eight. Our parents were alive and well.

But despite Muhammad's anxiety, I was the one who thought often about death. These thoughts were not due to four of the children crowding around me laughing, while Muhammad held the fifth. Rather, I kept coming back to the image of the coat hook in our bedroom. It was not behind the door but on the wall next to our bed, so I could stretch out for my dress from bed each morning. For some reason, I kept imagining myself in an emergency, rising from the bed and pulling on the dress. I told Muhammad about my daydream and begged him to stop driving the car. It wasn't that he didn't try to be safe. Unlike other more experienced drivers I'd seen, who kept one hand on the steering wheel while the other held a cigarette, Muhammad kept both hands glued rigidly to the wheel. I worried just the same.

Unbelievably, the dreadful day arrived. I reached for my pink dress with white circles that hung on that hook, wailing as I took it down. The four children, waiting for their father to come home, began bawling with me. The baby Muhammad Kamal clung to me for dear life. It was a holiday, but Muhammad had gone to the office for a couple of hours, as they'd managed to catch a notorious smuggler. He'd said he wouldn't need to stay long and asked me to make sure the children were ready so he could take them for a ride when he returned. But his car had skidded on the wet road on his way home. He was taken to the hospital.

Muhammad was unconscious for a while, but then he came round.

'I skidded,' he said when he saw me. 'Thank God the children weren't with me!'

The doctors did their very best for him. I kept thinking that death had already snatched away my sisters Manifa and Raoufa, and Umm Fawzi. I begged God to forgive Muhammad for firing his revolver into the sky that recent night, when he'd gathered his children around him. I begged him to forgive me for trying to poison my ex-husband and Ibrahim with salt. I begged his forgiveness for telling Muhammad to wait until my husband died for us to marry; I reminded him how I'd got to know and love Muhammad before I'd found out I was to be married to my brother-in-law.

For hours I sat beside Muhammad's bed. He was in pain, drifting in and out of consciousness. His bed was enveloped in tubes. Blood from his kidneys and heart showed up in his urine. I meditated, begged God's forgiveness, asked for his mercy, prayed and wept. I asked God not to respond to Mother's old prayers, asking for revenge on Muhammad for stealing me away. Once again I reminded God that I already knew and loved Muhammad before I was married to my brother-in-law. If I were to say, 'It's in accordance with your will,' I asked myself, would he forgive everything and make him better? It was God's will that the dew should fall, but this time it had fallen not on roses and sweet basil but on asphalt. And so Muhammad had skidded in his car, then pressed the accelerator pedal rather than the brake.

When Muhammad awoke, he began to ramble. He held my hand, telling me there was 700 lira hidden in the desk drawer in his office. Seeing that Fatima never left my side, Muhammad asked me once why Hanan had never come to see him. I smiled at him and said, fibbing, that Hanan was visiting a friend in the north, and that she was planning to come to see him soon.

'Tell her to take an aspirin tablet to calm her down and to come see me,' he said. Though he must have felt that Hanan, as always, had seldom visited us. Then he told me not to forget about the 700 lira in the desk drawer; he told me I should go and get it before anyone else found it.

I sat with him. I blamed myself for not forbidding him to drive the car, in spite of my terrible premonition. I blamed myself for praying that he'd die whenever we fought; for wasting so much time; for making him wait so long before I got my divorce; for interrogating him whenever he returned from work; and for preferring to sleep, rather than stay up with him. Though Muhammad was conscious, he was delirious. He seized my hand and kissed it and asked me to run away with him through the window …

One of his sisters began to wail.

'The Angel of Death is here to take him away!' she screamed.

Muhammad tried to escape the Angel's clutches … but then he was taken from me.

I was still wearing my slippers as a throng of people gathered for his burial. The funeral ceremony turned into a kind of wedding feast, with crowds from all the villages in the south, sacrificed sheep, the Quran blaring from loudspeakers, and memorial speeches. Through it all I could hear Muhammad's own words whenever we argued and I wished him dead. 'If I die you'll want to weep blood all over me,' he would say. The mourners wore glossy shoes, chic tailored suits and expensive jackets with silk handkerchiefs in the breast pockets. In their fingers they carried prayer beads made of precious stones. They drove flashy cars, without crashing them on wet roads. Everyone came to bid farewell to my husband. There I stood among them, still wearing the slippers I'd put on when I'd heard about the accident.

Could it really be true that everything had ground to a halt, and Muhammad had become nothing more than a pile of bones? What of his ideas, feelings, plans, pain, memories, desires? His love of poetry? His sleepy ways and his laughter? How could all this come to an end just because his heart had stopped beating? How could he disappear without trace? Where was his longing for me? Where were the two feet that would leap from the bus as soon as he heard the word 'Bhamdoun', just so he could see me for an hour before returning happy to Beirut?

Amid all the weeping and wailing, I spotted Father. He was stifling a laugh and muttering something as he watched

Muhammad's mother riding on a donkey. The donkey had stopped and was refusing to move, while Muhammad's mother swayed to the left and right. I could understand how this sight had got the better of him.

When I fainted, Khadija and the other women tried to make me eat something. People said they saw a tear fall from Muhammad's eye when they brought our elder son over to bid him farewell.

An old woman patted me gently on the shoulder.

'Listen, sweetheart,' she told me, 'God gave him to you and now he's taken him away. You can cry and beat your breast all you like, but crying won't bring him back! Never mind, my dearie, some day you'll be together again.'

I knew she was doing her best to lighten my misery.

She started to mourn for the dead in her own family, but then she stopped.

She said instead, 'Come on, my sweet, get a grip on yourself, if only for your children's sake. They're still little. Come on, days and years will pass very quickly, and in the twinkling of an eye you and Muhammad will be back together.'

I didn't like the way she was trying to rush time forward, especially since Muhammad Kamal was not yet six months old.

'Preserve me from evil,' I muttered.

Muhammad's family home was crowded with wailing women. They kept pouring in. I heard one woman ask if my daughter Fatima, who was carrying Muhammad Kamal, was the dead man's daughter. The women whispered that she was my daughter by my first husband. They started gossiping about my divorce as if I wasn't there.

I had no idea where I was; maybe I was with Muhammad in his grave as odes rang in my ears. Khalil Roukoz – the famous poet whose work Muhammad had always loved and who had written a poem for Muhammad when Toufic was born, among many other occasions – recited these lines in a choked voice:

> You have departed, Oh Muhammad, from the life of this
>   world,
> When the burden of existence overpowered your eyes.
> This world of ours is a stage for meetings and departures,
> Not just for you, but for all of us, death awaits.
> Yet in your case you have spoiled the departure with a
>   fire,
> While still a young man, a life of promise still on your
>   cheeks.
> The tears in your widow's eyes fall two by two,
> So how were you able to close your eyes to them and
>   her?

Once again the old woman was at my side.

'My sweet,' she said, 'only remember: we all want to be with our beloveds. Woman is meant for man, and man for woman. When you go up to heaven, it'll be to paradise, God willing, because of all that you're suffering and will suffer. You'll cry out, "Muhammad, Muhammad, here I am!" and there he'll be, looking at you like the moon.'

My heart sank as I remembered that Muhammad was also my first husband's name, although nobody called him that. Was it conceivable that in heaven I would have to go back to the Haji? I decided I must talk to the oldest woman there, the one who was most religious and devout, and explain my fear that the husband I'd meet in heaven would be my first, not my beloved Muhammad.

She wiped my face with her hand, recited some verses from the Quran, and said, 'In the name of God, calm yourself, my dear. You want to be reunited with the deceased

Muhammad, because he's your real husband and your first husband has married someone else. Isn't that it? Be sure you never forget to pray and fast!'

I felt happier. But I could not help but wonder how it could be that this old woman, who'd lost all her teeth, was still alive, while Muhammad, a tall young man whose muscular body filled out his clothes, was dead. The feeling stayed with me from the very first day of the funeral rites. Every time I saw anyone old, male or female, I'd say to them, 'Here you are, old and haggard but still alive, and there's Muhammad, dead in the prime of his life. Do you call that fair?'

I only stopped doing this when Miskiah seized me by the hand.

'Unless you control yourself,' she said, 'people are going to think you've lost your mind.'

'But I have, I have,' I wanted to say. I still felt as if Muhammad was alive, but had gone away somewhere on government business. I was sure he'd be back.

His death had caused an earthquake that turned our lovely green field to a wasteland, then into a veritable desert. How were my five children going to live? Who would cut my fingernails and toenails?

'You Must Have the Wrong House'

T WO MONTHS AFTER Muhammad's death, my house in Beirut was no longer a home, but more like a mosque. Every day a Quran reader came to recite verses in memory of Muhammad. All kinds of people arrived as well: important people like politicians and civil servants, as well as the local doctor and teacher, relatives, friends and friends of friends. I felt the front door wide open. My five children, now aged eight months to eight years, spent their time making a racket, eating, crying and fighting. The littlest one cried and shouted constantly. 'Baba, Baba!' he called out. Muhammad had been both father and mother to him, bathing him, feeding him, and making him laugh. He would only go to sleep if Muhammad held him in his arms.

All my energy evaporated. As I sat there, collapsed, people poured into the house. They chanted Quranic verses that battled with the noise of the children. Soon I was desperate to close the door in the face of the Quran reader, but I hadn't the strength to ask him to stop coming, so I let him go on chanting while I lay prostrate on the bed. One afternoon, Ahlam rushed in to tell me that the blind Quran reader was asking after me.

I yelled out from my bedroom, 'Oh, I was just going to prepare you some herbal tea, but since you're leaving, I'll do it tomorrow.'

The day came when I did close the door in his face.

'Yes,' I asked when he arrived one morning, 'what do you want?'

'I'm the sheikh who's come to read the Quran,' he replied.

'Who?' I asked him again.

He hesitated a moment.

'The sheikh,' he said. 'The one who comes each day to read the Quran for the soul of your husband.'

'You must have the wrong house,' I replied. 'No one here has died. What are you trying to do, bring us bad luck?'

He kept on insisting, and so did I. Eventually he made his way back down the stairs, pounding his stick angrily.

I gathered up Muhammad's clothes and shoes, put them in boxes, and shoved them in the attic. I collected all his papers and diaries, put them in a bag, and stored them away in the cupboard. I found an empty cigarette packet among his things. Inside were 10 piastres, along with a scrap of one of my dresses with a pattern of gold circles. I couldn't remember a thing about the money; in fact the very sight of the coins and the little scrap of material saddened me so much it hurt.

The early rains arrived and I prepared the children for school. I felt as if I'd been sleeping in a garden with Muhammad's arm as a pillow. Now I had awoken to find him gone. Before me were five children, all clinging to my skirts. Four of them were yelling and screaming, asking me to write their names on notepads and books, to read their teachers' comments or help them with their homework. The fifth one wanted my milk day and night. I felt myself becoming the sixth child. Who would read me the letters from the bank requesting my signature? Who would explain money and contracts? Muhammad had taught me to sign my name, one letter at a time, but the veil that hung over a page of writing terrified me. Should I really be signing my name to all these pieces of paper? Now that Muhammad was dead, should I sign the inheritance document? I remembered how

Muhammad had written a will bequeathing me the lands he owned in his village. But then we argued and he tore it up; only to tell me he'd rewritten it once we were reconciled. I never knew why, but I didn't believe him at the time. I'd looked closely at the document, searching for my name. I found it, but I couldn't find the word 'land'. Then I looked for the name of his village, but couldn't find that either. When I asked him about it, he just hugged me tight.

It was as though the letters on the page were fighting one another, each one like an annoying fly that buzzed in my eye. Everything I'd ever learned, the small amount that Muhammad had taught me, simply flew away. I was at a total loss, surrounded by the swarming flies. Years ago, I'd compared the letters to nails on the page; now they were all confused in my mind, piling up, one on top of the other.

I hesitated before I signed my name. The civil servant handling Muhammad's estate paused. I'd already scribbled on three forms, but I couldn't pluck up the courage to admit I'd forgotten how to sign my own name. I felt so ashamed that I drew a rose, the same way I'd done for Muhammad, and then a bird. The man stared at me in disbelief and asked me to sign my name on another piece of paper, then another. When I drew the bird and the rose on every single sheet he told me it wouldn't do and suggested that I make my thumbprint instead. Suddenly I was back in the Nabatiyeh market, watching the blacksmith lift the horse's hoof to hammer the horseshoe in place. I remembered the wife of Shorty the falafel seller back in our old neighbourhood in Beirut: every time she was given a bill, she put her thumbprint on it, as though she'd been born with a jet-black thumb. I would never use my thumbprint. From that day, I told the man, my signature would be a rose and a bird, since I wouldn't forget how to do it. And so the civil servant took the forms and stamped the seal on them.

I followed the instructions of one of Muhammad's brothers and used the government compensation we received for his death to buy an apartment that I could rent out. I deposited some of the money with Salsabil, a woman in the village who invested widows' money and paid them back a year later with a good profit. I handed over more money to a shoe seller from Muhammad's village who owned a shop in downtown Beirut, so he could invest the capital and pay me the interest. Finally, Muhammad's brother-in-law was appointed our guardian, so he could collect the monthly stipend on my behalf and meet our household expenses.

I couldn't help thinking that Muhammad was still working for us, even though he was buried in the ground. At least we were eating, drinking and sleeping in our own home, unlike Mother's experience after her first husband died, which left her penniless. The thought made me hug myself. I imagined I was hugging Muhammad and smiling at him. 'Thank you, Lord,' I said. But then I remembered that Mother was thirty-four years old when her husband died, widowed at the same age as me. The thought made me shudder.

'I am Abu al-Hinn, the Tiniest of Birds. What's the Point of Shooting me?'

M Y HOME BEGAN to attract all kinds of butterflies and bees, those who brought nectar and those who were in need of it: miserable wives, spinsters in search of youth, divorcees. They were like movie heroines calling at my home, their hearts filled with songs and merriment. I heard detailed anecdotes about their passions and secret rendezvous; discussed complaints about distance, separation and overwhelming love; and participated in fortune-telling sessions, all over endless cups of coffee. It was as if my house had become a heart hospital, a rest home or a convalescent centre. Through me these women sought refuge from their brothers, husbands or even mothers. Regularly this crowd included my two older daughters, Hanan, now fifteen, and especially Fatima, who was now nineteen. She spent most days happily in my house, away from her father and his shrewish wife.

But I was still afraid. My fear spread to my five younger children, Mother, my friends and everyone who crossed my threshold. Muhammad's family (the men, that is) sat in silence like fishermen, waiting for me to make the tiniest mistake to trap me in their nets. Muhammad's three sisters were so upset by their brother's death that one of them stopped visiting us and left our district altogether, while the other two never stopped weeping, beating their chests and clutching us to them.

Muhammad's brothers did their best to control our daily lives, as if we belonged to them. They weren't happy that I'd managed to recover from the tragedy. They didn't like that I'd pulled myself together; that I was relying on my own resolve to take care of myself and my children. I felt certain that, if we'd been in India, they'd have decided to burn me alive alongside Muhammad's corpse. The brother who'd betrayed me to the Haji once slapped me. He was offended that, only forty days after Muhammad's death, without waiting for the end of the six-month confinement typical for widows, I'd left the house with one of his sisters to present our condolences when a relative died.

Another brother, Ali, fell in love with me. Amazed, I wondered how he could dare to come to the house every day reciting love poems, when not even a year had passed since Muhammad's death. He decided he was the man of the house and kept a close watch on everyone who came to visit; he began spying, following me wherever I went.

When I rebuffed him he replied, 'I'm free, I can do what I want. This is my brother's house!'

'*I* am free, *free* to live the life I want!' I shouted at him. 'Do you understand?'

Unlike Muhammad's brothers, however, my 'guardian' brother-in-law avoided me. I had to stalk him like a cat after a mouse. When I asked him for money, he ran off as if I was seeking a loan. He insisted on knowing about every single purchase, big or small, even down to a box of matches. I felt certain he was following the instructions of Muhammad's family: 'Make her beg for every single penny!'

Why was it that in-laws behaved like this, both in films and reality? The only way out of the situation was for me to go to court and receive an official order removing my brother-in-law's guardianship and restraining Muhammad's domineering brother Ali. But the ears of the official I saw

were stuffed with stones. They reverberated with the sound
of his own voice, as he pontificated on the law and what was
permissible behaviour.

This experience reminded me of the story of the bird
called Abu al-Hinn, a tiny fledgling. Seeing a gun aimed at
its heart, it begged the hunter not to shoot.

'Dear hunter,' it said, 'I'm Abu al-Hinn, the tiniest of
birds. What's the point of shooting me? You'd be better off
with a slice of bread and some onion!'

These words softened the hunter's heart and he left the
little bird alone and went in search of other prey. The bird
flapped its wings in sheer delight, and was so thrilled by its
powers of persuasion that it got ahead of itself.

Spotting another hunter, it rushed from its nest.

'I'm Abu al-Hinn,' it said again. 'One of my thighs is
enough to feed an entire household.' With that the hunter
shot it dead.

When I went to the shariah court, I was just like the
conceited bird. I was used to Muhammad's love and status
protecting me, so I had stepped into court assuming that
justice would be on my side. Now the official's rejection –
his complete unwillingness to listen – had turned me back
into Abu al-Hinn, the tiny bird that trembled as it entreated
the hunter not to shoot it.

Once more I resorted to trickery and cunning, with
the little bird Abu al-Hinn as my guide. I decided to seek
another appearance with the sheikh in the shariah court. I
asked him to cancel my guardian's power of attorney and
make me responsible for my own children; and to put a
stop to Muhammad's domineering brother Ali's amorous
harassment. He replied that the guardian had been selected
because of his love for my deceased husband and his fidelity
to Muhammad's memory. The behaviour of his brother Ali,
the sheikh told me, was caused by the brother's awareness of

society's failure to protect widows, for whom there was little sympathy, particularly if they were young. (He didn't add 'and pretty'.)

I decided I needed a new tactic. I hurried to Kamil's house to ask his beautiful green-eyed wife to help me by accompanying me the following week. At first the sheikh tried to repeat what he'd said on the previous occasion, but I told him again that I didn't believe an outsider such as Muhammad's brother-in-law was an appropriate guardian. I was my own person, in charge of myself, not the property of my dead husband's family. I also complained again about the lewd advances of Muhammad's brother Ali.

As I wept before the sheikh, my sister-in-law was equally busy batting her eyelids at him. The sheikh promptly signed the papers, acknowledging I was the primary guardian of my children. At that point my friendship with Kamil's wife – which stemmed from our own mothers' friendship – was firmly cemented.

Muhammad Betrays Me

ONE OF MY husband's female relatives told me her son had once been in a car with Muhammad when they stopped to pick up a woman, a foreign hitchhiker. I felt a stab of jealousy, as though Muhammad were still alive. I took off my shoe and threw it at his photograph, but missed. As soon as the relative left I stood in front of the picture, accusing him and demanding to know the truth. But his smile never changed. I banged on the picture. When neither frame nor glass broke, I moved it to face my own photograph, so that way he was looking at me and I could give him the cold shoulder.

I couldn't sleep that night. Could it be possible that the entire time I'd been exhausted, pregnant and raising my children, Muhammad was flirting with some foreign woman? Maybe they'd even had an affair! I told everyone who visited about Muhammad's betrayal. Without fail they laughed at me and pointed out how funny I was, unable to believe that such an innocuous incident could make me so unhappy. But anger gnawed at me. I decided I had to know exactly what had happened between Muhammad and this foreign woman.

A neighbour heard of my fury and told me about a friend who'd confided in her that Muhammad had been unfaithful. This woman had asked him for help on an official matter and he'd invited her to have lunch with him. When she'd turned him down, he'd flirted with her and tried to persuade her to change her mind.

I stormed out to see the woman, a schoolteacher, and demanded she tell me exactly what had happened between her and Muhammad.

'I'll show him!' I yelled at her, as if Muhammad were alive. 'I'll show him!'

She swore by the most solemn oath that she and the neighbour had made the whole thing up, as a way of getting me to take off my mourning clothes and begin to enjoy life again. It was now a year since Muhammad's death. I didn't believe her. Instead, I pictured Muhammad at his desk as the woman came in carrying her handbag, her chic outfit indicating that she didn't have to spend her days at home, cooking, washing and cleaning. Not only that, she could actually read official documents. I imagined Muhammad noting how well educated she was, his intellectual equal. There she was enjoying life to the full while Kamila was stuck at home with the babies.

I got out the bag in which I'd stored his papers, wondering whom I could get to read them to me. I needed a discreet friend, not someone who would take malicious pleasure from my situation. I remembered Leila, my neighbour who used to tell me the plots of the novels she read. Leila would understand.

We sat down together over dozens, if not hundreds, of pieces of paper. I told her how Muhammad had betrayed me, repeating what the old woman in Muhammad's village said whenever I visited my husband's grave.

I used her accent as I recited, ' "Oh, how I burn with grief for you! Your husband was a king, with a pistol on each hip." '

She would point to either side of her waist.

'Listen to me: when my husband died, I wept and wept, even though I had to reproach him. "You left for Beirut," I would say, "and rode on the trams. You left me behind to take care of the cattle. Now you're gone, and I don't give a damn." Come, come, Kamila, it's better to live through a funeral than see your husband marry another woman. After all, who can say? If my husband were still alive, maybe he'd have married someone else.'

But as I looked at Muhammad's writing, I fell in love with him all over again. I saw the letters I had made my daughter Fatima write to him. I saw the bird, the nest and the roses I'd drawn for him. I also saw notebooks divided into paragraphs separated by red ink. These were his diaries, Leila said, but what I wanted to find were the letters he'd received. Leila's eye fell on the words, '*Bonjour, mon ami*!' written in both French and Arabic. But this was part of a story about a love affair between two students. The boy took the girl, named K, on a picnic:

> We reached the hills to the east of Beirut. On this side the city bends like an old woman resting her back against a solid wall, or a child cradled by its mother.

With summer, the boy's beloved K went to Bhamdoun. Life became a burden and nothing seemed sweet any more. One day, he took a walk in the streets where they had strolled together, and spotted her at a tram stop, trying to cross the street. Hardly able to believe his eyes, he cried out to her in sheer delight. She turned and ran towards him. But the passing tram refused to wait till she'd crossed. Alas, her final view of him was from beneath the wheels of the tram, which crushed her and ended her life. The horror and grief stopped him in his tracks and he turned into a statue. There he stood for ever, his soul contemplating what had happened beneath those wheels.

When Leila finished reading, I was devastated. Had Muhammad really felt so utterly desperate when I married the Haji that he'd wanted such an end for me? Had he really wanted me to die so his torture could end and he could turn into a statue? Now he was the one buried underground and I was turning into a statue. It no longer mattered if I stumbled on evidence of his infidelity.

Muhammad's papers transfixed us. We were bewitched. Leila was eager to keep on reading. I left her for a moment and went into the kitchen. When I came back, she was still poring over the pages, shaking her head, clutching her heart or copying parts she'd found.

'God sent him to you from above,' she said, 'so you could taste the sweet flavour of love. The vast majority of women are destined to live and die, but the only sensation of physical pleasure they will ever experience is when they pee, or in their dreams.'

Leila started to read again, then stopped and covered her face in embarrassment. She was not yet married, though over twenty-five. She carried on reading till the end, crying out in her Beirut accent, 'Good grief! What next?'

Soraya's Complaint

Soraya complained about me to my parents,
Saying, 'Your boy has done me wrong.
'He has quaffed wine till his passions took wing
'And he has fondled my breasts.
'He has tasted the savour of my mouth against my will;
'He has encircled my neck and bitten my cheeks.
'He has sucked at my honey and fondled my rose,
'And his hands have toyed with my pomegranate.'
Soraya kept exaggerating and weeping,
And her cries caused my parents to weep as well.
Father spoke to Mother about her boy
And asked her why I persisted in such sin.

She said, 'He will sober up, and I shall offer him my
   counsel.
'His only sin is to be on fire.
'When he arrives, let me be alone with him in my tent.
'I shall rub his cheeks between my hands,
'And suck from his mouth the wine he has quaffed.
'Gradually he will sober up from his drunkenness.'
Soraya now said, 'If that indeed is to be his cure,
'Then leave him to me.
'I am the most skilful at sucking what has been quaffed,
'And my lips are the only ones to which his mouth is
   accustomed.'

We had a good laugh at this risqué poem, which
Muhammad must have copied from somewhere.

Next Leila read a letter from a male relative of
Muhammad's, telling him that he'd find some really
gorgeous French girls with stunning breasts, tiny waists and
fantastic behinds at a cabaret in Beirut. 'I work my way in
among them like a bird under its mother's wing,' the writer
said. 'Oh, how I wish you could be right here at my side,
since you're the chief when it comes to this particular area
of expertise!'

From the letter's date I could tell it was written when
Muhammad had been transferred to the Silk Valley, at a time
when our love was at its strongest. There was no reason to
believe he had been unfaithful. This calmed me down a lot.
I started putting all the papers back in the bag. By now I
was convinced Muhammad had never betrayed me. I poured
Leila a cup of coffee and lit a cigarette, something that from
then on never left my hand.

Six months later I took the papers out again so they could
be read by a new friend. Two sentences from his diaries
made me very upset: 'My darling Kamila no longer keeps

me warm.' And: 'After the four years I've spent with K, I've started to visit those girls, but they're always out.'

I'd known that, before I got my divorce, Muhammad had sometimes visited two sisters who had the reputation of being flirtatious. I remembered a dream I'd had after we were married, in which he went back and visited one of them. Muhammad was away on business for a week or two, and when he called I told him about my dream. He just laughed and then sent me a letter describing a dream one of his sisters had had after she ate some lentils too close to bedtime. In her dream the lentils grabbed her and dropped her in the saucepan.

I put all the letters and other papers back in the bag and left them in the cupboard again. I decided I must put those two sentences right out of my mind. Instead, I concentrated on the dozens of words of beauty he'd used, words that had lifted me to the very heavens. I let all those women – the relative who told me about the hitchhiking foreign girl, Leila, and my new friend who read to me about the flirtatious sisters – believe that their strategy had worked. As they'd hoped, I shed my mourning clothes and took Fatima with me to buy a nice colourful sweater. Then we went to the hairdresser and I had my curly hair straightened. On the way home I took a detour through our old neighbourhood, hoping that I might run into the boy next door. Our old house no longer had its open roof; three apartments had been built on top of it. As I passed the boy's balcony, I didn't stop; I just smiled and continued on my way.

I had found the will to live again, but Mother still aggravated my fears. She was afraid of Muhammad's family and of our creditors. She was scared for my young children: afraid of them playing on the balcony or near the gas oven, afraid that they'd be hurt crossing the street, afraid that they might catch her eye disease. But all those worries paled compared to her concern over my youthful desires. If she saw me standing in front of the mirror, doing my hair, she would try to stop me. When I laughed, left the house, or sat on the balcony with a neighbour or female relative smoking a cigarette, she'd glare at me.

'You're drinking coffee as if it comes free from the spring! Your coffee is taken from the mouths of those orphaned children,' she scolded all of our visitors.

When Muhammad's brother Ali arrived, she expected me to retire to my room. And although she loved my children, she was forever arguing with my daughter Ahlam, trying to stop her from playing, skipping, or standing on the balcony. She wanted her to be like the girls from our village in the south, doing endless household duties and looking after her younger sisters and brothers.

Mother's aggravation, annoyance and intense sadness were at their worst when Father came to visit. She made it clear that he was the one she hated and despised – not his wife, her rival and replacement. She sat there darkly as he told us funny stories about the women in his village, who constantly sought his help and advice. They'd complain to him about how badly they'd been wronged and he would sympathise with their plight. He described how he patted one woman on the shoulder or pinched the cheek of another. From this, we'd know that he'd been flirting. These women had never met a man like him before; he appeared so open and friendly that they'd find themselves telling him all manner of intimate and personal details. Often their problems involved sex with their husbands. Father gave them this piece of advice: 'If your husband wants you and has sex with you, you can put it right out of your mind that he plans to take another woman as a *durrah*.'

I'd always assumed the word *durrah*, or second wife, was derived from the word *darar*, meaning to hurt or harm, since the second wife caused much distress to the first, subjecting her to great cruelty.

Father always made a variety of suggestions, confident they'd be of little benefit, but would somehow serve for his personal profit. As payment, he'd ask for whatever the woman could hand over without her husband's knowledge: dried tobacco leaves, eggs, yoghurt or flour. One woman offered him a chicken and a pail of yoghurt. In return, Father gave her one amulet after another, promising they would make the woman's husband return to her bed and have sex with her again. The woman kept placing amulets under her husband's pillow, but the result was only more frustration and annoyance.

She complained to Father that his amulets weren't working.

Father lost his temper.

'Look, woman!' he told her. 'We've eaten your yoghurt and grilled your chicken. If your husband doesn't want to fuck you by now, he's never going to do it!'

Father was trying to get Mother to laugh.

When she remained stony-faced, he yelled harshly at her.

'God damn your ugly face!' he shouted.

In vain I tried to stop him, and so, to my surprise, did my stepmother.

'One peep or complaint out of you,' he said, pointing to my stepmother, 'and you'll go the same way as her!' He pointed back to Mother.

I tried to change the subject, but Mother silenced me with a single sentence.

'Have you forgotten how he left us with nothing?'

I bit my lip and shared her pain. I'd have preferred her to go and stay with one of my brothers when Father visited, but I didn't dare suggest it. She only felt safe and relaxed at my house; she wanted to be close to my children.

I'd watch her as she dozed off on the sofa. No one had ever helped her, not for a single day of her life, since the moment her first husband was killed. Her silence and sorrow had grown with the years. The buzzing inside her head grew worse, especially when she was lying in bed, tossing and turning, unable to sleep. 'The buzzing has started again!' she'd mutter. This buzzing meant her fears for all her grandchildren, old and young. She would listen to their complaints and problems and to each one she'd make the same offer: 'Why don't you take my gold ring and earrings and sell them?' Then she'd lift the edge of her headscarf to show us where she kept all her worldly possessions, tied together with a knot.

Sometimes I'd get her to watch television with me, in an attempt to inject a little joy into her heart, but she'd just start urging me to deal with whatever was happening on the small screen.

'Tell that girl she shouldn't believe him and get in the car. He'll chuck her tomorrow!'

If the heroine began to weep and Mother asked why, I'd say it was because her beloved had abandoned her.

'Serves her right!' was Mother's reaction. 'Didn't we tell the girl not to trust him? It's her fault. Why didn't she listen to us?'

At the sight of a male newsreader, she'd grab a headscarf and throw it to me, shouting, 'You should cover your head!' She'd duck out of sight and make sure her own headscarf was firmly arranged around her face.

Three years after I lost Muhammad, Mother died. We took her body back to Nabatiyeh to be buried next to my two sisters. When we arrived at the home of her brother the cobbler, he refused to let us in. His son had been married not long before and he didn't want to attract the ill-omen of death to his home. I wept and screamed. My poor mother was denied sympathy and refuge even in death.

Out of respect for the past, Mother's childhood neighbours offered their own house, even though they hadn't set eyes on

her since she'd left for Beirut. My aunt, the one with the
snake in her stomach, arrived to mourn. Her weeping seared
my heart. We buried Mother in the ground, and for one last
time I asked her forgiveness for the day, long before, when I
bit her as hard as I could. I told her that I had forgiven her for
marrying me off so young, because she didn't know better.

The Money in your Pocket is more Beautiful than your Heart's Desire

B Y THE SEVENTH year after Muhammad's death, many things had changed. I was dodging my creditors. I'd started watering the frangipani at night, rather than during the day, for fear one of my creditors might spot me on the balcony – the butcher, the baker, the greengrocer, the owner of the banana shop, the furniture shop, the textile shop, even the electricity-meter reader. Muhammad had planted the frangipani in a small pot, where it neither grew nor shrivelled but simply stayed as it was, producing a few flowers. Muhammad had always meant to transfer it to a larger pot, but had died before he got round to it.

When creditors knocked on our door, my young son opened it. He protected me like a suit of armour. Though he was only seven years old, he was quick-witted and able to take control of the situation. If a creditor was particularly angry, tears would pour from his eyes as he explained, 'Mama has gone to the doctor. He says it's something serious.' If the creditor went into a rage and insisted on waiting for me, he would change his story. He'd say that I'd had to go back to the south because a relative had died, and that he was waiting for his cousins to take him to their house. He even told one stubborn, merciless creditor that I had died, and wept on his shoulder.

Of all the people to whom we owed money, I liked the electricity-meter reader best. He was a sweet young man.

One day he told me very shyly that he'd been a schoolmate of Fatima's, so I promised I'd tell her to come and see him. Then I had an idea.

I asked if I could postpone payment until the end of the month.

He looked very nervous but replied, 'Certainly.'

So I asked him if he would lend me 10 lira to buy books for my children. I said I would pay him back when the electricity bill was due next month. He thrust his hand into one pocket, then the other, scraped together the money, and gave it to me. My request had obviously shocked him; we lived in a large house. Fatima wore pretty dresses, went to dance parties, and was regarded as one of the nicest girls in the class.

My efforts to keep track of the household expenses were an utter failure. Each cup of coffee came with its own costs: beans, sugar, gas, coffee pot and the cup itself; not to mention washing-up liquid and sponge. My kitchen was a coffee house for my female friends, who came to sip coffee each morning, noon and night. It became a café at lunchtime: 'Time for lunch! Have some lunch!' The saucepan and the *Kibbeh* plates were always emptied. When the children got home from school, the dirty plates and empty saucepan told them what they'd missed. They'd ask for sandwiches, making it clear how hungry and angry they were, and I'd give them money to take to the corner shop. I made a blacklist of words that swallowed money: 'sandwiches', 'rubbers' and 'pencil sharpeners', the latter two being steadfast foes that disappeared constantly from my children's hands.

No matter how hard I tried, I couldn't manage to arrange things so there was food waiting for them when they got home. And if ever I did succeed, they were soon hungry again anyway. They'd rush off to buy those same sandwiches, followed by their very favourite dessert. When the shopkeeper told me he couldn't hear their requests over the roar of traffic, he and I agreed to mount a bell on our balcony. When we rang it, he'd come across from his shop, and we'd then place our order in a basket that we lowered down to him.

The stories about the ways I managed to dodge my creditors made everyone laugh. Once, I didn't have time to run to the bedroom, so I hid behind a curtain in the sitting room, and then realised I was holding a lit cigarette. I put my hand by the edge of the curtain for fear of causing a fire, and the rising wisp of smoke gave me away.

Another creditor didn't believe my little boy when he said I'd gone to the doctor, and decided to inspect the sitting room. Again I hid behind the curtain.

'By God, I can see you there! I swear I can see you,' he shouted.

I remained motionless, convinced he couldn't see me but was trying to trick me.

'I can see your feet,' he said. 'I swear to God! You're wearing red slippers.'

Very coyly I pushed the curtain aside and put my hand to my mouth.

'Hush, hush,' I said, 'make not a sound. I'd never have hidden if I had even a piastre!'

'God alone has the power and glory!' he muttered, and began laughing out loud.

My little son joined in the fun, dancing and jumping all over the sofas and throwing himself on the floor.

It wasn't enough that I had to avoid my creditors. I also had to deal with my youngest son, who had inherited my cunning personality. I had nursed this son of mine well beyond the age of five. As soon as he got home from school, he'd throw his books down on the floor and shout for me, even if I was surrounded by women friends, and point to my bosom. I'd take him into the bedroom and uncover my breasts. Still in his school uniform, he'd stretch out and nurse with his eyes closed, like a tiny baby. He'd nurse even as I was putting on my stockings or shelling peas.

And now he began blackmailing me.

'Give me a lira,' he'd demand, 'or I'll tell Uncle Ali where we've been.' Muhammad's brother, who was still in love with me, continued to stalk us.

'Give me a lira, or I'll tell,' my son would repeat in a low voice. Was my own son trying to wheedle money from me?

Ali was often there, loitering as usual. He narrowed his eyes when he heard Muhammad Kamal's threat.

I yelled at my son, 'Go on then, tell him!'

He ran away, but in the distance he started singing, 'If you don't give me something, I'll say that we went to Ba, to Ba.'

He was too scared to say the actual word 'Baalbek',[22] where a female neighbour and I had taken the children without a male member of the family as chaperone. I screamed at my son, I screamed at Muhammad's brother, I screamed in rage at having allowed myself to be pushed around. I felt as if I was swallowing a knife.

Without warning, Ali took out his revolver and pointed it straight at me. The children huddled around me, crying. My neighbour's son called the police, who came and took him away. The terror reminded me of the old embattled Kamila, who'd survived through trickery and hypocrisy, defiance and shouting.

Afterwards, I tried to get things back to normal, but Ahlam was terribly upset by the gun incident. She stopped going to school, saying she wanted to protect me. I brushed her concern away, telling myself she was just being lazy. My eldest son insisted on transferring to a school closer to

22 The site of the famous Roman temple to Jupiter, situated about eighty kilometres north-east of Beirut.

home, because he too wanted to watch over me. I tried to
get support from the other members of Muhammad's family,
but apart from Miskiah, all of them – men and women alike
– believed that I was no good at managing the children or
the household. They thought I was frivolous and selfish. And
even Ali's arrest after threatening us did nothing to diminish
his ardour. His behaviour became even more domineering
and obsessive.

Standing in front of Muhammad's photograph, I shouted,
'For heaven's sake, come down and get me out of this! Deal
with your brother!'

As my financial situation deteriorated, I was forced to seek
out the women and men with whom I'd deposited money.
First I visited the woman called Salsabil, who invested the
savings of widows. Her name meant 'a spring' and she lived
up to it, avoiding me and running away like water. When
I did finally manage to confront her, she denied that I'd
given her anything, since there was no written agreement.
The truth emerged: she regularly squandered the money
of widows. Next I went to see the shoe seller and asked
for the entire amount I'd deposited, instead of the slippers
and shoes he'd been giving me in lieu of interest. He
swore I'd already got the better of him on the deal. When
I approached the man who sold lovely nightshirts – with
whom I'd deposited Muhammad's annual bonus for fear
I'd spend it all – he produced a detailed account showing
I'd bought things costing the entire amount I'd handed
over: silk nighties embroidered with lace and satin ribbons.
I didn't argue with him, even though, whenever I'd tried
to withdraw some money, he'd muttered that the market
was sluggish and offered me his goods instead. I'd taken
nighties for me and my daughters, even though they were
so young still. We would put them on and strut around. I'd

been coming home month after month with ever prettier and more expensive nighties.

The only solution was to start selling off my jewellery. It pained me to pawn a gold necklace for a mere 100 lira, particularly when I discovered that the jeweller had tricked me. The necklace was worth nearly 1,000 lira.

I informed all the shopkeepers that they weren't to sell anything to my children without getting my signature first. Naturally the children began faking my signature, still a flower and a bird. When I decided I couldn't afford to buy them new clothes for the feast celebrations, Muhammad visited me in a dream.

'What's going on, Kamila?' he asked. 'Have you forgotten how important the feast is for young children? Have you forgotten how you felt when your family wouldn't get you a new dress for Eid?'

In spite of our desperate financial situation, I continued to give generously to beggars, even asking one of them to break the one lira note I had left, so he could keep half the amount. If my purse was completely empty, I'd tell the beggar to call on us at the start of the next month, and then I'd sing him a song and send him happily on his way.

Once I tried to pay a taxi driver his fare when neither of us had any change. I took a picture of Father out of my handbag and handed it to him with a smile.

'OK,' I said. 'Take this picture of my father.'

The driver stared at me in alarm, thinking I was mad.

'Go on!' I said again. 'Take this picture of my father instead.'

'What am I supposed to do with a picture of your father?' he asked in a low voice.

'What do you mean? He comes from one of the best families in the south. He's a sheikh. Just hang his picture up in your home, and you'll –'

But the driver wouldn't let me finish.

'How's this picture supposed to feed my children?' he asked. 'How will it help me send them to school?'

I asked him to drop by my house the next day to collect what I owed, and gave him directions by suggesting he ask for Kamila.

'Everyone in the quarter knows me,' I assured him.

But he didn't believe me.

I insisted I wasn't mad; it was just that, every time I had any money, it grew wings and flew away.

When I told Father about my plight, the only advice he offered was, 'You must stop thanking God, you know. If you keep doing so, he'll assume you're all right and stop providing for you!'

Being constantly broke did not prevent me from doing whatever I wanted. It certainly didn't stop me from taking a trip to Syria to visit my half-sister Camelia in Damascus. We had become close since Muhammad died, and she had started visiting me in Beirut.

When we were en route, my children and I were stopped at the Syrian border. Cars were speeding across into Syria, except for the one in which I was travelling. Our taxi driver couldn't believe I had absolutely no money in my purse, nor could the Syrian customs officer. He stared at us, utterly astonished at my attempt to cross the border without paying customs fees and bewildered at my insistence on telling him about my situation. I explained that I'd been reduced from wife of the Bekaa region bureau chief to a widow in financial distress. When it became clear he wasn't going to let us across, I started to get angry.

To show my desperation, I climbed out of the car, stood on a rock and yelled some lines from the Quran, ' "As for beggars, do not rebuff them; as for orphans, do not oppress them." ' Pleased with my skilled oration, I began to imitate the radio announcer at the beginning of a news broadcast: ' "Brothers in Egypt, in Syria, in Iraq, in Algeria ..." '

The customs official stood there, flummoxed. My children reacted to my behaviour in different ways: some were laughing, others were telling me to shut up.

'Mama,' they said. 'We're so embarrassed! Stop it!'

But I carried on until I saw the official disappear inside the office and emerge with his supervisor.

Spotting the braid on the shoulder of the supervisor's uniform, I started up again in classical Arabic: ' "Brothers in Egypt, in Syria, in Iraq, in Algeria ..." '

The supervisor came over and listened to me. I could see that he understood what I meant, that Arab countries claimed to be united, one nation, yet all demanded an entrance fee. Taking my identity card from the junior official, he went back into the office and stamped it.

As my debts grew more and more out of control, everyone gave me advice about how to economise. The first suggestion was that I stop smoking cigarettes, because they were so expensive, and smoke a hookah instead. So I started having an occasional puff, until one morning I awoke to the delicious smell of frying potatoes. Thinking it was coming from the restaurant next door, I got up to investigate. To my horror, I discovered that the smell was coming from the sitting room. A coal from the bottom of the pipe had flipped out and set fire to the edge of the Persian rug. I was so upset; Muhammad had bought that rug, and I had kept it in perfect condition for years. Now it was ruined.

The second piece of advice I received was that I should marry again. Then someone would provide for us and I wouldn't need to keep borrowing money. More than one man came to seek my hand, despite the five children crowding around me. But they all looked like characters from an Egyptian comedy. The sight of each one made me imagine Muhammad shaking his head in sorrow. How was it that these characters were so certain of my answer that they were prepared to propose? I managed to get rid of them quite easily, except for one. He was a man with such an enormous head that I had to bite my tongue to stop myself from asking if the barber ever complained he'd been paid too little after a haircut. He worked with associations and charities that dealt with orphans' affairs. Before long we nicknamed him Marble Man, because on one visit he complimented Muhammad Kamal for not playing marbles.

'I can't stand children playing marbles,' he remarked.

Who do you think you are, holding forth like that? I thought to myself.

The next time he came calling, there was a bag of marbles waiting for him. As soon as he sat on the sofa my son (prompted by me, of course) emptied the bag on to the carpet and began to play with them. 'Tric-trac, tric-trac,' he kept repeating, until the marbles were knocking against the man's shoes. He even pushed the man's feet apart to search for a marble that had gone under the sofa. I could see Marble Man getting more and more annoyed, but he tried desperately to keep calm.

'Hey there, boy,' he kept saying. 'Take it easy!'

Eventually, unable to bear it any more, he left and never came back.

None of these suggestions eased my financial worries. To make matters worse, I was well aware of conversations amongst my family and Muhammad's about me. 'Kamila's no good at managing things,' they'd say. 'She's completely disorganised. All she thinks about is gossiping and drinking coffee.' But once I'd finished cooking and washing dishes and clothes, what else was there to do in those long days and nights but welcome female friends, chat, sip coffee and smoke cigarettes? How else was I supposed to forget about love and Muhammad, other than by turning my home into a café?

'Baba's Here, Baba's Here!'

O NE DAY, THE landlady from our house in the Bekaa Valley – where we'd lived during that fateful summer when Muhammad died – paid me a visit. Just the sight of her brought back feelings of overwhelming grief and loss. But I cheered up as I remembered those days, when I'd been revered as the wife of the bureau chief. She invited us to spend the summer with them again, free of charge. The thought of going back to that summer made me happy; it was as though Muhammad might return to me after a long absence. Also, to pass the summer in the Bekaa Valley would be far more affordable than remaining in Beirut.

So, with the arrival of summer, my children and I got on the bus and headed for the Bekaa Valley. But, as soon as we travelled through the mountains and down into the valley, my head began to pound and I bitterly regretted my decision.

'Where did Baba crash?' my children kept asking. 'Was it here?'

Only Ahlam remained silent, closing her eyes to stop herself fainting. When I entered the house I expected Muhammad to appear from one of the rooms; or look down from the balcony; or emerge from behind the leaves of a tree in the garden. When I saw the hook on which I'd hung my dress, still there on the wall of our bedroom, I burst into tears.

'Oh, Muhammad,' I whispered. 'Why did you have to die so young?'

As the days passed, things became easier. I managed to convince myself that I'd turned the page on my life with Muhammad, that he was finally gone. How wrong I was!

One day all five children came rushing in, yelling, 'Baba's here, Baba's here!' I ran out after them, my heart in my mouth. A car just like Muhammad's Volkswagen drove up. Out of it stepped Hanan, followed by one of her male friends, who'd been driving the car. I was rubbing one hand against the other, chiding myself for thinking like a child.

'I can understand why the children thought it was him,' I told Hanan. 'But what about me? How on earth could I rush out, believing Muhammad was back?'

I began to rent the same house each summer, bringing my widowed friend, Umm Bassam, whom I'd met through another widow. She had become one of my very closest friends. We became a large extended family, both in Beirut and during summers in the Bekaa Valley, ferrying our children with us everywhere. Umm Bassam was my exact opposite: competent and good at keeping track of her money. She taught me how to play cards. To avoid gambling with money, we used packets of bread to lay stakes. No matter how hard I concentrated on the cards, she always won. It aggravated me so much that I once dreamed that I asked her to show me how to win, just once. 'Wet your pants,' she answered, 'and I'll let you win!' It didn't seem particularly strange in the dream. But the next morning when I awoke, I discovered I had indeed wet the bed.

The Widows' Club

EACH MONTH, WHEN I went to collect my benefits, I was struck by the similarities between my complaints and those of the other widows. We all shared stories of how people took advantage of us, exploiting our situation and our loss. So I decided to found the Widows' Club. It quickly grew to include divorcees, like my poor friend Fadila, who'd been married for just two months before her husband divorced her. We allowed unmarried women to join as well. It became a club for women who felt they were in the way of their married friends and a burden to their families. I was constantly astonished at how many widows and unmarried women there were in Beirut, and how many men there were seeking their affections!

Unlike most of the others, I kept myself aloof from men. There was not a man alive worthy of taking Muhammad's place in my heart. Each time I rejected the advances of a man who came asking for my hand, I'd think to myself that I'd successfully managed to build a barrier between myself and men. But I'd soon discover how wrong I had been. Wherever I went, male eyes watched me, flirting, like when I was married to the Haji. As a widow, I had the attraction of forbidden fruit; men also saw me as neglected and thirsty for attention. It would only have taken a broom to sweep away all the amorous glances, but I have to admit they made me proud that I was still attractive. I secretly welcomed them. I started to feel like a teenager again.

The days rushed past and responsibilities for the house and children gradually grew less burdensome. There was a song by the singer Najat that went, 'He lives close by, and I love him, I love him!' It caught my imagination. A younger man had started paying me attention, and for once I felt interested; he lived in a nice building just a few yards away. I liked the fact that he lived so close and could hear our voices and see us from his apartment; I could hear him on the telephone, his television, even the sound of his refrigerator door opening. But then I saw that he was making eyes at our neighbour's daughter as well. In a fit of vanity I took out my identity card. I added a tiny stroke to the number 2, changing my date of birth from 1925 to 1935. When I had to show my ID card to collect my pension, the altered date was spotted immediately. The matter was referred to an officer, who made a big deal out of it. I tried to explain, but the officer refused to listen to my excuses.

'Madam,' he kept insisting. 'This is forgery, do you understand, forgery!'

'Listen,' I said. 'Someone wants to marry me. Don't you see: I've got a fiancé! That's why I've lowered my age. That one little stroke could change my entire life. Please understand how hard things are, with five children, responsibilities and high prices … One little stroke, what difference does it make?'

That had him laughing.

'OK,' he said. 'This time I'll let you off, because you've made me laugh!'

Going out with a younger, educated man proved difficult. When we went to the cinema, I had my eldest son come too. He read the Arabic subtitles out in a loud voice so I could follow the film. I didn't want my friend discovering that I couldn't read or write.

A few days later I spotted him at it again, this time flirting with another neighbour's daughter. In a fury I painted over the window so he couldn't see us and we couldn't see him. When I relented and scraped off the paint, I discovered he'd already moved, disappearing into the vast city of Beirut.

With him gone, I reconnected with Beirut and its clamour; with the children, their schools and their friends. My friend Fadila took me with her when she went out with the man she was in love with, a spiritual healer. We'd go to restaurants or cafés, sometimes with a group of the healer's friends. I loved it. It was clear to me now that I hadn't been living a cinematic life, the life I'd imagined I'd had with Muhammad. In the end, what use had it been to me that Muhammad was acquainted with ministers and Members of Parliament, that he could recite love poetry by heart? What use had Muhammad's huge office been to me, with assistants left and right? During our marriage, my endless pregnancies and exhaustion had left me isolated from friends and relatives. I'd seen the world through his eyes. After his death, it was as if I started out all over again. I had to learn how society was constructed and what went on in shops and offices by dealing with the humdrum business of everyday life.

My favourite times were still the summer months, when we went to the same residence in the Bekaa Valley and I could look out over the hills, meadows and mountains. I also enjoyed the attention we received while we were there; the local men liked the fact that we were from Beirut. Once, when I was out walking with Umm Bassam, I saw a young man gesturing at me from a balcony. The Bekaa Valley was famous for strong summer winds and they were making his clean, loose-fitting white shirt billow. Overcome with delight, I tidied my hair and stared back at the young man. I whispered to my friend, gesturing towards the balcony and warning her not to move forward in case it made him even more eager. But Umm Bassam burst into laughter; she laughed and she laughed.

'You're blind as a bat!' she said.

The young man I had seen was only shirts and sheets hanging on a clothes line.

The Marriage Season

SOON AFTER HIS wife passed away, Father became the first in a series of people to marry. He sent me a proverb as a message: 'Although he was old and wise, he had far from repented.' From this I understood that he had married a much younger woman, and she was young indeed, even younger than me.

The second marriage was Hanan's. The joy of heaven descended on me when Fatima told me that Hanan had married. Hanan had never confided in me or told me what she was up to. But I consoled myself with the knowledge that she had taken after me and done what she wanted, defying the family and her society to marry a Lebanese Christian.

I had always known that Hanan resented me for divorcing her father and leaving her behind. Fatima had suffered too, yet she remained close. I saw less and less of Hanan, who had spent a number of years living in Cairo and was now back in Beirut, absorbed in her work as a journalist.

The third to marry was Fatima. She introduced me to her fiancé, making me feel respected and content, as a bride's mother should. I was so relieved that both my daughters had found husbands – not because marriage, especially for women, would ever provide security, but because I had feared that having a divorced mother would stand in their way. Before her marriage, Fatima had been in love with another man. His parents came to meet her – and her family. They arrived at the door, expecting to be entertained by the mother of the house, only to discover that I no longer lived there, and that there was a stepmother who also wasn't home that day. Only Fatima and Hanan received them but, had their stepmother been home, the prospective in-laws wouldn't have seen things in a better light. They left in disgust and convinced their son that he must not marry Fatima.

Finally, my daughter Ahlam, who was barely eighteen, married a Palestinian student who'd been living opposite us, exactly where the young man I'd admired once lived. Although she'd been so young, Muhammad's death had affected Ahlam the most. Finding love was what she desired. She went to live with her husband in Kuwait. Meanwhile Toufic, my eldest son, decided to go to London to study computing. I had to sell our two apartments to fund his trip and college fees. Only then did I discover that my brother-in-law, our 'guardian', hadn't paid taxes on either apartment since I'd bought them. I had to pay back taxes, which left very little profit from the sale.

So now it was just me and Majida, Kadsuma and Muhammad Kamal.

Five years after her marriage, Hanan gave birth to her first child, a boy. At the age of forty-eight I'd become a grandmother. Her private-hospital room faced the sea and, as I entered, I saw her lying in bed surrounded by bouquets of roses. I was overjoyed. Here was my daughter, living the way I'd always wanted to live – with scented flowers everywhere and her husband's family gathered around her offering her boxes of chocolates and presents. I watched as Hanan chatted affectionately with her mother-in-law. For a few moments I felt jealous, but I pushed the feeling away. Hanan hardly knew me, nor I her. But I loved her dearly and knew that she loved me too, in her own way.

By the time Hanan gave birth to her second child, a girl,

two years later, we had grown much closer. She was keen for me to visit her; or she was until I started bringing a neighbour or friend with me to see the baby. I had to make myself ignore − superficially at least − her clear annoyance at these extra visitors. She didn't like my friends − they weren't as sophisticated as she'd have liked and I think they embarrassed her. In my heart I was critical of her too, because the only people from my world she wanted to see were her brothers and sisters. She didn't understand my need to show my friends that my daughter had married up and lived in one of the best districts of Beirut.

She had never, not even for a second, put herself in my shoes. I came to her from a home bursting at the seams with neighbours, children and visitors, with brewing coffee and clamouring creditors. I lived in constant anxiety: that the electricity might be cut off because I couldn't afford the monthly bill; that the gas cylinder would run empty; that the television would suddenly stop working and need to be repaired. Did she ever wonder, I thought, how I managed to pay the fare when I came to visit? Did it occur to her that I struggled to work out which button to press in the lift that took me to her floor?

Once, I visited Hanan in her apartment. There was a cage with singing canaries that could bathe in a little water tray. In another cage, a mouse Fatima had bought for Hanan's little boy jumped on a wheel and started playing; then it went into its little house with sawdust on the floor. The little mouse stuffed its mouth with seeds until it looked as though it had the mumps.

Hanan was at her desk, writing.

'I'd like to be that mouse!' I told her.

'It's called a hamster!' she said with a laugh.

'OK, then,' I replied, 'I wish I could be that hamster. He plays and jumps, eats, drinks and sleeps, oblivious to everything going on around him.'

Hanan laughed even harder.

'He's lucky he has no debts,' I said. 'Or electricity and gas bills to pay!'

I thought she might get the hint and slip some cash into my handbag this time. But she only laughed some more, then went back to her own world, to her writing, to the canary and her two children. I don't think it occurred to her that I was asking for help.

1975

IN THE SPRING of 1975, the Christian Phalangist militia killed some Palestinian refugees on a bus that passed through Christian neighbourhoods. Muslim–Christian disturbances rocked Beirut all over again. Like everyone else, I expected it all to blow over quickly, as it had in 1958.

I saw a photograph in the newspaper of the Prime Minister, Rashid Karami, wearing a polo-neck jumper.

'The crisis must be over,' I cried, 'or he'd be wearing a black suit.'

I looked at pictures of Druze, Shia, Maronite and Sunni leaders, all smiling, and assumed everything would be OK. But the leaders became like blind men with swords, thrusting at everyone around them, as each formed a militia and took over different quarters of Beirut. There were dead and wounded, explosions and demonstrations all over the city. My women neighbours and I kept our ears glued to the radio, listening to the newsreader Sharif al-Akhawi, who became to us the only trustworthy Lebanese. He told his listeners which roads were safe to use. Life as we knew it ground to a halt, replaced by another kind of existence: standing in line at the bakery, at the street water tank, at the petrol station. It was as if I was nine years old again, and had just left the south for Beirut. One day, as I watched a mule pulling a kerosene tank amidst the noise of car horns, I was reminded of my years as the stone-bearing donkey.

Thoughts of that unhappy time also brought back memories of Muhammad. If Muhammad were still in the same job, I thought, he might have been bureau chief of all Lebanon by now. I tried to figure out how old he'd have been if he were still alive and with a sob I realised he'd be fifty-seven. But when I remembered the threats the Nasserites had made to him in 1958, I was glad he was no longer alive to face this new crisis.

My house was crammed with relatives and acquaintances whose homes lay on the border between warring neighbourhoods. They included my friend, Umm Bassam; Kamil and his family; and my nephew, Maryam's brother with the wooden leg, who'd returned to be with his family after living on the streets. Our house became a hostel. We huddled on the porch, in the sitting room, kitchen and bedroom – even in the corridor outside the bathroom. There was a perpetual din of throat-clearing, laughter and coughing; farts echoed forth and secrets were revealed. Toufic, who had returned from London and was working for an international airline at Beirut airport, got up one night to record the snoring. When everyone was asleep, he played the tape at top volume. Someone awoke and prodded the person sleeping next to him, assuming he was the snorer. By the time everyone had prodded everyone else awake, they were all cracking up with laughter.

There were days when we didn't dare walk in front of the window. We tried to keep laughing and joking, but our fears grew and grew. My fear was so intense that, when Toufic tried to sneak out of the house to meet his girlfriend one day, I pointed his hunting rifle at him.

'Better for me to kill you,' I told him, 'than have someone else do it! At least I'll be able to bury you and know where your grave is.'

The situation deteriorated to the point where people started calling the events outside the war. The streets were deserted. I was forced to stop visiting Hanan and Fatima. If there was a lull in the fighting for a few days, people would make travel plans, desperate to leave. Hanan took her two children to London, followed soon after by Fatima and her husband. Toufic travelled to America to join his girlfriend and they decided to get married. Majida and Kadsuma went to Kuwait to stay with Ahlam. I remained in Beirut, worried sick that Muhammad Kamal, now sixteen years old, would decide to join the neighbourhood militia, a group made up of Palestinians, Sunnis, Shia and Druze. They regularly fought the Christians,[23] like so many teenagers and young men in Beirut. Eventually I took him to Kuwait, hoping we would soon return home. But it was in vain, because the war only escalated.

In spite of this exodus, my house in Beirut was never empty. Friends and family stayed on, and the door remained open to anyone who needed shelter from the fighting. It became a place of refuge for many and dozens of people held the keys.

---

23 At that time there was no Hezbollah – i.e., no Shia militia.

Battuta's Daughter[24]

I T WAS FEAR that made me leave Lebanon. I wanted to be with my children and to keep Muhammad Kamal safe. So I abandoned my friends, my street, my neighbourhood, carrying with me the secrets of those who'd stayed in my home. I was devastated that I had to leave, and full of anger at the way Muslims and Christians were fighting against one another.

In Kuwait we stayed with Ahlam. The climate there — boiling hot, sandstorms, humidity — was so extreme that it crushed me. The only time I felt at all relaxed was in the evening, when the wind blew. Then I could open a window and breathe real air, rather than what came out of the air-conditioning vent. As the wind carried the scent of vines and figs to me, I tried to imagine I was at our summer home. But each morning, once again, I would feel as if I was choking, from the dust and sand stirred up by the wind. The dust covered us in a fine white layer. We looked like fish sprinkled with flour, ready to be thrown in the pan.

In Kuwait we never sat out on the balcony to watch the passers-by, and Ahlam's lovely house felt like a prison. I took on the task of cooking, preparing elaborate dishes. At first my new role excited me. If only Muhammad could have been there to see me being an exemplary mother and grandmother! But before long the pressure of obligation took away my initial enthusiasm. Once I roasted a chicken

24 Ibn Battuta, a fourteenth-century Arab traveller and explorer.

and, when I took it out of the oven, it was nicely browned and delicious-looking. But when my son-in-law started carving he revealed, to my mortification, that the small bag containing the giblets was still inside the bird.

I missed Beirut and the Widows' Club terribly. To console myself I started watching a television soap opera called *The Head of Goliath*, about a Bedouin man who is on the run. I became utterly engrossed in his tribal world and began creating friendships with the characters. I got so involved that I even postponed my departure for Beirut for several months. (I would return periodically during a lull in the fighting.)

Meanwhile Majida and Kadsuma each fell in love with Lebanese men and decided to get married in Kuwait. Then Muhammad Kamal went to join Toufic in America. I felt that my responsibility to my children was coming to an end. After a while I followed him from Kuwait, intending only to be in the US for a short visit. On the plane, I asked myself how it was even conceivable that I, Kamila, a woman from Nabatiyeh who'd never even learned how to read and write, could really be going to America. My heart was in my boots as the plane winged its way across the sky. Terrified, I looked around and spied a man who seemed to be Arab.

'Tampa?' I asked him. 'Tampa?'

A few hours later I asked him the question again.

'Look, lady,' he told me impatiently. 'You're in a plane. Suppose it was going to Brazil. Do you think we could make it change direction?'

Then I got angry too.

'OK,' I replied. 'But remember that our ancestors travelled by donkey and camel, not by plane!'

When we arrived, I was desperate to conceal from the other passengers that I was illiterate. I pretended that I couldn't find my glasses and asked someone to fill out the immigration form for me.

The sheer size of America astounded me. Travelling in the car with my son, I couldn't help wondering why the earth hadn't split beneath the weight of the trucks, trains and skyscrapers. I was astonished by the goods on offer in the shopping malls. The shops and supermarkets were miniature cities in themselves. I felt like a voracious locust, eager to buy and buy. But, I reminded myself that, as the proverb went, while the eye may look it's what's in the hand that counts. I had to make do with purchasing reduced items, not worrying if the edge of an ashtray was chipped or if a blouse had red lipstick on it. America was one gigantic market; they even used parks to sell things.

What I liked to do best was to go to the fairground. It thrilled me to win a toy bear or a dog. I'd return home triumphant, clutching my trophy to me. I used my suitcase to store my collection. I called my bag the big whale, and in it I kept things like McDonald's aluminium ashtrays shaped like leaves; and from the aquarium, a shell shaped like a star, though I was completely unaware it was still alive.

Before long, just as I had learned to pronounce Tampa, Toufic and Muhammad Kamal moved to San Diego, where Fatima lived. I went with them. When my other three daughters also moved there, I was delighted. San Diego reminded me of Beirut. It had nearly the same weather and nature. I loved the zoo. All the animals I'd heard of in stories I saw for the first time. I loved picnicking in the park with Fatima and her American husband. Once I found myself dancing to music I hadn't heard before and I was told it came from Cuba. I danced a mixture of the charleston, belly dancing and *dabke*, the Lebanese folk dance.

But I soon realised that two of my daughters, Majida and Ahlam, were unhappy in their marriages. I was determined, though, that they would not consider divorce. I did not want my grandchildren to suffer, even though to most people divorce now seemed no more significant than taking a sip of water. But their unhappiness tore at my heart. I could see that their husbands were never going to change. I tried hard not to do it, but I found myself interfering, blaming, cursing, fighting, and soon even encouraging my daughters to file for divorce. 'You could always come back with your children and live with me, just like when you were children yourselves,' I told each of them.

My bitterness towards my sons-in-law and my obsession with seeking revenge against them was compounded by my troubles with Muhammad Kamal. Recently, he had joined a group of hippies living in the neighbourhood. I started spying on him and his group day and night. Ahlam tried to stop me, but I couldn't help myself. I needed to know he was all right. I found that I was really alone, far away from the world, cut off and helpless; while in Beirut, I could ask for help from the electric pole or the door or the wall.

Eventually Majida and Kadsuma returned to Kuwait, but all this family upheaval made me profoundly unhappy. I saw a doctor, who prescribed various pills. Whenever one of my children showed concern at the quantity of medication I was taking, I defended the little round capsules. I believed that the effort of the many people who had produced each pill could only mean that they were greatly beneficial to my health. Still, I continued to feel restless and lonely, especially when Toufic was at work. I tried to strike up conversations with people. I'd always imagined I could communicate with everyone, even a group of chimpanzees. But I failed in America. Aren't these Americans my relatives? I asked myself. Aren't we all descendants of the same father and mother, Adam and Eve? Why can't they understand me? If I sigh, it means I'm unhappy. If I smile and say good morning, it means I'd like to chat.

Once, I approached a female neighbour. I smiled and held up a coffee cup, gesturing that I could tell her fortune. All she did was smile back briefly and disappear inside her house.

Such misunderstandings caused great amusement within my family, but they only added to my vexation. I couldn't believe that language could form such a barrier, even with a dog. A huge dog managed to get into the house one day, and my daughter-in-law and I were terrified and hid. All day the dog simply slept on the sofa, until my son got home and shooed it out with the simple command, 'Go!'

One day I saw the old man next door weeping as he talked to Muhammad Kamal's girlfriend. I clutched my chest, terrified that something had happened to one of the children. But Muhammad Kamal's girlfriend explained that the old man was only recalling how his wife had suffered from cancer and eventually died. I began crying with him, sharing his grief. The elderly man asked her why I was crying, as he was sure I hadn't met his departed wife.

A few days later the news came of my own father's death. I visited our neighbour and tried to let him know that my own father had died, hoping he'd shed some tears with me. But he hadn't a clue what I was trying to tell him. I wept all the more, because I was so far away. Not even my children would weep along with me.

'Come on now,' I urged them. 'Shed just a few tears. Feel a bit sad with me! After all, he was your grandfather. He was my father and now he's dead.'

My children thought it strange that I could feel this way about Father, after he'd neglected me when I was little. As I'd grown older, I told them, things had changed. We'd started talking to each other again and I'd seen how I'd inherited some of his character. He loved me, and my love and loyalty meant a lot to him. I wouldn't dwell on all the misfortunes buried in the past. Instead, I focused on the things I loved about him: his knowledge and the poems and proverbs he'd recite.

If Father had not so often recited to me a poem by Imam Ali, how would I have known about the five benefits of travel?

Leave your country in search of enlightenment.
Travel, for in travelling there are five benefits;
Dissipation of worry, the gaining of enlightenment,
Science, literature and the company of the honourable.

The War has Ended

I TRAVELLED BETWEEN AMERICA and Kuwait until the war ended. Then, after sixteen years in exile, I returned home. Whoever God allows to travel is indeed fortunate, I thought to myself. Here I was, alone in Beirut, while my seven children continued their lives abroad, exiled from their country and culture by war. The sixteen years of war had made me angry and remorseful. The people who finally ended it were the same people who had started it. And what had they achieved? I realised, with bitter irony, that I had arrived home with sixteen pieces of luggage.

I stored the suitcases in one corner of my sitting room. But seeing them there, unopened, made me terribly depressed. I hid them under a sheet. I think I felt horrified by the excess. A few days later, after my head had stopped spinning, I opened all the suitcases and scattered presents on the floor.

I took what I wanted, then called to my neighbours and some relatives and shouted, 'Go ahead, help me get rid of everything.'

When only a few items were left, I went out on to my balcony and called to some young children playing below, 'Hurry and come up and take whatever you want.'

And the children gathered round, snatching things from each other. I saved a child's white umbrella from Disneyland to give to Hanan's daughter. When I finally did, on one of Hanan's visits to Beirut, we laughed for a long time. Although I had seen Hanan and her family every couple of years when they visited – in Kuwait and then in America – my granddaughter was much older and taller than I remembered.

In Beirut I reverted to my old routine: entertainment, laughter, and fortune telling. I was happy to be back among neighbours, relatives – my two brothers Hasan and Kamil – and friends. I was delighted to be back in the thick of things. During my period of exile, I'd ceased to believe I'd ever get to sleep in my own bed again, or that my house would be there waiting for me when I returned.

I converted part of my balcony into a miniature garden filled with potted plants, just as Mother had done in our garden plot at Nabatiyeh. I visited Father's grave in the south and offered my condolences to his widow. I asked her about Father's library of manuscripts, some of them handwritten, that he had bequeathed to Ahlam. Each time Father went back to the south after a visit, he'd take with him some books he found lying around in our house, unaware that most of them were actually Ahlam's school textbooks. He'd loved reading Khalil Gibran, the author of *The Prophet*, and Mikhail Nuayma. His widow told me she'd given them all to the *husayniyya*.[25]

'But why, if they were willed to Ahlam?' I asked her, in great disappointment. I reminded her that Father had inherited his library from his father and grandfather.

'I thought you were away and were never coming back,' she answered.

I wondered whether the presiding sheikh had stumbled across some of the stories and notes Father slipped between the pages of his books – stories of love and erotic passion. His widow told me what Father said to the doctor in his last days.

'So, Doctor, you see these four children standing before you? They're all from his excellency's factory and there is a

---

25 A gathering place for the community next to the mosque in Shia neighbourhoods.

fifth one in America.' Then he looked down and went on, 'I could make a lot more too. If you let me get up, I'll prove it to you!'

Gazing at his red fez, I couldn't help chuckling as I imagined the scene.

After his death, I decided I must close the book on the distant past and the war. But it wasn't easy. I felt like the monkey I'd seen on television, who would lift a stone and then faint at the sight of a snake cooling beneath it. As soon as he recovered from the shock he would hurry back to the stone, lift it, and faint again.

I no longer felt the pleasure I'd experienced when I first returned to Beirut, a pleasure that came from simply being at home, on the balcony, in my own bed. Now it was as though being back had reawakened the dormant past, rekindling feelings of guilt that lay buried, deep in my subconscious. I became exactly like Mother, unable to stop the buzzing. I focused on the pain I had caused Mother, Hanan and Fatima; and the insecurity and uncertainty that my five younger children had suffered after Muhammad's death. And last but not least, I worried about my grandchildren and their troubles in America.

The more the doctors prescribed pills, the less I slept. It was as if the vividly coloured pills were a microscopic lens that projected bruised old stories and memories in the tiniest detail. In the end I sought peace, confronting Hanan at last with my past, asking her to write it down. Only then did I start to see its wrinkled layers gradually turn smooth, with each word I uttered, with every place I remembered.

'One Stone Takes You Away, Another Brings You Back'

I'D BEEN THINKING a lot about Mother, my old home in Nabatiyeh, and my childhood there, so Hanan suggested we visit the south together. We travelled down to Nabatiyeh in a Range Rover. I told Hanan it made me feel like a contingent of army or police. Gradually I got used to travelling in that big car; it made me feel protected against car sickness, shortness of breath, and the heat. Hanan asked me not to joke around and embarrass Ali the driver. I tried hard to keep quiet, but my tongue got the better of me and I found myself singing a famous popular song, 'Ali, Ali, the oil vendor!' We all laughed.

'Mama,' Hanan said. 'You're really very funny!'

We were heading for the house in Upper Nabatiyeh where Mother had raised me with tender care. I'd once mentioned to Hanan that I'd like to see the house again; I hadn't set eyes on it since we'd left for Beirut when I was just nine years old.

As we turned off the coastal road I exclaimed, 'Good grief. How on earth did your grandmother – God have mercy on her soul! – manage to walk all the way from Nabatiyeh to Beirut to see her children, even if she did stop for one night in a hostel? It's a long way. If only I had the strength and will to walk such a distance!'

On the outskirts of Nabatiyeh, I got out of the car and tried to find the hostel where travellers stayed. I also looked for the market in the square: where we'd chased after Father, where

I had seen gold at a jeweller's for the first time, and where my uncle the cobbler once worked. Hanan remembered the Nabatiyeh market too. She remembered being there on Ashura Remembrance Day, and seeing women spitting on the unfortunate actor playing the accursed Shimr – the man who delivered the fatal blow that killed al-Hussein the Prophet's grandson.

The poor man was trying to defend himself.

'Hold on!' he yelled. 'This is only a re-enactment. I'm not the killer Shimr, I'm Mustapha the baker!'

We drove on towards Upper Nabatiyeh, where there are still tobacco fields. Hanan looked for the house of Abu-Ghaleb, the Haji's childhood friend, but she couldn't find it. We stopped again when we saw a woman standing beneath an olive tree, shaking the branches so the green olives fell on to a coloured sheet she'd laid out on the ground. Hanan went over to the tree, but I hung back; I wanted to smoke a cigarette in the quiet serenity of the place, beneath the blue autumn sky.

Hanan recognised the woman at once.

'What?' Hanan exclaimed to her. 'Don't you know me?'

'Come closer,' said the woman. 'Then I can give you a hug and kiss and smell you. I'll recognise you!'

'I'm the girl who used to drive you crazy!'

The woman came over to Hanan and they embraced.

'You're Hanan!' the woman cried, after gazing at her.

They embraced again, a real hug this time. Then Hanan introduced me to Samira, one of Abu-Ghaleb's daughters, but she corrected Hanan's introduction.

'Didn't you know that I had reverted to my real name, Amina? I'm Hajja Amina now,' she said. She explained that as a child she'd hated her name.

By now Hajja Amina was almost seventy, a little younger than me. As we walked, she began to talk to me about how her mother had loved Hanan and Fatima, and how she always felt sorry for them.

' "It's a shame," my mother used to say,' Hajja Amina told me. ' "Poor Hanan needs her mother and her home. Go and buy her some chocolate. Get her a drum and some bangles." ' Hajja Amina went on to tell me that she remembered how once Hanan had started to cry, wishing that she could go to Beirut. Hajja Amina's eldest sister stood up and told her, 'OK, go ahead. You can catch a ride on the pussy cat; she'll take you to Beirut.'

I left Hanan and Hajja Amina talking and walked in the back garden, smoking another cigarette. I felt as if my heart was torn in two, contracting all over again. Concerned, Hanan came to find me. I tried to make light of the pain I felt, but when she pressed me I told her that Hajja Amina had been speaking about her as if she had no mother.

'Good heavens,' I told her, 'I don't know what happened to you in 1958. I had no idea where you and your sister were then, I only saw you that one time at the house of your Uncle Ibrahim, when the troubles were just starting. I was stupid enough to imagine you were both all right. How did you manage to get by in life, all on your own? What happened when you had your first period? How did you manage to clean yourself and cope with the pain?'

'There was no problem,' Hanan responded. 'I was happy when I got my period. What you should be asking is how I remembered to clean behind my ears or inside my navel!' She gave me a big hug. 'Stop it, Mama!' she said. 'You have to live in the present.'

She raced back inside, eager to see the kitchen, the back yard and the tent where the family used to thread tobacco leaves on skewers. Hanan had mentioned to me in the car that she had used Abu-Ghaleb's house and lands as a setting in her novel *Beirut Blues*.

As she had done so often since I had come back into her life and she into mine, Hanan tried to ease my guilt and pain. I recalled how we had first been reunited, how I'd come to feel closer to her. Fifteen years earlier she'd asked me to have dinner at her hotel in Beirut, where she and her family were staying on a visit from London. I was sitting with her in a room overlooking a sandy shore. As we chatted, I began to understand why she'd wanted to see me alone. It was very rare for us to be alone together; usually when we met we'd make small talk, remain silent or eat, and that was it. This time she made me feel that I was her children's grandmother and her husband's mother-in-law, as she insisted that they come and sit with us. I wondered whether her delight at seeing me, and the love she was showing me, might sweep away all the sorrows buried in the past.

As we sat together, Hanan kept looking at me. I knew that in me she saw herself. She came close and put her face next to mine, asking her daughter, who sat near by, if we looked alike. I got the impression that Hanan had made up her mind – that I was indeed her mother, who gave birth to her, contrary to what she used to say, that she had found herself on the surface of life with her father.

We took Hajja Amina with us to look for our house. She turned down the driver's offer of assistance, instead leaning on Hanan as she tried to get into the car.

'What's the matter?' Hanan asked her. 'Is it because he's a stranger that you don't want him to help you?'

'The Devil's the only stranger,' was her reply.

Again we set off, and all at once there were the chinchona trees and the vines. I started shouting and almost tumbled out of the Range Rover window, determined not to miss the street again.

'This is it,' I finally cried out. 'This is it! Ali, please stop. Stop here!'

We all got out, but I struggled to find the right house. I began to feel like a swarm of bees that had lost touch with its queen and was buzzing about aimlessly. Hajja Amina pointed to a dilapidated house with a painted lintel over the door. No, our house hadn't been at the top of the road, but more to the left, I told her. I took a few steps in that direction, and felt myself begin to remember the way my feet had moved in the old days, how I had to steady myself so as not to topple over in my wooden clogs.

Standing in front of a house, I shouted, 'This is the one! The gate put me off. There was no gate when we lived here.'

Two women on the flat roof saw us talking and came down to open the door. Hajja Amina told them I was looking for the house where I'd been born. They welcomed us warmly and we went inside.

'There's the lintel,' I exclaimed. 'And the window!'

'The proverb is right on the mark,' Hajja Amina proclaimed. ' "One stone takes you away, another brings you back"! Beirut took you away and now your old house has called you back.'

'There were fig branches hanging outside that window,' I cried out. 'Mother would pick figs from exactly where I'm standing. What happened to the fig tree?'

I turned to the two women, as if expecting them to answer, as if some sixty-six years hadn't slipped by since I'd left. Hanan wandered over to the window ledge with its carved geometric patterns and two central columns.

'Mama, I never realised you grew up in such a beautiful house with such lovely features,' she said.

'My son left the columns and window the way they are because they're antique,' one of the women explained.

The two women insisted we sit with them on the balcony so we could look out over part of the back garden and road. Behind us was the garden where I'd once played. In front of me the stones of the wall remained jagged, as though someone had put mortar between the cracks.

We drank coffee and I couldn't stop myself saying, 'My God, life is so wonderful down here! If only I'd stayed here to live, I'd never have had to take any medicine, let alone Prozac.'

The women looked at each other and Hajja Amina looked at Hanan, not understanding what I'd meant.

'Everyone loves Mama,' said Hanan, trying to make light of what I'd let slip. 'Every day she takes a pill so she can cope with all the people who come to see her.'

Where was Mother now? I wondered. Where were the cows? Where was the donkey, my friend Apple and the other girls? How could the world have taken me away from this place, to Beirut, Ra's al-Naqurah, Syria, Kuwait and America?

We left the house and headed for the cemetery. I wanted to recite the Fatiha, the opening words of the Quran, in memory of Mother and my two sisters. We searched for their graves in the wild grass but couldn't find them. Hajja Amina offered to read, or to teach us how to read, the Fatiha; it would make its way to the souls of Mother and my two sisters, she told us, even if we couldn't find their graves. I wanted to ask Mother's forgiveness for all the times when I'd refused to make her *Kibbeh*. I wanted to tell my elder sister that I'd been forced to marry her husband and had then divorced him. I wanted to tell my other sister that all her children were living in America, even the son with the wooden leg, who'd gone there to join the rest of his family.

Hajja Amina recited the Fatiha, seizing each of us by the hand as she did so.

'Now, my dears,' she said. 'Let me follow it with a supplication guaranteed to reach your dearly loved departed:

> Let their souls cleave the graves apart,
> And soar o'ertop the highest castles,
> And smell the sweet scent of ambergris and incense.
> Bring them to the garden of bliss,
> And free them from the fires of hell,
> Oh Lord of all Mankind,
> Lord of the Prophets,
> And best of trustees.

'I dedicate this to your late mother and two sisters.'

I was beginning to feel very fond of Hajja Amina and invited her to visit us in Beirut so she could have some fun with us.

'God willing,' she replied. 'But you never know …' With that she seized our hands again and recited a poem:

> If everyone knew themselves better
> And made themselves an object of study,
> There would be no fighting in this world
> Nor any idle chatter.
> Then the judge could close his prison.

'Never forget, my dears: the tiniest drop of oil can solve even the biggest problems.'

On our way back to Beirut, Hanan told me that Hajja Amina had taken her aside when I was smoking a cigarette.

'Why does your mother bury her head in her hands?' she'd asked. 'Why is she so upset about that house? There are thousands of homes much nicer than that old heap.'

I started to cry and Hanan held my hand. She asked if the night, descending about us as we drove, was making me weep and long for the past. Today was actually her birthday, she reminded me. She snuggled close to me, making me cry even harder. I moved away; I didn't want her to smell cigarettes. Then I was afraid she'd think I didn't want her to hug me.

'I smell of cigarettes,' I explained.

'Mama,' she replied. 'I love you, so why are you crying?'

I think she had realised that I was crying because I wasn't sure she loved me.

'Tell me honestly,' I asked. 'Do you love me still?'

She gave me another hug.

'Mama,' she repeated. 'I love you a lot, even more since we have begun to talk. I feel guilty that I waited so long.'

'But how can you love me when I abandoned you as a little girl?'

'That doesn't matter. The important thing is that you had to leave Father. In any case, it's ancient history by now. Think of the present, not the past!'

But how was I supposed to make light of my pain after this trip south? Our encounter with Hajja Amina had made me see more clearly the enormous mistake I'd made in abandoning my two daughters.

Hanan began listing the advantages she'd enjoyed because I'd left home when she was a child.

'Mama,' she said, 'I let the other children feel sorry for me. I used to tell the teacher lies when I hadn't done my homework. I'd say we'd had to go to court so the sheikh could ask us whether we wanted to live with our father or our mother.'

Not even these white lies could make me laugh.

'You and your sister are two little jewels,' I said. 'And I threw you in the dirt.'

That made Hanan weep. I pulled myself together; I didn't want to upset her. But then Hanan lifted her head and told me she was crying, not because I'd left her as a little girl, but because every time she heard me trying to speak classical Arabic, she was reminded of the fact that I'd never been given the opportunity to learn.

'If only you knew how to read and write,' she said. 'You, not me, would be the writer!'

Hanan had always told me what she was writing. I'd give her a proverb or simile to add: 'When you're full of gloom, visit a tomb'; or 'Every time there's a new moon, it reminds me how short my life is.' She'd put these things in her stories and read them back to me. I was proud she was so fond of my ideas and images, but what I really wanted her to do was write my life story.

Whenever Hanan talked, she revealed my own self to me. Without thinking about it, I knew that the present is the past. I almost felt as if I'd taken on her personality and become Hanan. Wasn't that exactly what I'd been thinking about when I went with her to see the house where I was married, and gave birth to her? After the Haji died, we stood side by side, contemplating the old quarter and our neighbours. It was sad to see how the house had been demolished. The beautiful gardens had disappeared and in their place tall apartment blocks rose.

'Here's where I used to stand,' I told Hanan, 'to look out for the boy next door.'

The staircase was still there and we looked at it together before I climbed it slowly, holding on to the black railing because my knees hurt.

I entered my old room.

'Here's where I'd listen out for Muhammad's footsteps; he'd leave me roses on that second windowsill,' I told Hanan.

We moved into the lounge, where I stopped in front of the hat stand (which we used to call *boor shaboor*, meaning *porte-chapeaux*) and the piece of art deco mahogany furniture that had been my pride and joy. I remembered how I'd always meant to put a light bulb under its glass shade, but had kept putting it off, and then I'd left the house for ever. I decided I would ask my nephew, Hussein the Ideologue, if I could have it; he'd been pardoned and had returned from Africa, where he had escaped after his attempt to assassinate a judge. I picked up the shell we'd used as an ashtray, which was still in the same place. I was amazed when Hanan put it to her ear, just as she always had, listening to the sound of the waves trapped inside. Then we spotted the photograph of the Haji, with my nephews and Fatima in the centre, still hanging in its usual place. Their hair and faces looked ragged where the photograph had been eaten by bugs. We laughed because my nephew Ali's eyes seemed huge.

'They're bulging,' Hanan said, 'because he was staring straight at you, hoping to catch you out when you filched some cash from Father's pocket!'

It wasn't, in fact, the first time I'd been back to the house since my divorce. I visited the Haji once, when he was bedridden. His wife was there too, though I'd never liked her because she'd sometimes been cruel to Fatima and Hanan. By then the Haji had gone blind, but hadn't admitted it to anyone.

'I'm the pest, tarred and feathered,' I announced. 'The woman who gave you nothing but grief and trouble! Do you remember me?'

'You're as beautiful as a moon,' came his reply.

A week later he was dead.

Hanan and I went to visit my brother Kamil and his family; and my brother Hasan, who was very ill, but still managed to sing that song from *The White Rose* he'd sung to me all those years earlier. He sobbed as he sang:

> Oh thou rose of pure love,
> God bless the hands that have nourished you!
> I wonder, oh I wonder, oh I wonder.

Finally we visited Ibrahim and Khadija. I was relieved that we had, because two weeks later, Ibrahim was gone too. Dead. Ibrahim kept asking Hanan who she was and he spoke to me in French, a language that neither he nor I had ever learned.

I told him, 'Oh brother of mine, how I wish you had conversed with me in French, instead of making my life hell.'

Everyone laughed, except Ibrahim, lost and dejected, who continued to ramble.

How is it, I wondered, that, as we grow older and our desire for life fades, we can reconcile ourselves to the past? How does it come about that our past and present lives blend and become a kind of ragged patchwork, like the clothes worn by my aunt with the snake in her stomach?

We went home and Hanan took my address book to copy the pages. Each time she visited me in Beirut, she would comb the book to see what drawings and numbers I'd added. I'd long since devised a way of writing things with pictures: I'd draw a picture of a person alongside their telephone number. A man holding a pack of cigarettes was the man who sold us cheap tobacco; two fat balloons alongside the number of a friend were her two fat sons; a mouth wide open was Fadila singing; a plate with a banana and apple was the local restaurant; an aeroplane was drawn beside the number of a relative whose husband was a pilot; a water jug and washing machine depicted the repair company; car wheels represented the number of Hanan's mother-in-law's driver; a man surrounded by fire was the number for a woman friend whose son was a fireman.

When Hanan came to the electrical-repair man, she

paused, almost hitting herself as she laughed. She asked about the way I'd drawn his teeth. I said he had huge teeth like a shark, as well as a big mouth. Then Hanan spotted the dove I'd drawn next to her name – because she was always flying off somewhere. She smiled and drew a rose alongside my own name, which I'd written in my own hand, next to my telephone number.

HANAN

Kamila (back left) and Hanan (centre)
with two of Ibrahim's daughters

'It's not that, is it?'

WHY DID I draw that flower next to my mother's telephone number in her book? Why did I decide finally to write her life story?

I kept asking myself these two questions, after Ahlam called me from San Diego to tell me that Mother was terribly ill, too ill to travel back to Lebanon on her own. Ahlam would accompany her.

Two months earlier, during my last visit to Lebanon when we made the trip south together, Mother talked endlessly about visiting Ahlam, Toufic and Fatima in California. I tried to persuade her not to go, reminding her how unhappy she felt when she was in San Diego, witnessing Ahlam's misfortune. Since her divorce, Ahlam's life had deteriorated and it made Mother feel utterly helpless. But she was as stubborn as ever, my mother, and listed for me the reasons she should go. She was trying to convince me, or maybe herself, that this trip was a test of strength, now that she was an old woman, as to whether she was still fit and well enough to leave her sofa and her balcony in Beirut and hop on a plane.

'Go ahead, Hanan,' she said, 'ask me why I'm full of energy and hope. I have never felt so light, so content, because I have dumped my life and strife on your shoulders and we have finally bonded. Oh! Telling you my life story was better than a hundred Prozac pills.' She went on and on like this, finally throwing the last dice. 'What I really need is a break from everyone in Beirut.'

Fatima and I were critical of Mother for constantly receiving and entertaining friends, relatives and especially women neighbours, even one woman whom she disliked because she was aggressive and jealous. Whenever I dropped by I would sneak into the kitchen, so Mother and I could exchange a few words in private. The visitors would pour into the living room and occupy the sofas from early in the morning, still in their dressing gowns, to wait for the nurse whom Mother had befriended and showered with gifts so that she would come each day to check her pulse and blood pressure. I remember once visiting Mother in the morning to see that all of the women were lifting their sleeves, ready for the nurse, as soon as they heard her footsteps on the stairs. Over the years, Mother had changed the name of her Widows' Club to Patients' Club, and her café to clinic. She would offer her visitors – alongside tea, coffee and food – pills from her 'pharmacy' – a big plastic bag containing all sorts of medicines in packages and bottles – for cholesterol, headaches, diabetes, stomach ulcers, even Prozac. The women were free to take anything except the pills for her angina, or Orangina, as she called it.

Mother went ahead with her plans and took the seventeen-hour flight to San Diego. As she landed safe and sound, she congratulated herself on meeting this great challenge. But an hour later, at Ahlam's flat, she began to feel terrible.

She described what was happening during a telephone conversation.

'I feel as if I am a eucalyptus tree, shedding the smooth, light bark of my trunk to reveal dark layers like blood.'

To add to her discomfort, she told me, Toufic's wife, whom my mother had known since she was fourteen and to whom she had been both a friend and mother over the years, had stopped calling her Mama and become impatient, making her feel unwanted. I tried to tell her that all daughters-in-law become irritated with their mothers-in-law. I found myself suggesting that Mother give Toufic and his wife a break and visit Maryam, who now lived in Detroit.

Mother snapped back, 'Visit Maryam? Do you think I have the energy or heart to see her, a feather shaking in the winds of Detroit? After what her husband did to her? When he became ill and was dying of cancer, he wanted her to die with him, pointing his gun at her day and night, while the children tried to protect her. Eventually God was the one who protected her, by finishing him off.'

Although Mother was taken to the doctor many times, it was only when she began to choke when she ate or drank that the doctor took her seriously. Then he stopped insisting that she was merely depressed and that her symptoms were psychosomatic. He carried out some tests, but Mother didn't want to wait for the results. She decided she must return to Beirut, where she could take refuge in her home and be cared for by her own doctor.

With Ahlam at her side, she clutched her heart for the entire seventeen hours she was on the plane, convinced that it was her heart that was making her choke.

Back in Beirut, she was admitted to hospital and diagnosed with an inflammation of the thyroid. The doctor suggested making an incision in her throat to help her breathe, an idea she rejected. During one of our telephone calls, I tried to persuade her to listen to the doctor and let him go ahead with the operation.

'So you want me to be like that man in our neighbourhood who had to press a button at his throat every time he needed to speak, his voice emerging from the pit of his stomach, as if from the cave of Ali Baba and the forty thieves? People would feel only pity for me.'

I called the doctor in Beirut. He explained to me that

Mother was suffering from thyroid cancer and had only a few months to live.

'It is not fair,' I found myself crying. 'It is not fair.'

Why had I drawn that flower in her telephone book? Why did I finally agree to write her life story? Why hadn't I remembered that one of my friends had been struck down with cancer as soon as she finished writing her memoir?

I took a flight to Beirut and went straight to the hospital. There I found my four sisters and two brothers. I tried to be normal and casual with Mother, and very strong. I sensed that she was like a hunter, trying to detect among us any tiny quiver or flutter, in our eyes or our voices. We all assured her that the radiotherapy she was having was simply a laser machine that would cure her thyroid infection, just like the laser that had cured her afflicted eyes a few years earlier.

When she was released from hospital for a few days, we all – children, relatives, neighbours and friends – celebrated her return home. But she wanted to go back in – she only felt safe in the hands of doctors and nurses, surrounded by medicines and machines, blood-pressure gauges and heart monitors. She felt peaceful there, removed from her house and the constant chatter of the neighbours and well-wishers, and the sound of the television. I don't think she realised how far her health had deteriorated until one of her visiting neighbours got into a huge argument with her daughter, and the daughter threatened to throw herself off Mother's balcony.

'If you want to throw yourself off a balcony, then go home and get on with it!' the mother yelled at her. 'Can't you see how ill Kamila is? She wouldn't be able to deal with the police.'

Was it conceivable that Kamila, doyenne of coffee cliques, head of the Widows' Club and instigator of all kinds of fun and games, had become Kamila the invalid? Was it conceivable that she couldn't come up with tricks to play on her own body, couldn't force it any more to stand up, sleep, drink, eat, walk, think, laugh and sing songs? But it was as if she could instantly read my mind.

She suddenly asked me, 'Will I always be this way, or will the nightmare pass, so that I can go back to being the Kamila of old?'

In many ways she remained that Kamila. As she lay in her bed, one doctor uncovered her, another turned her over. She drifted in and out of consciousness, but came to as a nurse was inserting a catheter. She broke into song:

> I hid you, I hid you,
> And we've kept you safe.
> Now everyone's looking at you …

Her fear of death made her refuse to keep flowers in her room, insisting that they be put out on the balcony. Flowers were only for the dead or dying.

'What are they trying to tell me?' she said.

When Ahlam arrived wearing a black top one morning, Mother grabbed her by the hand and told her to take off her black clothes. It was too early, she said.

One morning, as she and I were sitting on the balcony of her hospital room, she demanded an answer.

'Why do I still choke every time I try to eat or drink? Why do I have to sit there, half-naked, shivering with cold underneath a huge machine while its rays work their way inside me? I insist that you tell me the truth. It's not that, is it?' Mother didn't want to utter the word, so she said it in English: 'Kinsir.'

I busied myself arranging her sheets, pretending that I hadn't understood what she was asking me. Trying to raise a smile, she asked me if the word 'kinsir' was derived from the Arabic word for eagle, *nasr*, or from the verb meaning to be broken, *inkasar*. I gathered my courage and spelt out the word in English, the first vowel being an 'a': 'Cancer.'

Clasping my hand, she asked me again if what she had was cancer.

When I asked her why she wanted to know, she replied, 'I need to know how I am going to live from now on.'

I found myself confessing that yes, she had cancer, but I assured her she was getting better.

'Just one more session,' I said, 'and it'll all be gone. It'll be like you've been through a long nightmare.'

Immediately I regretted telling her. I sensed how her heart sank and saw her knees begin to shake.

'No, I don't believe I have that illness,' she said. 'I want to run away from it, from that eagle so eager to pluck out my life spirit. Ever since I fell ill, I've been telling myself it might be cancer and all of you around me have denied it.'

I hugged her as she moaned, 'Heaven help you, Kamila.' Then she took her head in both hands as she muttered to herself, 'What has become of you?'

By next morning she'd come to believe what I'd told her, that she was getting better – one more session of radiation and the cancer would be gone. I think she'd convinced herself that, if it hadn't been the case, I'd never have dared tell her what the disease actually was.

She made me promise not to tell anyone about her illness. She felt that it marked a weakness in her, as embarrassing as poverty itself, or leprosy; like someone with bad breath or head lice. She was afraid the news would give her enemies malicious satisfaction – especially the neighbour who so terrified her.

The fact that the doctors and nurses paid so much attention further convinced my mother that she must be on the road to recovery. If she was heading for the grave, surely they wouldn't have bothered so much with her? They had even tried, unsuccessfully, to stop her from smoking, something she could never give up. The fact that Mother still craved cigarettes gave me hope that she was still healthy. She used every trick she knew to get hold of them: flattery, bribery, anger. 'OK, goggle eyes,' she'd mutter under her breath when a nurse took away her packet of cigarettes. She even asked a hospital cleaner to sell her just one cigarette. He was sympathetic, agreeing with her that cigarette deprivation was worse than any illness, and he nicknamed her Madame Cigarette.

She enjoyed smoking most of all from the balcony of her hospital room, watching the pigeons on the roof. Once, she saw the boy pigeon kiss the girl. Then the two of them took off and flew away, only to return and start all over again. She began singing Asmahan's song, 'Once I entered the garden …' She sang it as if she was on her own, as if she was taking a walk in the gardens opposite. She sang for all she was worth, happy her shortness of breath had not yet cut off her voice.

I rushed from the room as I heard her voice, still so young and melancholic. It took me back to the time when she was in love with Muhammad, and would sing to him as we played near by during one of their rendezvous. Her voice released the tears I'd been suppressing for more than two months; they ran with great force down my face, gushing down to my weeping heart. Only when I had managed to get hold of myself did I return to her room.

I knew she could tell that I'd been crying, but she said nothing, only asked why I thought we'd finally made the visit to her childhood home in the south just six months earlier and didn't find her mother and sisters' graves. Had they been calling out to her? Why had I finally agreed to listen to her life story? Why was she suddenly so desperate for me to hear it? And why had Fadila burst into tears when she'd first visited her, saying, 'I thought you'd died. They told me Kamila had died!'

My mother gradually withdrew from the life going on around her, although once she roused herself to beg the husband of a patient who had entered her room by mistake to lift her up and carry her out to the balcony so she could smoke. She reflected at length on many seemingly unrelated subjects, but in fact they all had one thing in common: death.

'How is it our body lets us down? How come in the Egyptian film *Night of Life* we sat there and admired Fatin Hamama's dress as she lay sick and dying, listening to someone sing 'Life's pleasurable moments are few ...' to her?

'Why did I laugh at my uncle the cobbler when I heard him moaning in pain, 'I am hurt, I am hurt,' the whole night through, even after I suggested he change his words or add something like 'Oh God' or 'Please help me'?

'Make sure you all give me a decent funeral in Muhammad's village ... How I regret all the lovely shoes I haven't yet worn ... Someone should water the plants on my balcony. I am going to miss them!

'So that's the way it is, Kamila. God help you, cancer's got you. And all the time you thought it was your heart.'

During her illness, we, the five sisters and two brothers, would take turns visiting our mother from the four corners of the earth. The day Fatima appeared, my mother raised her head excitedly. She tried to speak, but couldn't. Her eyes spoke and her mouth moved, but no sound came out. The doctor suggested that we bring her a pen and paper so she could write down whatever she needed to tell us. We stood mute, hesitating, none of us willing to tell the doctor that Mother couldn't read or write.

After that day, she drifted in and out of consciousness. When Toufic and Muhammad Kamal, visiting from San Diego and Kuwait respectively, came and sat beside her, each holding a hand, she opened her eyes and realised she was in the intensive-care unit. Then she kept staring at me, and at my hair, which I'd put up with a hairband because Beirut was so hot and humid.

I knew exactly what she wanted to say.

'Your hairband's great, it's *dah*!' That was how she'd described anything new or beautiful when she was a child in Nabatiyeh.

To our surprise, and to the surprise of the doctors, Mother would regain consciousness from time to time and engage with us, gesturing and smiling. Her curious eyes would follow us around the room. One afternoon, she registered the anger and disapproval on the faces of the nurses in intensive care as they gathered around the television set. All Mother could make out were explosions and collapsing buildings. With her hands, she asked a nurse what was going on. Ahlam told me later that the nurse was amazed that Mother could focus on the television in spite of her sedation. The nurse turned off the television, not wanting my mother to be upset, but she kept gesturing, demanding an answer, until the nurse finally explained.

'Some planes have flown into buildings in New York,' she said.

Mother relaxed, relieved that the catastrophe couldn't have affected any of her children or grandchildren.

Her eyes closed. I watched her as she finally entered a sweet world of unconsciousness. I reflected on how she'd hugged herself in the hospital in the early days of her sickness, refusing to allow one of us to spend the night with her. Though people might sleep next to their loved ones, she told me, ultimately everyone is on their own once they fall asleep. Mother wanted to count the number of nights she'd slept since her birth. Ahlam worked it out for her – twenty-seven thousand, three hundred and seventy-five nights. She did not know that people were still coming to visit her; we clustered in the room next to the intensive-care unit, her seven children gathered around her. Why hadn't the seven of us gathered when she could still jump up and sing? Why was it only now, when she couldn't be with us, that we were going out to restaurants together and warming ourselves with each other's company? My sisters and I praised her snow-white body, and Ahlam complained to the nurses when they cut her hair without our permission and clipped the long fingernails that were my mother's pride and joy.

When I saw my Uncle Kamil in the intensive-care unit I rushed to him, and hugged him tight as if he was still a child, pouring the lentils into his djellabah before he and Mother ran away from their father and stepmother. I felt a strange urge to shake Mother awake and plead with her to laugh with Kamil, to see Khadija, who came to visit even though she was very old, and listen to Fadila, as everyone else did, as she made her way from the hospital foyer to Mother's bedside, saying, 'Kamila, Kamila, let someone else die, not you!'

Fadila wept as she entered the room, but then she would dry her eyes and hurry to the bed.

'In the name of God,' she'd begin, 'Kamila, listen to me. I've prayed two *rakaa* for you, the Prophet's own family. Dear beloved friend, may they greet you one by one, especially Sitt Zaynab, and caress you!' She would rub my mother's face with her hands, as if sweeping up wheatgerm left to dry on the roof.

One day Fadila told us we must not lose hope, we must keep trying to save Kamila. She instructed us to copy the text of the Sura al-Waqia from the Quran ten times, boil the pages in water, sift them, and scatter the pieces in a plant pot. We should then bring the water containing the Quranic verses and give them to my mother to drink: this would cure her. Fadila asked us to swear solemnly that we'd do it. But then Majida pointed out that Mother was no longer able to eat or drink, and was fed through a tube in her nose. Fadila suggested we feed the water through the tube. If the nurse was a Christian, we should tell her the verses came from the Bible.

She then turned to Cousine, one of Ibrahim's daughters.

'I beg you,' she said, seeking reassurance. 'We must bring my dear, dear friend Kamila back. She's been my friend since we were young girls. If she dies, then so do I.' She struggled to get a ring off one of her fingers. 'Please,' she went on. 'Take this ring. It's worth over 100 lira. God wants you to have it. Only promise you'll make those copies of the Sura al-Waqia!'

Fadila admitted that she couldn't read or write; if she could, she'd have copied the verses herself.

'You mean you're just like Mother,' said Majida. 'No one taught you either?'

She started to sob.

'If only I'd been able to make out one letter from another,' she lamented, 'I wouldn't have been robbed of my property and land by one of my relatives who asked for my thumbprint on the ownership papers, pretending that he had found a way to exempt me from paying taxes.'

Majida hurried home and copied out the Sura al-Waqia ten times and took the bottle to the hospital, but she didn't do anything with it, just tucked it away in her handbag. And that was the way we left Mother that evening, just as usual. We all dined together; then I went to my hotel room, leaving my clothes laid out as I did each evening, in case the hospital rang in the middle of the night. That night they did, and I was the first to arrive. Why did I draw a flower next to her phone number? Why did I agree to write her life story?

I went into her room.

'Mama,' I whispered, as I ran my hand over her coldness. By now she was as cold as ice, even though there was a light aimed straight at her and she was completely enveloped in blankets, coverlets and hot-water bottles.

'You're a white angel,' I found myself telling her. 'Now here come the other angels to take you away in your lovely gown and your new shoes. Now you can play with them – jacks, catch and skipping – and you can rub citrus fruit against the wall so you can put salt on it and eat it. Thank you for your tiny womb that was my home, for giving me my name and character. And thank you, because every time I think of you I find myself smiling and laughing.'

I uncovered her feet. They looked like pure white porcelain, as if she had never walked on anything but silk, as if she had never run barefoot in the wilderness of Nabatiyeh.

Life's Journey

MY MOTHER LEFT the hospital in an ambulance, surrounded by garlands and bouquets of roses and sweet basil. Muhammad Kamal rode with her in the back of the ambulance; there he sat, looking wan and feeling sick from the powerful scent of the flowers or the smell of death itself. How strange! As a child, he'd been her ally in all her schemes and secrets, and now here he was accompanying her on her final journey, the most secret of them all. Roads can always be closed off, but not this one; the road to death lies for ever open. Men stopped in the street and stood still out of respect as we passed; some drivers got out of their cars. The din of car horns ceased. As soon as the ambulance swung up the road towards the Ra's al-Nab neighbourhood, to the old house where my mother lived with us before she left us and married Muhammad, Fatima and I could no longer control ourselves and burst into hysterical sobs.

How could it be that this young driver, who had no idea of my mother's origins, had decided to give her a tour to bid farewell to her life? It was almost as if he'd put his ear to the inner wall of her being, and that of my sister and me, and decided to take us all to the places where we grew up. We passed the grocer's shop where Muhammad had gone to send her messages and flowers through the boy who worked there. These were the very streets Fatima and I had sneaked through to visit Mother after she'd left. Here was what remained of our school where Mother would meet us after our father forbade us to see her as often as we wanted. Here were the same trees; and the rough wrought-iron grilles over the frosted glass of the doctor's surgery that I would look out for each time my mother took me to Muhammad's room. Here was the Prime Minister's house with its balcony, where Maryam had fallen in love, and the alley in which our old house stood. By now most of the cement had crumbled, leaving only the edge of the wall. I remembered how my mother and Maryam had once asked a boy to scramble up and get them a chunk of cement that had caught their eye because it was perfectly square, and then cracked it open with an adze. Inside the sandy stone we found a tiny piece cut out of the mosquito net we used when we slept on the roof. Years later my mother explained that this was the work of the mother of the boy next door, who had cast a spell to prevent her son from falling in love with my mother.

Now the ambulance came to Muhammad's house and the window of the howdah room where Mother and I once hid behind the door, trembling, waiting for Muhammad to return. The window was wide open and I pictured Muhammad inside, waiting for Kamila.

Finally, we reached my mother's house. As the whole neighbourhood rushed to the ambulance, our crying grew even louder, and so did that of Mother's female neighbours, the wives of the shopkeepers and everyone she knew in the quarter. A little girl asked her mother if this was the funeral of the woman who had brought presents from America. Now the wailing began in earnest. The ambulance came to a halt. The shopkeepers had swept the street and sprinkled water on the ground; they'd lowered the awnings on their shops and turned the radio to a station broadcasting the Quran. Everybody waited until Mother had had her fill of the quarter and the house she would never see again. What about we daughters? Could we bear to look at her balcony, knowing she wouldn't be sitting there, watching passers-by or watering her plants? It was hard for us to move on. The traffic waited patiently.

My mother left her home for ever, and then unexpectedly we passed by the house where my grandmother, Mother and Kamil had first lived when they arrived in Beirut. Then we drove out of Beirut, the city where Muhammad and Mother had met by the side of a fountain one day, and we headed to Muhammad's village, the place where she was to be buried under the verdant tree that looked out over the hills and valleys, next to Muhammad's grave. There we would bring them together again, just like two love birds inside a single cage, in the cemetery where my mother used to clean Muhammad's grave, leave flowers and recite the Fatiha, turning away from all the people who'd tried to separate her from the love of her life.

So, amid prayers and Quranic verses, she was buried by the men, as the custom dictated, while we women stayed in Majida's summer house and wept for her from afar, feeling that she had been kidnapped and hidden beneath the earth. Out of concern for Kadsuma, who had a heart condition, my sisters begged the professional mourner to read only the Quran, not stirring religious homilies or the Ashura rituals. Despite the request, though, the professional mourner started keening the sad and tragic tale of the Battle of Karbala, while the women swayed and wept.

She went on to fan the flames of grief by reading with great passion, so much so that she became like Sukayna, al-Hussein's daughter, when she first saw her father's horse without him, and lamented, 'Oh my father's horse, tell me, did he find water, or did he die thirsty?' This stirred all of us into a frenzy. We wailed and beat our chests. Then, although we tried to stop her, she ended the ceremony with political slogans praising the regime in Iran.

After that, the men joined the women. A sheep was sacrificed for the sake of Mother's soul. No less than fifty cats also assembled from the village and its environs; they sat waiting patiently on the terraced land encircling the house. A beggar – who used to know the moment Mother set foot in the village – stood with a few loaves of bread, wanting to contribute something to the sad occasion. Soon a tent was erected around her grave so the Quran readers could be with her for three whole days and nights as custom dictates; and to keep a lantern burning so she wouldn't feel lonely, especially during the darkness of the night.

Mother wasn't the only person to be buried that day. Muhammad's sister Miskiah, their emissary, had died the day before. We were told that years earlier Mother had asked Miskiah and other friends not to leave her to be buried alone. 'I'd like a friend to die with me,' she'd said, and they'd laughed.

At dawn the next morning we made our way to the cemetery, carrying incense and candles. Fadila sat by the Quran reader and asked him if my mother had been listening to his recital. Then she gave him some pastilles to suck so his voice would reach Kamila sweet and pleasant, not like that of the blind sheikh in Beirut whose voice made her and Mother close their ears and pinch their noses because of the foul smell.

I gathered around the freshly dug grave with my sisters and Muhammad Kamal. Toufic, who'd been flying across the ocean when Mother died, had been in touch. He was eager to get a picture of everything as it happened, moment by moment. His heart was racked with grief. We told him we had carved 'Kamila' on her gravestone above the phrase we knew she loved best: 'Most beloved of women'. We had brought the frangipani from her balcony in Beirut and planted it next to the grave. Majida's son placed a cigarette on the grave and called his grandmother Beauty Queen of the Graveyard; I knew he was wishing he had a joint of hashish to make him high. The tree giving her shade from above oozed a sticky gum that stuck to our clothes and shoes. We all laughed. Mother was still not willing to let us go without her, even though she would now sleep for ever, amid fragrant flowers and chirping birds, looking out over mountains and valleys.

We said goodbye to her on the seventh day, in the hope of visiting her again during Eid. But she visits us all the time, whether we are awake or asleep, happy or sad. Each one of us has lived to regret something they once said, or didn't say, to her. But Mother makes us laugh too, especially when we remember her friends arriving at her funeral adorned with generous presents from her, gifts originally given to her by us: one friend with a gold ring; Fadila carrying a snakeskin purse; and Leila a Hermès scarf – because Mother never did like its pattern of horses.

As I said goodbye to her, I thought of what she would have said if she were looking at her own grave.

'We go up and down; we run hither and thither; we roam here and there and everywhere and we end up exactly where we began. And here I am, back in my place near Muhammad, to be with him for ever.'

Epilogue

MY DAUGHTER IS married, and I feel as if my mother is sitting with me in the limousine, sitting behind my eyes, absorbing the noisy hum of New York. In my mind, she's wearing her blue-and-white suit, the one she wore whenever she wanted to look 'chic', as she used to say.

She scolds me, as I have not managed to buy a new dress for the wedding.

I tell her, 'How could I when I am mourning you still, with neither the energy nor the will to look my best? I only buried you a month ago.' I tell her how much I miss her and ask for her forgiveness for not telling her I was getting married thirty-three years earlier, for not sending word to her when I was about to give birth to my children.

She laughs with the bride and groom, and clutches the womb that gave birth to me.

'Look what my descendants have achieved: from a village in southern Lebanon to New York.'

I whisper to her, 'Your brave genes are in my blood. You are the source of my strength and independence.'

Two years after my mother died, I sat down to write her story. Majida had sent Muhammad's diaries and letters to help me. When I wrote, faded sheets, some as yellow as wilted gardenias, were scattered about.

Muhammad had written on school exercise books, pieces of cardboard, government paper and headed paper decorated with flowers and butterflies from a grand shop in Beirut, which I loved for its Venetian architecture. I felt a rush of nostalgia when I saw it. He wrote in pencil, black and dark-blue ink. Here I was, possessing the years from the thirties to 1960, the year Muhammad died, in his own hand; the lines, the colour of the ink and the pencil made me shiver. I saw my mother in her happiness and in her strife. I listened and heard Muhammad as he moaned, felt his despair, machismo and vanity.

Muhammad wrote full pages, not leaving one inch empty, as if he was writing from prison and paper was scarce. He wrote different poems on each of the eight sides of a folded piece of paper. He wrote plays and stories, three pages' worth of material on one page. It was as if he hadn't stopped to take a breath. I listened to his voice, guessed his moods, took his pulse. Love was on Muhammad's mind and on the mind of his friends and brothers. As I read their letters I saw that men also suffer because of love and betrayal. 'My love is as strong as rock,' Muhammad wrote. 'I love you more than I love life.' And after he married my mother, he always addressed her as 'darling wife'.

I found my name in one of his letters to my mother. A cup of coffee had scalded my face at the age of two; Muhammad was concerned, asking after me, wanting to see me. As I read this, I found myself touching my face, with no memory, or trace of a burn. Suddenly he managed to wipe away my jealousy, jealousy that was never stronger than when I once stood at their door after a quarrel with my stepmother. They were grilling kebabs and my mother tried in vain to persuade me to come in; Muhammad pleaded with me, but my feet were nailed to the tiles. I was jealous and felt awkward and clumsy. I wanted to be my baby sister in her pink pyjamas. I wanted to be included in that moment, but I didn't know how.

On a mangy page torn from a school exercise book I found a letter, addressed to Muhammad in a child's hand. Had somebody steadied my mother's hand and helped her to write this letter? As I read it my heart skipped a beat. It was the letter my sister Fatima wrote, as she and Mother hid in the bathroom. Reading it and observing the spelling mistakes and the hesitation of a child filled me with sorrow and regret. Did Fatima feel confused, or proud that she was able to write a letter for an adult?

And then I found a small piece of pale-pink paper with writing in red ink across it. It was my mother's will, written with Muhammad's help, signed by her very carefully, letter by letter at the bottom, as if written by a child. She left twelve bracelets to be sold to pay for someone to go on a pilgrimage to Mecca on her behalf; her wedding ring for my sister Ahlam; two sets of earrings, one for me and the other for Fatima; one half of her clothes for me, the other half for Fatima. The sofa, carpet, couches and cupboard were all for Ahlam. The will had been written just two years after her divorce. Had she thought of dying? Was she thinking of ending her own life? I asked around, but no one could give me an answer.

I found an official message from Jean Helio, French High Commissioner to the Lebanese people in 1934, telling them they were to vote to elect the first national assembly for an independent Lebanon, and assuring them that it would be an honest and fair election. On this address Muhammad had poured out his heart in a love letter:

Not a moment passes without my thinking how lonely I am in this life, even though the world may seem to keep it full, and all because I am so far away from you.

The minutes slip by so fast, as I sit here. My eyes sing them songs of emotion and tenderness, and they look at me as if to say, 'What you see before you is but a version in miniature of what is in my heart, my beloved!'

I have measured the days in terms of our two hearts, each of them filled with a violent passion. My beloved, whom I worship and adore, I have decided to set you apart for a long time, a time when my agony will be dire indeed.

As much as love is poured out on these fragile sheets, death is ever present on the torn and disintegrating paper. The writers, all dead now, speak of dying almost as often as they do of love, but their idealism shines through. This was a generation that believed in politics, in pan-Arabism, in the homeland and independence. Luckily Muhammad was not alive to witness the strife that enveloped Lebanon and still continues; and the exile and disintegration of his beloved family, as his children became immigrants in all corners of the world.

Muhammad touched me deeply as I read and understood how much his existence was tied to the written word. And yet he fell passionately in love with my illiterate mother, embracing with such ease that vividness of hers, which unnerved so many others. How I wished I was their messenger instead of the grocery boy, carrying Muhammad's heart to her even when he wrote when I was barely one year old, 'Shall I try to help you get a divorce or are you simply fooling about and passing time?' And how powerful a thing to have these words left to me, particularly since my mother didn't write.

The last thing I read was a letter from my mother, dictated to Muhammad Kamal and addressed to me but never sent. It had been written during one of her lengthy visits to Kuwait, after she heard me being interviewed on Lebanese television when I published *The Story of Zahra*:

Don't measure things by a past that is gone. It was sweet indeed, because I challenged the executioner and the chains that bound my wrists. I regained my freedom from all those virgin maidens who were sold without a price. But fate was stronger than I was, and it crushed me. It took everything I had, absolutely everything. I turned into a tree that had been stripped of all its leaves, leaves that jumped from pavement to pavement in the company of their friends, the breeze and the howling wind. I became a ship with no shore in sight. When I saw your lovely picture and heard the sound of your sweet, melodious voice, I received back my own beauty from yours and my intelligence from yours as well. That stripped tree once again started to sprout gleaming leaves, and they will stay that way just as long as life and capacity stay with me.

The minute I gathered all the papers of our conversations and sessions together, ready to work, my mother became alive, not in Beirut, or in the mountains, or in the south, but this time in my flat in London. She was living her life again for me. I saw her for the first time as a child, a teenager, a young woman, then middle-aged, and finally an old lady. I travelled into another world of emotions, stories, metaphors and anecdotes, sometimes reduced to tears and sometimes roaring with laughter. I was humbled by her frankness, by her courage as she spilled out what was hidden, as if she had lifted the lid of a deep, deep well. When I became too distressed over a certain episode in her life and couldn't go on, my mother's photo, which I had stuck on one of the notebooks, would cheer me up. In it, she was accepting a silver cup from an official, after one of my sisters was crowned Queen of Dance at the summer resort party. My mother had rushed over to him and asked him to pretend to give her the cup instead.

The day I started to write her memoir, I could hear protesters outside the nearby Canadian Embassy, demonstrating to save the seals. A tourist bus passed by. I could hear the guide's words: 'To your right is the memorial for 9/11, and to your left is the Italian Embassy.'

I caught myself muttering, 'And here is Hanan, writing about her mother, who loved and suffered, who ran away, who raised her fist against the rules and traditions of the world into which she was born, and who transformed her lies into a lifetime of naked honesty.'

I opened my first chapter with the words, 'I can see my mother and her brother, my Uncle Kamil, running after my grandfather,' and then I stopped. Or was it my mother who stopped me? I heard her voice insisting that she wanted to tell her own story. She did not want my voice; she wanted the beat of her own heart, her anxieties and laughter, her dreams and nightmares. She wanted her own voice. She wanted to go back to the beginning. She was ecstatic that at long last she could tell her story. My mother wrote this book. She is the one who spread her wings. I just blew the wind that took her on her long journey back in time.

ACKNOWLEDGEMENTS

Thanks to Margaret Stead, whose help I am ever grateful for.

A NOTE ON THE TYPE

The text of this book is set in Bembo. This type was first used in 1495 by the Venetian printer Aldus Manutius for Cardinal Bembo's *De Aetna*, and was cut for Manutius by Francesco Griffo. It was one of the types used by Claude Garamond (1480–1561) as a model for his Romain de L'Université, and so it was the forerunner of what became standard European type for the following two centuries. Its modern form follows the original types and was designed for Monotype in 1929.

ALSO AVAILABLE BY HANAN AL-SHAYKH

ONLY IN LONDON

As a flight from Dubai comes into London's Heathrow and hits turbulence, four people from different corners of the Arab world are thrown together: beautiful, lost Lamis, recently divorced from her wealthy Iraqi husband; Nicholas, an expert at Sotheby's on Islamic daggers; louche and noisy Amira, a Moroccan who lives off immoral earnings and the transvestite Samir, with a monkey hidden in a basket. Landing safely they go their separate ways, but from then on they find their lives are intimately entwined. *Only in London* is a funny, tender and sexy novel that uncovers a unique world in the heart of a big city.

*

'A fresh, amusing and surprising take on London, and on life'
THE TIMES

'A delightfully unfamiliar view of London, anecdotal and elegant,
with a freshness and sensuality in its language'
INDEPENDENT ON SUNDAY

'Behind Arabic signs spicing up London's Edgware Road there seethes an exuberant, passionate, mixed-up slice of the Middle East that Hanan al-Shaykh expertly and amusingly lays bare … You will laugh. I did'
DAILY MAIL

*

ISBN 9781408801925 · PAPERBACK · £7.99

B L O O M S B U R Y

I SWEEP THE SUN OFF ROOFTOPS

At the intersection of tradition and modernity, East and West, childhood and
adulthood, Hanan al-Shaykh's characters find their way through the shifting
and ambiguous power relationships that shape the landscape of the modern
Arab world. A woman feigns insanity to escape from an empty marriage, only
to have her plans backfire; a young Danish missionary finds herself slowly and
inexorably drawn into the world of the Yemeni village where she has been
stationed; and a woman's light-hearted attempt to contact the world of the dead
turns serious when she encounters the spirit of her late husband.

At once clever and evocative, *I sweep the sun off rooftops* is a collection of
great insight, wit and poignancy, placing Hanan al-Shaykh among the foremost
cosmopolitan writers of our time.

*

'Subtly nuanced and compassionate, the often intolerable conflict in these
stories are handled with a staggering lightness of touch'
THE TIMES

'Al-Shaykh writes with a pen that is neither East nor West but entirely her own'
LOS ANGELES TIMES BOOKS OF THE YEAR

*

ISBN 978 0 7475 6131 6 · PAPERBACK · £6.99

BLOOMSBURY

WOMEN OF SAND & MYRRH

Winner of the Elle Prize for Literature

In an unnamed Middle Eastern city, four women from different social and cultural backgrounds tell their story. There is Suha, an educated Lebanese woman brought to the desert by her husband; Tamr, who must fight against male rule to educate herself; Suzanne, captivated by the men and the mystery of the Arabian desert; and Nur, in fierce pursuit of lovers (male and female) and foreign adventures – but her husband has her passport. All four women struggle in a society where women cannot drive a car, walk in the streets unveiled, or travel without male permission. It is a society where sex, due to its constraints, becomes an obsession. These women are treated to every luxury except that which they truly desire – freedom.

*

'A masterpiece'
NEWSWEEK

'A powerful and original writer ... Her artistry in this memorable book lies in the way she tells about religion, sex, marriage, housekeeping and hundreds of other human activities as they really are in the great golden cage in the desert'
INTERNATIONAL HERALD TRIBUNE

'Al-Shaykh goes where few Arab writers have gone before: not just into a world of women but into their sexuality'
ECONOMIST

*

ISBN 9781408805909 · PAPERBACK · £7.99

ORDER YOUR COPY: BY PHONE +44 (0)1256 302 699; BY EMAIL: DIRECT@MACMILLAN.CO.UK
DELIVERY IS USUALLY 3–5 WORKING DAYS. FREE POSTAGE AND PACKAGING FOR ORDERS OVER £20.

ONLINE: WWW.BLOOMSBURY.COM/BOOKSHOP
PRICES AND AVAILABILITY SUBJECT TO CHANGE WITHOUT NOTICE.

WWW.BLOOMSBURY.COM/HANANAL-SHAYKH

BLOOMSBURY